INDIGENOUS DANCE AND *Dancing Indian*

CONTESTED REPRESENTATION IN THE GLOBAL ERA

MATTHEW KRYSTAL

UNIVERSITY PRESS OF COLORADO

Published by University Press of Colorado
245 Century Circle, Suite 202
Louisville, Colorado 80027

First paperback edition 2020
Manufactured in the United States of America

The University Press of Colorado is a proud member of
The Association of American University Presses.

The University Press of Colorado is a cooperative publishing enterprise supported, in part, by Adams State University, Colorado State University, Fort Lewis College, Metropolitan State University of Denver, Regis University, University of Colorado, University of Northern Colorado, University of Wyoming, Utah State University, and Western Colorado University.

∞ This paper meets the requirements of the ANSI/NISO Z39.48–1992 (Permanence of Paper)

ISBN: 978-1-60732-096-8 (hardcover)
ISBN: 978-1-64642-081-0 (paperback)
ISBN: 978-1-60732-097-5 (ebook)

Library of Congress Cataloging-in-Publication Data

Krystal, Matthew.
Indigenous dance and dancing Indian : contested representation in the global era / Matthew Krystal.
p. cm.
Includes bibliographical references and index.
ISBN 978-1-60732-096-8 (hardcover : alk. paper) — ISBN 978-1-64642-081-0 (paperback) — ISBN 978-1-60732-097-5 (ebook) 1. Indian dance. 2. Indian dance—North America. 3. Dance—Anthropological aspects—Cross-cultural studies. I. Title.
E98.D2K79 2012
781.62'97—dc23

2011035516

Author picture: The author at La Calera, San Miguel, Totonicapán, July 2010. Photograph by Frances Krystal, the author's six-year-old daughter.

for Mom

INDIGENOUS DANCE AND DANCING INDIAN

Contents

Figures

Preface

Ethnography and Ethnographer

It is Veterans Day weekend, and the gray and windy November weather, for the moment, is of little concern. We are sitting comfortably in the floor-level grandstands of the University of Illinois at Chicago Pavilion, a multi-use stadium on the near-west side of the city. The diversity of purpose of the facility is fully expressed today. The southeast end of the floor is crowded with powwow dancers, forming a continuous clockwise flow of humanity. Drum groups circle the dance arena, defining its border and providing musical accompaniment. The northeast end of the facility conforms more closely with the spatial norms of the surrounding city. Vendors of various sorts, social service agencies, and advocacy groups occupy tables and booths that are ordered in neat rectilinear rows and columns. Behind us, on a mezzanine that connects lower to upper level, reside more booths including, and of particular interest to my son, fry bread vendors. The hexagonal path of the mezzanine represents a compromise between the circle of the dance area and the generally rectilinear form of the building and its surroundings.

I am here, family in tow, out of personal interest, but also because I have assigned students from my Native Americans course to attend the powwow. Working as an anthropology department of one at a small liberal arts college has me moving beyond Mesoamerica, the region of my fieldwork and most of my training. After spending the summer reading and preparing for the Native Americans class, I am attending the powwow late in the term with an eye on generating questions and topics for classroom discussion. Although K'iche' Maya dance was the topic of my doctoral dissertation, I am here more as a professor than an ethnographer. It is during an intertribal dance (one where dancers of various styles and ages dance together) that I begin to shift from teacher to researcher. As I gaze on the arena full of dancers, I contemplate and compare K'iche' traditional dance and powwow and find that they are similar and different in interesting ways. Centrally, both feature indigenous dancers who perform for ethnically mixed (or at least potentially mixed) audiences. As my mind wanders through topics that we have been exploring in the Native Americans class, I recall that the University of Illinois (at its downstate Champaign-Urbana campus) features a most controversial form of dance. There a carefully selected white college student dresses in Plains regalia and dances as "Chief Illiniwek" during the halftime of football games. Reflecting on field experiences in Guatemala, I recall that traditional dancers also contend with representations in dance by ethnic Others. My mind wandering further, I visually survey the audience. It reveals profound ethnic diversity typical of this part of the city, and it becomes clear that various groups use dance to represent themselves. More interesting is how a variety of dances, familiar to me by a curious mix of intention and chance, feature aspects of indigenous life.

0.1. Composing a Circle. The Pavilion at the University of Illinois, Chicago, is readied for grand entry, November 2006. (Photograph by author.)

This book concerns the representation of indigenous life and culture in four varied forms of public performance identified as "dance." Specifically, it examines traditional dance performed by K'iche' Maya, folkloric dances presented in various communities, powwow dances of Native American nations, and the performance of Indian[1] mascots in sport. In some of these forms, indigenous people represent themselves. In some, Indianness is presented by Others. For example, performers of K'iche' traditional dance enact themselves and their own culture, occasionally representing ethnic Others as well. Indigenous[2] powwow dancers represent both the culture of specific Native nations and the shared political identity Native American. For immigrant folkloric performers, the connection between the status of the performer and the culture enacted in dance is somewhat ambivalent. Among sports mascots, dancers enact Others. Simple consideration of the diversity of performers generates two obvious questions. Why do Native performers feel compelled to represent their culture in dance, particularly to audiences that feature ethnic Others? Why do people who are not indigenous feel compelled to perform and consume images of Indianness? The simple answer is that these dances address the basic human need to construct meaningful and satisfying senses of identity. All the dances considered here deal, in one way or another, with the creation and contestation of identity in the context of intensive, globalized, cross-cultural relations. The *variety* of the forms presents an opportunity to consider various challenges of identity in multiple contexts. Taking public dance performance as a kind of secular ritual, in each case I explore how performers and audiences work on a common set of identity-related problems on a globe marked by rapid circulation of image and message and by relative ease of movement of people. In these struggles to dance meaningful and satisfying identity, common themes include the slippery notion of authenticity and persistent social inequality. In essence, the dance forms examined here construct cultural difference and, in doing so, assert authentic identity. How and why indigenous culture (or its likeness) is danced remains to be addressed in the following chapters.

K'iche' traditional dance, Native American powwow, folkloric dance, and Indian mascot performance do not make up a scientifically designed representative sample but result from the process of ethnography and the experiences of an ethnographer. My first gaze through a developing anthropological lens on representational dance was in graduate school. Witnessing a Mardi Gras Indian performance was part of the process that transformed me from a visitor into a resident of New Orleans. Paradoxically, these Indian dances presented by African Americans struck me as fundamentally authentic. The music and dancing expressed a uniquely New Orleans style, performed by and mostly for New Orleanians. The polyrhythm, the spontaneity, the joy, the localness all combined to produce an emotionally moving experience. At the end of the day, it was an interesting encounter, but not one that immediately converted itself into scholarly interest.

Indeed, dance became a scholarly interest through an indirect path. As I searched for a dissertation topic and research site, my main interest was in ethnicity and ethnic conflict. I hoped to make apprenticeship a part of my field method, so I began to seek production sites of material culture that somehow dealt with ethnicity. The Guatemalan *morería*—a shop that produces, rents, and maintains masks, vestments, props, and other equipment used in traditional Highland Maya ritual dance-dramas—fit the bill. One dance-drama outfitted by *morerías*, the Dance of the Conquest (sometimes called the national dance of Guatemala), expressed ideas about ethnicity and ethnic conflict in a variety of ways. On my first trip to Guatemala I found a *morería* in San Miguel Totonicapán that agreed to host me as an apprentice and I was off. At first, dancing was somewhat incidental to my project. Over time, this changed and fieldwork formed a lens of perception that focused on dance as an expression of culture and identity.

The intersection of dance and identity continued after fieldwork and graduate school. While working in a suburban Chicago English as a Second Language program, I realized that Latino (primarily Mexican) immigrants performed and attended representational dances quite similar to folkloric dances that I had observed both Maya and non-Maya Guatemalans perform. The more I asked about these immigrant folkloric dancers and dances, the more I encountered them within the college and its surrounding communities. I found students, teachers, and even an administrator who were performers or enthusiasts of folkloric dance, some finding it only after they emigrated.

After leaving the applied anthropology of ESL, I began teaching at a small liberal arts institution, becoming the only full-time anthropologist on the faculty. As a result, I was compelled to become a generalist. Work in ESL became a source of data and field experience as I found myself teaching on a wide variety of anthropological topics. As I described above, it was while attending a powwow that examining and comparing these varied forms occurred to me. However, the selection of dance forms examined here is not quite as personally random as the description above implies. There is good reason to consider and compare these particular four genres. First, the approach I take here reflects an ideal of ethnography embraced most famously by Margaret Mead. In *Coming of Age in Samoa* (1928), Mead turned the anthropological gaze on her own society. Mead contended that Samoan adolescence could tell us something about American[3] adolescence. Although better understanding of self through understanding of Other is implied in most ethnography, direct comparison involving the researcher's natal culture has not been a mainstay of anthropology. This partly reflects a healthy concern about ethnocentrism and a resulting reticence to make central the culture of the anthropologist. Changing theory and changing reality contribute as well. The notion of communities or cultures as well-bounded units was overstressed in early anthropology, and globalization makes it impossible to imagine a group as isolated and uninfluenced by international flows of images, people, and products. This is not to say that we all share a common culture; the global village imagined in the hubris following the collapse of the Soviet Union has yet to emerge. Rather, beliefs and practices are shared in social groups (from families, to communities, to nations) that have increasingly permeable borders. We engage Others and their cultures in various ways and with increasing frequency.

At the same time, we should not underestimate the power of intercultural discourse to sharpen the definition of cultural self and to invigorate the beliefs and practices that make a people distinct. Intercultural relations highlight relative identity markers, and for the people engaged in them, ethnic identity becomes primary. So, cross-cultural interactions, even those that are fleeting or "virtual" (and particularly those that are conflictive), can define and reinforce the notion of "us" and "them."

Therefore, the goal of learning about one's own culture by studying Others becomes complex in light of globalized relations. It is not simply a matter of what they do there and what we do here. Rather, it is necessary to treat the sites of interethnic relations as a series of particular *glocalities*, places where people construct and contest community and culture, responding to various forces and influence from beyond the immediate region. Considering representational dance in the U.S. means considering immigrant dances. Exploring K'iche' dance means exploring Maya identity and indigenous politics in general. In turn, powwow also must be considered in light of global trends in indigenous self-representation. Even the rural land-grant university finds its culture and its symbolic Indian contested, exposed to larger social and political forces.

In other words, social life of the twenty-first century is one in which transnational institutions and forces have an increasingly powerful role. As employed here, *transnational* has implications for material culture, space, performance, and identity. Large-scale and anonymous processes dominate the creation and distribution of food and objects in complex societies. Industrialized production for market consumption generates mass quantities of impersonal and identical objects (Carrier 1990). The initial steps in industrialized fabrication—resource extraction and raw materials production—have been global for some time. Recently, reductions in transportation costs, combined with the ever-present search for cheap labor, have further deterritorialized all dimensions of production (though the highest levels of management and finance remain concentrated in the wealthy core countries). In the past, one might express connection to one's compatriots by "buying American." Presently, such expressions are muted by the fact that many of the parts of a car assembled in the United States are made in multiple other countries and that Japanese autos are occasionally assembled in the States. In short, from raw materials, to parts, to finished product, processes of production transcend national borders. They are fundamentally transnational.

In terms of space, transnational emphasizes the permeability of borders that I described above. It challenges the notion of "nation" as a unit that occupies a concrete, bounded part of the landscape encompassing particular political, economic, and cultural forms. Although on unequal terms, people move among nation-states more frequently than before. Reflecting change, but also revealing disjuncture between dominant ideologies of nationalism and sociopolitical reality, *trans*nationalism suggests that major social forces and actual people on the landscape transcend the borders and policies of states. The notion that a country defines a clear territory and a particular culture, as appealing as it might be, does not correspond with reality.

In terms of identity, transnational suggests that an individual holds multiple ways of orientation of self to other. Beyond the layering of kin and gender, we have potential for multiple cultural and geographic bases of connecting to and distinguishing from Others. For example, a Native American person is at once a member of a particular Native nation and a U.S. citizen. At the United Nations building, the same person attending the Permanent Forum on Indigenous Issues expresses connection to an indigenous identity with people from all over the globe. Differing manifestations of nation and nationality express themselves depending on context. Transnational means multi-identitied, somewhat confounding conceptions of nationality and nationalism that insist that identity is one-dimensional.

Despite the above emphasis of permeable borders, the institution that maintains them is alive, if under some duress. The state, as a category of polity, still matters. Although real states contend more than ever with multinational corporations, multilateral trade entities, and transnational nongovernmental organizations, they remain preeminent in the maintenance of international borders. States typically labor to control the inflow of people and harbor ambivalence about the outflow of people. At the same time, according to the dominating ideology of international trade, states are to welcome the inflows of products, culture, and capital. Furthermore, under the neoliberal economic policies promoted by the United States and European Union, states are to surrender decisions about the allocation of resources within their borders to the mechanism of markets. Even the exercise of coercive force, the bread and butter of the twentieth-century state, is subject to privatization in the twenty-first-century state. Much of the traditional domain of complex polities is now subject to transnational entities and a borderless force (the market). Yet states demand loyalty and often promulgate ideologies that assert the necessity of cultural homogeneity within their borders. The bifurcation created by the ideology of nationalistic patriotism set against the reality of transnationalism and the policies of neoliberalism has profound effects on the construction of identity (to say nothing of economic life). It brings people, products, and images of varying cultural origins together in spaces that are theoretically culturally homogeneous. This comingling of culture occurs in the context of increasingly marketized and individuated competition in which one is expected to feel community through a state.

Allowing for an important (but not totalizing) role of the state in social life reinvigorates Mead's approach to better understand cultural self through cultural Other. The context for most of the dances examined here is the United States, a state society predominated by the descendants of immigrants, generally hostile to immigration, and largely ignorant of its first peoples. Viewed from this perspective, the set of dances examined in this work offers a glimpse into the construction and maintenance of an array of broad categories of identity within U.S. society. White and Latino are predominant ethnic labels and are both represented in dance that references indigenous culture, sometimes claiming ethnic Other as a part of self, sometimes using ethnic Other to define self through opposition. Too often ignored in treatments of U.S. ethnicity, Native culture (or imagined Indianness when deployed by whites) is the source material for these other categories of identity. Not surprisingly, Native people contest the use of their cultures in identity construction both in dance and in more direct political activism.

To make this discussion of identity in U.S. society truly anthropological requires some comparative outside reference point. In this case, distinct histories and radically different scale and power between Guatemala and the United States offer us an opportunity to compare similar issues in divergent settings. In these two countries that seemingly share little more than proximity, the nonindigenous deploy ideas about indigenous culture to construct satisfying identities, and the indigenous struggle with the representations of themselves and their culture by Others. White sports fans and elite Guatemalans find strikingly similar values in symbolic Indianness. In turn, American Natives and Guatemalan *indígenas* respond to their respective states and dominating societies in similar ways.

In this book I consider each of the above dance genres, exploring common themes of identity, authenticity, and globalization. However, before unpacking the dances specifically, some groundwork regarding definitions and basic theoretical framework is necessary. In Part One, I examine dance as a sociocultural phenomenon, how dance intersects with key dimensions of identity and power in globalized contexts. I also elaborate how I use the concept of secular ritual to examine dance. As the construction of *authentic* identity is a common goal of the dances in question, I analyze the concept of authenticity in Part One. Following these introductory chapters, in order, I treat K'iche' traditional dance, Native American powwow, folkloric dance inspired by Mesoamerican culture, and dancing Indian sports mascots.

MK

NOTES

1. I use "Indian" to describe the culture and society of Native peoples as imagined by politically and economically dominating Others.

2. I use the term "indigenous" to discuss Native nations and individuals from the European invasion of the Americas to the present. This term presents some difficulties but is superior to alternative terms and also, particularly as explored by Ronald Niezen (2003), has global implications. We find common state policies and common strategies in response and, perhaps most importantly, growing political cooperation among peoples of diverse aboriginal cultures. As such, it is used to self-identify and find connections with other peoples who have faced and survived similar histories.

3. By stylistic convention and for more substantive reasons, I am cautious with the term "American." Too often it is read as meaning white and mainstream, the cultural and social forms of the dominant socioeconomic group. While acknowledging that the United States, like other nation-states, produces distinct styles, worldviews, notions, and other cultural expressions, it also produces a diversity of such expressions. This variety and the contributions of various other peoples, classes, and groups to culture labeled "American" are frequently underestimated. Moreover, the United States shares the North American continent with two other nation-states and the Americas with many more. Latin Americans, who are apt to note that they too are Americans, deploy "Estadounidense" to identify their non-Canadian northern neighbors. The term, however, is a bit cumbersome to the English reader. "Gringo" serves as well to identify people, culture, and objects from the United States, but it is easily as pejorative as "Estadounidense" is unpronounceable. Accordingly, I use "United States" as the noun form and "U.S." as the descriptor. When referencing that collection of ideas and forms that garner a degree of privilege in mass media and are largely associated with whiteness, I use the term "mainstream." "American" is used, but in contexts where I deliberately problematize the concept.

Acknowledgments

Many contributed to the completion of this book. To thank them all is impossible, but I express my gratitude to the following. Munro Edmonson and Victoria Bricker provided both the mentoring and scholarly foundation that gave my interest in human identity focus and framing. Judith Maxwell introduced me to fieldwork in Guatemala and identified the community and institution that became central to my development as an ethnographer. My field consultants in San Miguel Totonicapán were gracious and patient hosts, collaborators who on various occasions sensed where my understanding was weak and helped me get it right.

I am also indebted to many colleagues at North Central College who encouraged and supported me. In particular, Donald McVicker provided wise advice and feedback that were crucial to getting this book off the ground. He was also an invaluable sounding board as I developed my ideas and labored to connect and compare divergent forms of dance. Additionally, Mara Berkland and Paloma Martinez Cruz read early drafts and provided vital encouragement and thoughtful critique. In addition to my colleagues, I am grateful to my students for their thoughtful questions and revealing comments.

Most of all I am grateful to my family, who frequently accompany me to the field and were more than understanding about "Daddy and his book."

And, finally, I express my appreciation to the dancers who made fieldwork interesting and enjoyable.

INDIGENOUS DANCE AND DANCING INDIAN

Part One

Introduction

One

Dance, Culture, and Identity

Peeking above the trees of Grant Park, the tops of some of Chicago's most famous buildings scrape a perfect clear blue July sky. The lakefront park is taken over by the Taste of Chicago, a mega-festival featuring cuisine from scores of the city's numerous and diverse restaurants. In addition to food, "The Taste" offers entertainment. The city provides a number of performance venues, and reflecting a strategy that embraces (and channels) ethnic diversity, it has invited the Mexican Dance Ensemble of Chicago to perform on the "Fun Time Stage." The stage anchors an open meadow lined by booths and tents oriented to children and parents and even a merry-go-round (but no beer vendors). The space and presentation construct not only ethnic diversity, but appropriate family fun as well.

As it is Sunday morning, the festival is lightly attended and the audience is small. The performance, however, is enthusiastic. Dress and props are carefully controlled, uniform. In one presentation, all the men wear identical pants, boots, and bandanas, although their belts vary slightly. The backs of their identical jackets are adorned with identical appliqués featuring the iconic Mexican image of eagle, snake in beak, perched on a cactus. In another performance, women's costumes are identical in form down to matching earrings, although their flowing layered skirts vary in color. This visual, near-complete sublimation of individual to group (and culture) extends to movement and sound. The dancing is crisp; bodies are coordinated tightly to one another and to the music. The effect is particularly dramatic in pieces that feature stamping. The perfect simultaneity of several dancers stamping in unison with the beat of the music overtly communicates precision of performance. Beneath the surface are more subtle messages about unity in the expression of tradition.

Viewing the performance reminds me of other forms I have been observing. Traditional K'iche' dance, partly because it is fundamentally narrative, features vestments, masks, and steps that vary by character but adhere to convention for each figure. Powwow dancers construct regalia and perform dances that afford a greater degree of personal expression within general aesthetic guidelines. All, however, to a varying extent, articulate individual dancer to dance convention.

1.1. Unity in the Expression of Tradition. Members of the Mexican Dance Ensemble of Chicago perform at Taste of Chicago, July 2006. (Photograph by author.)

I approach dance not as a choreographer or as a dancer, but as a social scientist interested in how people form, contest, and communicate culture (and particularly the culture of identity). However, dance is linked in the popular imagination to anthropology more than it is actually investigated by anthropologists. This is unfortunate as dance is instructive of cultural knowledge and social practice to insiders and outsiders alike. It communicates overt information about the current state of social affairs but also tacit information about the conduct of social affairs and even the nature of human experience.

However, before getting into dance as a cultural and social act, some attention to defining it specifically is warranted.

Dance is diverse and difficult to define, and the focus here necessarily favors depth of field over sharp clarity. At root, dance involves formal, intentional movement. This intentional movement, even in its "free" forms, involves some degree of bodily conformity to socially shared conventions. Music is common but not necessary to dance. Continuing the notion that individuals express connection to group and convention through dance, rhythm, an essential component of music, provides an auditory framework to organize particular (or particle-like) dancers into coordinated movement. As such, dance enacts the coordination of individuals to group through convention. It may help to employ a common metaphor articulated by early thinkers in social science.[1] If we take human society as an organism, dance provides a code for forming cells into organs and organs into organism. It is more complex, however, than individuals simply articulating themselves bodily to convention.

The commonality of dance across a wide variety of societies reflects a basic challenge of human social organization. Regardless of scale and complexity, societies must articulate individuals with self-awareness and self-oriented drives to group purposes. The degree to which human beings share knowledge and cooperate socially marks us as a species and is at the root of our adaptive fitness. Alone we are slow and weak, but together, sharing accumulated knowledge through symbolic systems of communication, we become the world's dominant species. In social *groups*, from families to communities to polities, the human potential is realized. Although it is clear that individual human beings survive and thrive in social groups, we do not generally follow the guidelines expressed in our cultures blindly or perfectly. Cooperating with the group necessarily entails sublimation of some individual desires, and we do not always go along happily or willingly. The challenge for any society, then, is creating schemes of social organization that compel conformity but accommodate individual needs and capacities. Varying by culture, history, economy, environment, and so forth, societies have developed a dizzying array of solutions to this fundamental human problem. This is not the place for an ethnology of individual and society, but a clear and logical pattern exists. Rigid structures that rely heavily on coercion foment social tension. Loose and fluid social organizations—the type typically found among foraging bands—afford a great deal of individual autonomy and defuse social tension. Most societies exist somewhere in between, requiring more persistent organized social structure than foraging bands but relying on a combination of avenues for human expression within group conformity. This balance is never perfect, and to get people to go along sometimes requires more direct articulation of ideology and use of force.

I draw a deliberate parallel between this diversity of articulation of individual to group and the diversity of dance form. This is not to say that foragers always have free and loose dance forms that reflect their economy and social organization or that stratified complex societies produce exclusively rigid hierarchical forms of dance. Rather, dance establishes concrete patterns of body conformity (in dress and in movement) and concrete patterns of spatial relations among individuals. It, in effect, enacts and works on that basic challenge of human social organization. When individuals dance they embrace or challenge tradition and express conformity or individualism. It may complicate or make the picture more interesting to point out that, varying by genre and context, dance allows the individual to do all of these things at once. A dancer can follow tradition and innovate while expressing individualism that conforms to the norms of the group. As such, dance is about two basic human tensions: between cultural continuity and cultural change at the collective level and between individual expression and group conformity at the personal level.

Accordingly, dance is an ideal context for members of a society to express, to contest, to contemplate how individuals should be articulated to group. If we accept this basic premise, dance then informs an array of related topics that are governed by the culture of social organization. Most obvious among these are the norms of social interaction. Perhaps more than specific rules, dance asserts the notion that human social interactions are rule-governed. It may tell us how men and women are to interact (e.g., who is to "lead," in the common English metaphor taken from dance) but the constant is that these relations are not random. Rules that govern who does what and when they do it exist in life and in dance, sometimes clear, sometimes tacit.

So enters the topic of social status, those categories of interaction that organize individuals into social structures. Rules of social discourse are informed by roles connected to social statuses held by individuals that are activated in particular social settings. Statuses and associated roles may be hierarchically arranged, and dance can embrace and enact or challenge and invert rank. Accordingly, dance is about rule-governed social behavior, social statuses inhabited by individuals, and the arrangement of these statuses (hierarchical or otherwise). How it fits individuals into group says something about the nature of personhood itself. In dance (as in society) people come together and follow, bend, or break the conventions of social life. Dance sets itself apart from more common activities by doing all of this in an overt and formalized fashion. As such, the anthropological definition of dance that I propose is as follows: intentional, formalized movement of bodies that expresses and contests shared ideas about social structure (including its norms, statuses, and notion of personhood) and the articulation of individuals and groups to social structure.

At this point I begin to narrow the focus to a specific category of dance. The forms I described in the opening paragraphs are *representational* dances. To define representational dance, some exploration of *representation* as a concept is necessary. Representation is a heavily loaded term whether employed by social scientists or other social actors. It has social, cultural, artistic, and political dimensions. Basic to human culture are the variety and intensity with which we use acts and objects to stand for or signify concepts and other acts and objects. We experience life through systems of symbols. A combination of sounds represents, by convention, an idea; representation is linguistic and symbolic. Moreover, in language and particularly in art and performance, representations are multivalent. Acts and objects represent multiple ideas, some explicit and highly conventional, others tacit and circulated in subsets of a society.

Representation, however, is about more than symbols and meanings. It has clear political and material dimensions as well. Politicians in democratic societies (ideally) represent their constituents. In disputes, attorneys represent their clients. Beyond the ideals of democracy and peaceful resolution of conflict, social inequality is reflected in representation. A given segment of society (e.g., men) may be overrepresented among formal governing bodies or in the organization of economic production. Others (say, women) may be underrepresented in politics and economy. Compounding problems of underrepresentation, minority or marginal peoples are frequently *mis*represented either by well-intentioned but ethnocentric advocates or by compromised but official bureaucrats and politicians.

The point of stressing the complexity of representation is to bring to the surface how a given act can have both symbolic and political dimensions. Particularly useful to the present discussion is Terrence Turner's (1992, 2002) treatments of Kayapo (Xingu River Basin, Brazil) use of audiovisual technology as a medium of self-representation. Turner responds to critics who assert that the incorporation of high-tech video equipment undermines Kayapo culture because its origin is outside of their horticultural and foraging lifeway. Turner counters that it is not the medium of expression or the stabilization of expression in repeatable images that matters as much as the relationships among those who represent. Through shot composition, editing choices, and other technical aspects of filmmaking, the Kayapo have made video their own. They indigenize technology in two ways. They use it to express a distinct Kayapo worldview but also to effect political power and protect themselves from the "developmentalist state" of Brazil (Turner and Fajans-Turner 2006:3). As such, the resulting video products are complex technically and in the audiences that they attempt to reach. Turner terms the consequent multiplicity of messages (some available only to some members of the audience) "polyphony" (2002). Kayapo leaders contest and construct power through their use of complex metaphorically loaded speechmaking that is compelling to other Kayapo. Video aimed at and circulated among wider audiences serves to shame state officials and state institutions and thus undermines attempts to realize developmentalist policies. Turner (2002:246) concludes that "power is an effect of representation," not the other way around. Kayapo motivate one another to action, build alliances with other indigenous groups, and reach sympathetic nonindigenous outsiders through acts of representation that are symbolically compelling in multiple ways. Kayapo video, then, is representation of concepts through symbols and images that also seek to effect and protect collective political autonomy or self-representation.

What, then, makes a dance representational? Drawing on the work of Nahachewsky (1995) and Trimillos (1995), Anthony Shay, in *Choreographing Identities*, discerns between "representational and social modes" of dance (2006:27). However, as I outlined earlier, it is clear that dance is inherently social *and* representational. If the premise that dance is cultural behavior is accepted, then all dance represents a myriad of ideas about social life. What sets representational dance apart is its emphasis on deliberate representation, what it attempts to represent, and how it does so. First, representational dances are performed publicly, with a clear division between performers and audience. They intentionally construct images and messages intended for viewers who do not directly participate in the dancing. Although representational dance is performed in a context of socializing and socialization, it is not social in the sense of a prom. Just as a video recording of a political meeting is not actual decision making, courting may be referenced in representational dance, but the performance is not a part of actual courtship. Although distinct forms exist, Shay is careful to avoid reification of the categories of dance that he deploys, favoring instead the concept of "parallel traditions" (2006:9–14). Forms coexist. A dance presented in a formal venue in front of a paying audience may draw on several forms that are danced "in the field" (Shay 2006:9). Field dances, in turn, are enacted on various social occasions, at weddings, as rituals, and so forth. Shay rejects the evolutionism that has plagued the social sciences, recognizing that "dances in the field" and representational dances coexist. The modern does not replace the traditional but re-creates (or re-presents) it in novel settings. In short, representational dance is distinguished among various other dances by its *overt* theatricality.

Representational dances also differ from other forms in the relationship between audience and performer. First, as indicated above, an audience is necessary for representational dance. This is not to say that other kinds of dances are never observed. Rather, whereas representational dance requires an audience, social or sacred dancing can occur without spectators. Without an audience, representational dances are rehearsals. Second, dance forms vary in composition of performer and audience. Where social and sacred dances are generally performed within social groups, representational dance, particularly in the global era, is performed with audiences that include insiders and outsiders. Indeed, as I will explore below, sometimes the whole point of representational dance is to perform for outsiders. As such, it is appropriate to consider what a representational dance can say about collective identity as well as individual identity. In short, *what* representational dance works to construct is a unique cultural tradition, the foundation of identity. Similar to video described by Turner, representational dance is an intersection of politics and image, wherein performance works to influence and even compel insiders and outsiders.

DANCE AND ETHNICITY

Don Diego was a familiar client at the morería of my apprenticeship. He organized a dance group that performed the Dance of the Conquest, and his young son was learning traditional dance by taking a child's role in the Dance of the Mexicans. He had become comfortable enough with my presence that he invited me to an event he was hosting at his home. Although I did not know it at the time, that day on Don Diego's land would become one of the most important in my fieldwork. I would learn that a form of popular theater that I saw primarily as a tale about politics was as much about cosmology and mythology. I would come to better understand the effect of manipulating symbols in ritual and to learn of the power of kuux *(clandestine liquor distilled from fruit). As with much of my fieldwork, I cannot claim such a day resulted from intentional "research design" or the like. I am fairly certain in retrospect that Don Diego invited Chepe (one of my teachers) with me, to ensure that I would attend. Lest the ethnographer from the States get lost or forget, Don Diego arranged for an escort. He seemed to have had an interest in my getting the significance of traditional dance right. He may have had a sense that we ethnographers, who pride ourselves on interpreting meaning, sometimes miss the point.*

On that morning, during a ritual in celebration of the day of the Holy Cross, I learned that the red-masked Ajitz, a religious practitioner in the Dance of the Conquest, represents east, the traditional association of red in the Maya color-direction cosmology. The character and the dance had whole other layers of meaning that I was just beginning to grasp. While this play about the military defeat of the K'iche' was still about ethnic conflict, it was also about a particular Maya ordering of the world.

Ajitz was not the only character that would become more layered that day. I had come to realize that the white-masked Monacho character represented a particular strategy for dealing with powerful ethnic Others. This indigenous character, in some versions of the dance, assists the Spanish, guides them, and even betrays K'iche' military plans to the invaders. I had read Monacho as a symbol of betrayal, of placing self-interest above community, of how not to be Maya in a general sense. Chepe made clear just how salient the character was as a lens for contemporary events. In the woods, away from the road, away from Don Diego's house and milpa, Chepe steered our conversation to Monacho. It seems that the character more than represents sixteenth-century division among the Highland Maya. Chepe explained to me that through Monacho we could better understand the behavior of people at specific events. In fact, the stories in the paper about a military officer implicated in gross human rights violations were also stories about an indigenous man who had been led astray by the promises of power and wealth offered by the powerful ethnic Other, just as Monacho had been.

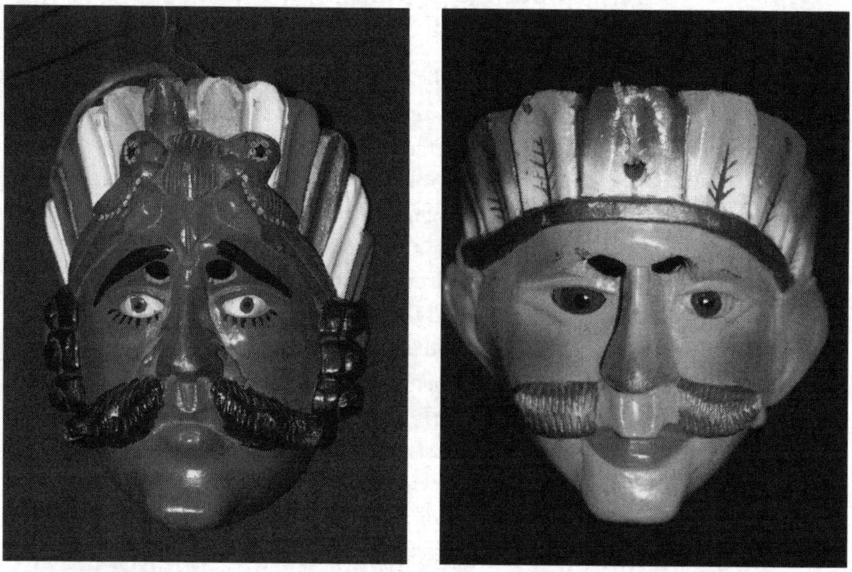

1.2. Treason and the Traitor. Masks for Monacho from the Guatemalan Dance of the Conquest reflect changes in the character's approach to the invading Spanish. Monacho begins the conquest story loyal to the Maya (left) *but eventually aids the Castillians* (right)*. Collection of the Morería Nima' K'iche', December 2007. (Photograph by author.)*

Interestingly enough, dance in the modern popular imagination is a common marker of exoticism. From the mindless movie entertainment of *Krippendorf's Tribe* to the operatic art of Bizet's *Carmen*, we imagine and present Others as *dancing* Others. While dance in general says something to members of social groups about their shared notions of personhood, social order, norms of interaction, and so forth, representational dance, by definition, is observed by outsiders as well. So we enter the domain of identity relative to Others.

More specifically, we address forms that dwell on how we are different culturally from them. That is, representational dances are frequently about ethnic identity.

Anthony Shay has remarked that dance is a particularly effective way to represent ethnicity. "[D]ance constitutes one of the major vehicles for ethnic reinvention and the construction of ethnicity, identity, and heritage" (2006:56). As I outlined above, there are a number of features of dance that suit it well to constructing images and messages about ethnicity. A group of people dancing together necessarily speaks to the nature of human interaction in a larger sense. Adding music and specialized dress gives to presenters the means to construct complex ideas about tradition and culture in addition to tacit notions of social discourse. Moreover, the theatrical dimension of representational dance introduces the possibility of performing for a culturally diverse audience. It should not be surprising that ethnicity is frequently danced.

Beyond the qualities of dance to embody it, ethnicity has two basic characteristics that compel people to express it both through mundane social discourse and through art and performance. First, ethnicity is contested. It relies on opposition for its construction and is often a way to label actors in conflicts over wealth and power. Second, for a variety of reasons, ethnicity is difficult to conceptualize in everyday language. For present purposes, I define ethnicity broadly as categories of identity based on shared culture and history that are activated in social settings marked by cultural diversity. While some distinction among ethnic groups, indigenous peoples, and ethnonationalist movements is warranted,[2] here I focus on ethnicity as a principal mechanism of identity formation present in all people. Like race, ethnicity is a social construction. Both seek to sort and classify continuous human diversity into a limited set of named categories. Both are bound to the social contexts where they are deployed and both are dependent on social interactions in their creation and for their continuance. However, simply interchanging the terms confuses the matter. Ethnicity differs from race in that it emphasizes cultural and historical markers of identity over ones of *presumed* biological diversity. This is not to say that ethnic categories never reference "blood," skin color, or other outward features of human diversity. Rather, ethnicity subordinates biological difference to cultural, social, and historical differences.

Ethnicity does not always generate social conflict, but it is cognitively oppositional. In other words, ethnic identity cannot define itself without some sort of Other. Among people with whom we share identity, our ethnicity is not primary; ethnicity is activated in social discourse marked by cultural diversity. This is not to suggest that ethnicity is only about labeling and sorting of individual social experience. It also provides the material for the emotive connections of social bonding. Through the stuff of ethnicity—shared symbols, practices, experiences, and memories—human beings form social groups. Human social groups, no matter their basis of composition, instill a sense of identity and purpose in individuals. When social groups operate in economic or political realms, they function to produce, protect, and compete for wealth and power. Given the degree to which persistent and growing social and economic inequality dominates globalized relationships, it should not come as a surprise that ethnicity often becomes the means through which stratification is constructed and contested. At times popular notions of progress attribute the accumulation of wealth and power to particular cultural features. Others disagree and point to social privilege obtained by virtue of ethnic inequality. Social stratification is both justified and challenged in terms of ethnicity. As is the case with most social relations in a world marked by inequality, power matters in ethnic relations.

Attachment to ethnic identity is founded on more than actual social groups and contemporary cultural diversity. To share ethnicity with someone is to share a particular history, and that shared memory generates a sense of connection rooted in the past. Histories of conflict deepen our sense of connection and may generate actual conflict. Defeats become sources of grievance, memories that rally people to social action and commitment to the group. Victories become sources of pride, but they also provide privilege that must be justified, protected, and defended. Although academic discussion of ethnic conflict often emphasizes the suffering of the weak, the need of the privileged to justify their positions and their fear about losing such advantages also drives ethnic conflict.[3]

The process through which the powerful justify power and by which the weak are subordinated generates negative stereotyped notions of the weak (that are worked through class, caste, race, or ethnicity). In the process, stereotypes both confirm and extend social inequality. Accordingly, the ideology and images of ethnic identity are highly charged foundations of power and stratification. The powerful insist that the weak are stupid, simple, natural, and so forth. The weak challenge and invert ideologies of the powerful, even as they seem to comply with them. Accordingly, this realm of interethnic relations is a social domain that takes on a culture of its own. In sustained relations, this interethnic culture becomes regularized, building its own set of norms of interaction. This is not to say that the symbols and behavior of border maintenance are the culture as a whole. Particularly in conflict or in persistent and gross inequality, interethnic relations manifest symbols and conceptions of the source cultures that are distorted and often oversimplified. The weak appear subservient and simple or even fulfill more specific stereotypes of the powerful as a matter of survival. To take unequal ethnic relations as the entire culture of the weak is poor social science, prone to reiterate stereotypes.

Actors in ethnic conflict do not always directly address material and political issues. As shared history is a fundamental element of ethnic identity, the past itself is contested. Not only what happened but what it meant are subject to debate. Thinking of ethnic relations as potentially conflicted and of this conflict having both material and ideational dimensions helps explain why ethnicity is danced. The semi-integrated global economy raises the stakes and puts actors in close real and virtual proximity. Contestation of power and wealth manifests in the usual channels, in public policy debates, in protest and strikes, and in capital's pursuit of low wages. It also plays out in *image*. Representational dance is evocative and effective in the creation of ethnic images. Its performance provides a venue to assert and contest ethnic ideology.

Beyond the overt politics of inequality, ethnicity is danced because it is part of a difficult area of human society: social identity. Human beings need to classify and make order of every dimension of experience. Identity in general is about just this process of categorization of social reality, of ourselves and the various Others that we encounter. Within tightly knit social groups and communities, we sort such experience primarily through gender, kin, and age. Outside of intimate settings, we create and employ other systems of classification: caste, class, race, ethnicity. Categories of social identities, across cultures, form along various composites of these axes, and an individual's identity is rooted in a collection of such positions. As a result, even in small-scale societies, individual and group identities are complex and multilayered. Ethnicity, then, works to classify and sort experience within the larger and untidy domain of social identity.

Three dimensions of ethnicity make it a particularly complex level of identification. First, interethnic relations present challenges to social discourse, bringing together people whose norms of social interaction may differ substantially. Second, ethnicity is conceptually slippery, employing multivalent and unstable symbols to represent identity. Third, ethnicity has the potential to generate abstract cover categories of identity that become remote from actual social relations.

As norms of behavior are culturally conditioned, some accommodation is necessary in intercultural relations. Sometimes we simply read the Other through our own culture and fumble along. In sustained relations more regular adjustments are made. Even in stable interethnic relations, where interethnic relations form a regular social domain and acquire their own culture, how we act and understand ethnic Others involves a degree of uncertainty not present in our relations with those more familiar.

Ethnicity is a muddied concept not only because it works in an area of experience that is already difficult but also because it is inconsistent in the symbols it deploys. Sometimes religion is a primary marker of ethnicity. Other times it is language, and at still others it is economic practice, such as the role of corn farming in marking a Guatemalan as indigenous. Moreover, these various labels may be referenced inconsistently, depending on social context; not all Maya are corn farmers. In fact, at times, ethnicity goes unnamed. It is unactivated in settings where we interact with folks with whom we share culture. However, social instability and social inequality both raise the potential for competition and conflict, and ethnic identity that has gone unmarked can become primary.

As not all ethnicity is marked by the same kinds of symbols, not all groups with ethnicity are the same. Groups who share culture and history include small, politically marginalized indigenous groups and large, yet still marginalized, indigenous groups, and even wealthy Native nations. Ethnic groups can be minorities within larger states but majorities in some regions of the same state. Some ethnic groups are less territorialized and more integrated, but not necessarily on equal footing.[4] So, a variety of human groups and identities form around notions of shared culture and history.

Just as ethnicity is part of a larger system of human identity, so is ethnic community subject to a range from real to imagined social connection. Some social groups we inhabit require little imagination as we encounter the members of the group regularly in real face-to-face interactions. Other communities, more remote from face-to-face social discourse, are more difficult to conceptualize. Nationality and the nation-state require us to imagine ourselves as members of what Benedict Anderson (1983) termed "imagined political communities." In such imagined communities we share membership among large masses of people, the vast majority of whom we will never encounter in face-to-face interaction. In other words, some of our layers of identity are expressed in concrete social spaces with corporeal human beings. Other parts of identity are abstractions, broad categories that cannot be experienced in actual social interaction. As a species, however, we evolved and have spent the vast majority of our time in small face-to-face social groups. Consequently, we tend to find the actual social group more satisfying than the abstract imagined one. Larger, abstract levels of identification require something more to make them socially meaningful.

Beyond issues of scale of identity group, broad categories present cognitive challenges. Broad categories of classification inevitably encompass significant diversity, whatever domain of experience they attempt to sort. In classifying social reality, high-level, abstract categories imply that widely varied individuals are essentially the same. The inevitable divergence of particular human beings from the expectations entailed in generalized labels of identity presents certain cognitive and social challenges. As the gap between actual experience and high-level abstract categories widens, the likelihood of cognitive dissonance, that uneasy feeling when our conceptual framework fails to make order of what we encounter, increases. Not surprisingly, broad categories of identity are often the subject of political discourse and art. Which characteristics are associated with a given abstract level of identification are frequently contested.

Expansive nationalist identity categories are not the only ones that demand abstraction and imagination. Pan-ethnic classifications also subsume a good deal of human diversity under broad categories. Often the product of colonialism, pan-ethnic categories group peoples inhabiting large geographic areas together based on general shared history or culture. For example, one may be classified as Asian by virtue of living in, coming from, or having ancestry in a wide variety of countries, many of which themselves are profoundly diverse. The pan-ethnic classification Latino, which I will explore in more detail later, reflects similar wholesale lumping. The countries of Latin America are culturally, linguistically, politically, and economically diverse, reflecting varied histories, geographies, and so forth. Within their borders additional diversity abounds. Yet, a person (or her descendants) born and raised in any of these varied places upon arrival in the United States is classified, usually primarily, as Latina.

The obvious question is, why do we form categories of identification that are so general? In the case of Latino (or Hispanic) some of the answer lies with the bureaucratic needs of states (here, specifically the U.S. state). States, one way or another, count, sort, and classify people and in such processes are seldom interested in highly refined systems of classification. The breadth of such categories also reflects the political power of the dominant sectors of a given society. To be able to decide how people are sorted and identified is an exercise of power. Those who enjoy social privilege enjoy the ability to encounter social reality with a simple system of classification—us and them—with a few superficial refinements. In the process, certain kinds and a limited degree of diversity are made official, while other diversity goes unnamed. Representational dance is used to express ethnicity but in a multitude of ways, sometimes presenting localness, and uniqueness but at others stressing broader, more imagined political communities. As such, the identities constructed in dance considered in this work are connected by form as well as by content. White, Latino, and Native are all rather broad, abstract identity categories. Each classification, in its way, subsumes regional, class, and cultural diversity under one label. In one of the cases considered presently, whites who adopt Indian sports mascots assert their ability to define the image of a politically marginalized Other. All Indians are (at least partly) Plains Indians in the world of sports mascots.

However, state and social power only partly explains the persistence of occasionally confusing pan-ethnic classifications. Those who are grouped together have reason to maintain their categories as well. For Latinos and Native Americans political voice and power are found in embracing a label that unifies peoples of various nations and cultures. There also lurk, however, in broad pan-ethnic identities, the twin dangers of overgeneralization and inaccuracy. Not every Native American is a Plains Indian and not every Latino is Mexican or Puerto Rican. (Nor, for that matter, is every white person wealthy and powerful and every African American poor and marginalized.)

The prolific (if unequal) circulation of people and the mass distribution of image so characteristic of globalization create an unprecedented multiplicity of cross-cultural interaction (real and virtual). The underlying complexity of human identity only further complicates matters. Construction of twenty-first-century ethnicity is multifaceted and shifting work. Similar to our cognitive work in spiritual life, it deals with something that is quite difficult to conceptualize and express in everyday language. Also, like religion, in certain circumstances ethnicity can be totalizing, the only level of identity that matters. In the following section I will endeavor to explain the roots of the power of representational dance to express this confusing but salient feature of life on the twenty-first-century globe. In doing so, I also establish a conceptual framework through which I will analyze specific forms of dance.

REPRESENTATIONAL DANCE AND SECULAR RITUAL

As my wife drops me off a block east of Memorial Stadium, it occurs to me that it is a beautiful day for football. The sky is clear, the air warm with a pleasant cooling breeze. As impressive as the weather is the similarly enveloping effect of the social environment. The deployment of the color orange in t-shirts, hats, flags, tents, stadium seat cushions, bumper stickers, and so forth is pervasive enough to make me self-conscious of what I thought was an unexceptional blue t-shirt. The messages carried on these varied fields of orange are often not about what brought me to Urbana-Champaign, the main campus of the University of Illinois. As a result of concerted and sustained local and national activism, the National Collegiate Athletic Association (NCAA) has banned Chief Illiniwek (the "honored symbol" or "racist mascot" of the U of I, depending on perspective) in image and performance. His continued presence has meant that the university will not be allowed to host NCAA championship competitions. At the moment, it appears that this may be the last football season to feature the dancing Indian manifestation of the "Fighting Illini." Retirement of the Chief has not come without considerable resistance from a broad base of students and alumni as well as members of the board of trustees. Beyond the campus, Speaker of the U.S. House of Representatives Dennis Hastert sponsored legislation to prevent the NCAA from implementing its ban on Indian mascots. (His tenure would end before the bill reached the floor.) As a consequence of this vigorous contestation, I expect there to be a proliferation of "save the chief" t-shirts and activities. While the iconic Indian-head image with its solar-like war bonnet appears in all sorts of contexts and the word "Chief" boldly fronts a fair proportion of t-shirts, it seems that just as many messages and symbols identify folks with the university without specifically referencing the imaginary Indian. Moreover, the raucous (and perhaps uncivil) marketplace of ideas that I anticipated with petition drives, protest signs, shouting, and the like is not present. Rather, walking around the stadium in narrowing circles from tailgate/parking areas to entrance gates, I encounter an innocuous marketplace of stuff. I find multiple opportunities to sign up for a University of Illinois credit card and buy t-shirts, hats, programs, food, and beverages, but I do not find a place to sign a petition (to save or retire the Chief).

What impresses most before, during, and after the game is the multiple ways that individuals connect themselves to the university and its various social groups and communities. These expressions of identity mute individuality and emphasize group unity. The sea of orange t-shirts in the student section (magnified by the fact that the opponent is Syracuse) is only one marker of communal identity. Pregame activities include a parade complete with a uniformed band marching in unison. In fact, uniforms of one sort or another are everywhere. Sheriffs who direct traffic, students who offer courteous assistance to visitors, event staff who coordinate parking, ticket takers, cheerleaders, trainers, coaches, and, of course, athletes all wear distinctive clothing that sublimates individual diversity to specific, game-related activities.

It occurs to me that my preconceived ideas about how to approach and understand Chief Illiniwek need modification. The context of athletic contest (particularly football) merits more attention than I had been directing at it. By the end of the day, I conclude that a more complete picture of the Chief emerges when his performance is understood as a secular ritual within a large complex of secular rituals dedicated to community through uniform and formalized behaviors.

To determine what makes a ritual a secular ritual, comparing sacred and representational dance is useful. Representational dance is similar to sacred dance; the latter can be public, and ritual specialists are performers in a sense. Representational dances, however, deal less directly with matters that are beyond the five senses than do sacred dances. As I will describe later, the sacred (or the rituals designed to access the sacred) are sometimes referenced in representational dance but are not central to performance. However, this is not to say that representational dances do not have ritual-like qualities.

What, then, is ritual? For present purposes, I will define "ritual" as symbolic action that is designed to access an order that is not available to the

1.3. Articulation of Individuals to Group Purpose. The University of Illinois marching band performs at halftime, September 2006. (Photograph by author.)

normal five senses. I further note that such symbolic action is routinized to a varied extent. Certain rituals demand precise execution of procedure; others provide actors a degree of room for improvisation. Rituals also typically carry a sense of obligation that sets them apart from other routine human behavior. To miss work is one thing; to fail to conduct a necessary ritual can carry spiritual consequences. Moreover, ritual involves heavy symbolic loading of act and object. It can demand that we rigidly control our bodies and dedicate concentration on extraordinary material culture. Special objects not seen in everyday life are displayed, or regular mundane objects are infused with intense meaning. Moreover, in this environment rich with signification, a given sign often references multiple meanings. Rituals are moments of particularly polysemous symbolic actions and objects. Ritual accesses an unseen order, but it also creates a sense of time and space that transcends everyday mundane experience.

With the exception of individualized forms such as meditation, rituals are highly social behavior. Participation can define one as a member of a congregation, a community, or an ethnic group. Often abstract, difficult-to-express notions and symbols are presented to the group and shared. Much as does good art, good ritual expresses that which cannot be expressed in normal mundane language. Also as does good art, ritual can give people a sense that they have encountered and understood, if only briefly, something profoundly true. Even for the ardent skeptic, expression of nonbelief in the moment of ritual can be exceedingly difficult. Similarly, even the dedicated individualist will find connection to community difficult to deny. As such, effective ritual establishes bases for both conformity and social solidarity.

Developed to apply what anthropologists had learned about ritual in small-scale communities to complex, industrialized societies, the concept achieved some currency following the publication of *Secular Ritual* (Moore and Myerhoff 1977). For reasons not completely clear, secular ritual as a conceptual tool has had a diminished presence in anthropology since the early 1990s. A complementing concept of *civil religion* enjoyed currency among scholars of religion during approximately the same period. Michael Angrosino (2002) has argued for reinvigoration of civil religion as a theoretical framework in anthropology. I agree with Angrosino but favor here the emphasis that ritual places on behavioral culture (whereas religion focuses on the ideational). Moreover, its attention to public representational activities (sporting events, political rallies, concerts, etc.) makes the concept of secular ritual readily employable here.

If a religious ritual is a formalized behavior designed to influence or access the supernatural or sacred, then what is a secular ritual? After all, clear in standard definitions of ritual is the notion of an unseen order, something beyond the five senses. Modifying ritual with *secular* directs us to things more ordinary. The distinction then between secular ritual and other mundane activities is a matter of degree in three areas: the nature of symbols employed, the sociality of performance, and the effect on participants.

All human behavior is symbolic. From speech, which obviously carries messages, to something as simple as donning a hat, what we do is read and interpreted by others. Moreover, these acts carry multiple ideas. *How* one speaks—tone, register, accent, and so forth—tells the listener and audience something about one's identity in addition to the content of the message. What I label "secular ritual" is particularly symbolically loaded behavior that does not make reference or connection to an unseen primary order.

Secular rituals, like sacred rituals, deploy symbols to work on the abstract, sometimes contradictory dimensions of belief and enact them. Both deal in areas that are difficult to express in everyday language. Sacred rituals concern cosmology, the relationship between human beings and the divine, unseen orders. Secular rituals are more rooted in social reality but nonetheless deal with concepts difficult to express in routine speech. In some cases the difficulty derives from political oppression and the associated fear. That is, the messages are unspoken because powerful outsiders deem and make them dangerous. Sometimes messages are unspeakable because they are abstract, contradictory, contested, unresolved, or all of the above. How to be a good human being and locating the social unit in which to be that good person are fundamentally challenging in an era marked by intensive flows of culture and gross inequality. Secular ritual is a way to address this problem of self and communal perception. It is identity in globalized, stratified social settings that necessitates the cognitive work presented in representational dances.

Secular rituals express what Sherry Ortner has termed "key symbols" (1973). Key symbols are particularly salient and loaded symbols that people put to broad use across a wide array of domains of experience. Ortner distinguishes between summarizing symbols and elaborating symbols. "Summarizing" symbols deal with abstractions unifying concepts, the stuff of cosmology, fundamental structures that classify experience. The flag for Americans and the crucifix for Catholics are such symbols; they are powerful and carry an array of meanings that transcend ordinary language. As such, summarizing key symbols present and reinforce the basic shared framework for interpreting experience. They provide the mechanisms by which a group of human beings puts order to a continuous and chaotic reality. "Elaborating" key symbols, particularly "key scenarios," provide schemes or scripts for behavior in contexts beyond their ritual enactment. Where summarizing symbols form the foundation of systems of sorting and understanding experience, elaborating symbols help us *construct* behavior. Key scenarios give our action a reference point and provide us a way to act that makes sense. Not surprisingly, lore, from folktales to creation myths, often constructs key scenarios. Evangelical Christians who cite the Bible and K'iche' Mayas who recount episodes from the *Popul Wuj* both deploy key scenarios to understand, justify, influence, or explain actual behavior.

The representational dances considered here have multiple means to symbolize ideas and moods, such as music, movement, and dress. All are well capable of carrying more than one idea. Music can evoke a feeling; a familiar tune, a whole set of ideas. The stylized dress of representational dance places people in time and place and references all sorts of ideas about "tradition." Coordinated movement, as I explored above, communicates all sorts of ideas about social discourse and social structure. In combination, music, movement, and dress provide a robust, multilayered means of expression. Dance performance, accordingly, expresses at once history, identity, culture, and community. How these ideas are read and what meanings are available, in turn, depend on the cultures and experiences of the audience. As I will detail in later chapters, representational dance constructs elaborating symbols when it deals directly with ethnic identity. It presents notions of how to be a particular kind of person that are transferable to actual interethnic and other social relations. As I examine specific forms of dances more closely, it will become clear that traditional K'iche' dance and Native American powwow also construct key summarizing symbols.

In addition to their symbolic complexity, rituals are social and secular rituals are particularly social. Indeed as I mentioned above, the secular ritual lens has often been used to examine events that feature large audiences or crowds. We social scientists, after all, are as interested in the shared behavior and culture of the group as we are in personal or individual ritualized behavior. In the present case, representational dance is performed for audiences. The coordinated action of dancers and the presence of the audience are all highly social behaviors, some regulated deliberately, some guided by tacit norms. In the process, dense messages of culture and identity are constructed and shared. In the end, to perform dance or to attend representational dance is to engage one's own community and perhaps the communities of Others.

Finally, secular rituals, drawing on Clifford Geertz's often cited definition of religion, work to create "long-lasting moods and motivations" in people (1973:90). Everyday movement in society provides opportunities to behave and observe behavior. These actions, while instructive of culture and identity, tend to reinforce rather than elaborate primary models of behavior. It is ritual that lays out symbols and ideals to contemplate beyond the performance and apply to other settings. As the term "moods" suggests, these are not strictly rational or rationalized norms that are presented and enacted, but ritual, secular or religious, has a strong emotional component. Effective ritual moves people emotionally but also provides rationales for believing and acting. So rituals (sacred or secular) provide cognitive frameworks and bases for embracing particular models of construction of behavior and interpretation of experience.

DANCE AND MYTHS OF IDENTIFICATION

Framing representational dance as secular ritual necessarily introduces the topic of myth. When we consider the relationship between myth and ritual within the domain of the sacred, myths are stories that necessitate and explain rituals, and rituals in turn make real or enact myths. It is in telling myths that the conceptual content of symbols circulates and takes particular form. In some cases dance enacts the myth directly. K'iche' traditional dance, for example, features a clear narrative, telling a story about the past that helps people understand the present. In other cases representational dances of identity deploy symbols of a mythic story or theme, leaving it to performers and audiences to discuss and circulate more general stories.

Long a subject of social science, philosophy, and theology, myth is a common form of storytelling that resists easy definition. A standard introductory cultural anthropology text, *Humanity*, defines myths as "stories that recount the deeds of supernatural powers and culture heroes in the past" (Peoples and Bailey 2003:399). Spradley and McCurdy (2009:300), editors of a widely used ethnographic reader, add that cosmology explains how the world is at present, while mythology explains how it got to be the way it is. These are workable approaches, particularly when we focus on beliefs and practices that are obviously religious in nature. However, human beings tell whole ranges of stories about the past that fall somewhere between the history of documented events and the past of the supernatural, otherworldly, unseen order. Realms of human discourse lie between myth as defined and employed in anthropology texts and history as an evidence-based recounting and interpretation of the past. I retain the notion that myths concern how the world arrived at its current state and that they involve the extraordinary, but I also contend that myths are not exclusively confined to the supernatural.

To illustrate the point, consider two related types of myth: creation stories and origin stories. Both tell us something important about where it all began. The former often include the creation of the cosmos, of important natural features, of the order of nature, of life in general. The latter tend to focus on us, the human component of creation. Moreover, our origins do not end with our creation. We may wander, struggle with the gods, or fight with other peoples before we arrive at who we are. Dennis Tedlock (1993, 1996), in his exploration of the K'iche' Maya *Popul Wuj*, reveals that a story recounting the creation of people also chronicles the rise of the K'iche' as a political force in southern Mesoamerica. The primordial K'iche' enter into a special relationship with Tojil, granter of fire and demander of sacrifice. Later, K'iche' political power is explained and justified by their particular relationship with the supernatural. Conrad and Demarest (1984) note parallels in Aztec mythology. The rise of the Aztec state and empire is tied in myth with the rise of the Aztec patron Huitzilopochtli. Myths of human origin can also be stories of ethnic and political origin.

The obvious question then is how can these various stories of the past be sorted? What are we to make of them? First, let us dispose of the notion that the past is knowable in a strictly objective sense. As popular as it is to demand that historians "teach the facts," the past is an abstraction; only the present is concrete. This is not to say that all stories of the past are equal in purpose or in objectivity or subjectivity. Distance of time and emotion and mode of recording shape the nature of the story. What begins as a shared oral story about the origin of a community can, with time, become a myth explaining the creation of all of humankind. A moment important in local history can become crucial in the construction of stories of national origin.

Such shared history, while possibly rooted in events, derives its power of identification and motivation to action in its telling. As such, it should come as no surprise that myths of origin are told in a way that emphasizes the positive in self and the negative in Others. For example, in telling their communal history, Zapotec Ixtepejanos emphasize victimization of Santa Catarina Ixtepeji by neighboring communities. Events in which they visited suffering on their neighbors are deemphasized (Kearney 1972:37–41). An effective myth of beginnings constructs "the good" and finds it in collective self. So we arrive at a refined definition of myth (or of a particular type of myth). Myths of *identification* are stories about the distant past that create, share, and reinforce positive, meaningful, and satisfying identities in the present. The task of the historian is to determine which stories of the distant past are supported by documentary evidence (and to figure out what constitutes good written evidence). The task of the social scientist is to explore how origin stories are used by social actors at present. The boundaries in practice, of course, are not as clear as I imply. To fully understand a given myth requires a bit of both.

The mainstream story of the first Thanksgiving is a particularly salient example of the representation of indigenous culture in secular rituals. Familiar to anyone who attended primary school in the United States, the first Thanksgiving story relates the past with both historical and mythical dimensions. Celebrated at grade-school pageants across the country each November, the tale is replete with a ritual-like set of standard symbols and artifacts. Turkeys, hats with shoe buckles, and (most germane to the current discussion) pilgrims and Indians crowd gyms and auditoriums. Common narrative elements include the initial pilgrims' struggles to survive, indigenous assistance offered to struggling pilgrims through subsistence knowledge and technology, subsequent bountiful pilgrim harvest, and a feast marked by pious thanks to God and harmonious interethnic relations.

In terms of history, it is clear that the early seventeenth-century Northeast was co-occupied by various indigenous societies and a rapidly expanding population of European colonists. Some colonists were indeed on the continent to escape religious persecution (or at least end their role as victims of it). Others were soldiers, merchants, entrepreneurs, or bureaucrats, among other things. Also true, Algonkian and Iroquoian peoples of the Northeast did (and do) make offerings of thanks at various harvests (or "appearances"; Tooker 1975), a central theme of ritual. Certain also is the success of Northern European colonization of first the East Coast and eventually the entire continent.

In terms of myth, the first Thanksgiving is a loaded text that makes choices, as all myths do. In artifact, Natives are frequently designated by feathered headdresses more reminiscent of Plains peoples than of northeastern Algonkians. Accordingly, the myth references a generalized image of Indianness. How the Europeans are represented also involves some interesting choices. The notion that the first such feast can be narrowed to a particular place is difficult to verify. Indeed, it seems likely that countless bountiful feasts that included ritual giving of thanks were shared between European and Native trading partners before Puritan pilgrims sat down to break bread with their Native neighbors. Trade relations preceded direct colonization and settlement, and the mutual trust necessary for trading partnerships are commonly cemented by ceremonial gift exchange and feasting. Moreover, the strong material incentives to maintain good relations with trading partners created a more convivial atmosphere than Puritanical religious ideology. Although it is not strictly knowable, the first Thanksgiving almost certainly did not include pilgrims (and more likely included French traders).

So why then does the myth select pilgrims? And why are two readily available alternatives not employed? Featuring traders or merchants would reference ambivalence about commerce and highlight the economic exploitation associated with colonization. Deploy soldiers and officers and we enter the sticky area of colonization through the violence of military conquest. The myth, instead, chooses victims of religious persecution to represent European colonists at the first Thanksgiving. Rather than material profit or imperial expansion, the pursuit of religious freedom is emphasized. That those fleeing persecution can be remembered as humble and pious makes pilgrims an even better symbol.

In effect, myth asserts as knowable the unknowable. The less knowable the past, the more latitude of choice available to the myth teller. In addition to choices of place, time, and attendees, the tenor of a feast shared by pilgrims and Indians is difficult to know. In addressing the unknowable, the myth chooses to emphasize peace and harmony. Given the nature of Puritan belief and practice, it seems unlikely that such a feast was not marked by considerable tension. It is difficult for the dedicated purist not to demand similar dedication from others. Would Puritan pilgrims have tolerated non-Christian sacred oratory or ritual offering? Recall that Christian settlers of similar beliefs occasionally drowned accused witches (members of their own communities) for not confessing witchcraft. Indeed, the whole notion of harmonious coexistence strains credulity. That the inheritors of the state that evolved partly from the colonies of these religious refugees would make religious conversion of indigenous people official policy is an unexplored backstory in the myth of the first Thanksgiving. These we see at the first Thanksgiving are tolerant religious Puritans.

So what does this myth do and why do people share and perform it at present? It is in effect a story of national origin. We see it as an important moment in the process by which the United States came into existence. That Native people offered assistance and shared in the feast implies strongly that they accepted (and now accept) colonial domination. By way of corollary, the legitimacy of Euro-American hegemony is asserted and resistance to it is denied legitimacy. All of it is accomplished by victims of persecution in pursuit of freedom, uncontaminated by greed or violence. The first Thanksgiving is indeed an *origin* story. It ends without much reference to the subsequent history. What happens after the feast is left unspecified. Least implied is the notion that Native societies would struggle to retain political autonomy and cultural distinctiveness. Other broader myths (explored later) take up the slack and fill in the blanks. The first Thanksgiving is a tale of beginning (a kind of *first* supper) that leaves the middle available for other myths of vanishing Americans, of self-conquest, of progress.

This myth of national origin is complex. While making choices that present the origin of white identity as uniformly positive, it also depicts aspects of Native culture positively. Dependence of colonists on Native subsistence knowledge and technology is recognized (and contemporary global dependence on myriad domesticates of indigenous origin is at least implied). Natives are cooperative, generous, and peaceful, more noble than savage. As a result of these positive elements, Native resistance has occasionally referenced the story. Seneca leader Sagoyewatha (Red Jacket) took elements of the first Thanksgiving story and put them to counter-hegemonic purposes in an address to the missionary Reverend Jacob Cram in 1805.

> Your forefathers crossed the great water and landed on this island. Their numbers were small. They found friends and not enemies. They told us they had fled from their own country for fear of wicked men and had come here to enjoy their religion. They asked for a small seat. We took pity on them, granted their request, and they sat down among us. We gave them corn and meat; they gave us poison (alluding, it is supposed, to ardent spirits) in return. (Ganter 2006:141, parenthetical note in original)

Based on a few positive elements of the text and their use in political rhetoric, are we to conclude that performing the first Thanksgiving "honors" Native Americans? Because mainstream formal education fails to realistically cover indigenous histories and cultures, does this myth become insurance against forgetting Native history? Is a myth better than simply forgetting? Is it better than self-critical remembering? What are we to make of contemporary Native Americans who contest the myth of the first Thanksgiving, some identifying it as a "National Day of Mourning" (Wilkins 2002:104)?

In this chapter I have explored the social and cultural dimensions of dance. In narrowing the focus to representational dance, I have articulated a common human practice to a common human challenge. Dance, in this light, works to construct identity within and between human social groups. Framing representational dance as secular ritual highlights and allows exploration of the difficult and compelling dimensions of identity. Stories of origin and myths of identification deepen meaning and justify and even necessitate performance.

I have emphasized that all of this takes place in a world marked by intensified circulation of people and images of culture. Given increasing global inequality, cross-cultural representational dances are performed in contexts that are marked by a paradox of familiarity combined with social distance. As such, not only are representations contested, but so is the *quality* of representation. Accordingly, before addressing specific dance forms in Parts Two through Five, the next chapter considers the ill-defined yet powerful notion of authenticity.

NOTES

1. Most notably Spencer (1988 [1877]).

2. This distinction is made by Niezen (2003:6–11) in detail.

3. See Green (1994:236) concerning how fear of the indigenous Other drives policies of state-sponsored violence in Guatemala.

4. Niezen (2003:4–9) and Maybury-Lewis (2002:44–45) agree that there are a variety of types of groups that form around culture and history, but they disagree on whether they can be grouped along a continuum (Maybury-Lewis) or if indigenous groups should be classed as distinct from ethnonationalist ones.

Two

Representational Dance and the Problem of Authenticity

In retrospect, I am convinced that some of the artisans and dancers saw my understanding of K'iche' representational dance as incomplete. I was, perhaps, too concerned with traditional dance, those forms that are performed typically during the fair in honor of the patron saint, that last several hours and have certain and clear roots in pre-Columbian practice. They likely sensed that I had a bias that favored traditional dance as more authentic than the folkloric dances, shorter theaticalized pieces that show a degree of influence of twentieth-century intellectual interest in "the folk." It was true that I had attended folkloric performances at local community events, but I pursued traditional dance performances outside of Totonicapán, sometimes traveling for days to do so. Time in Toto was spent largely in the morería *talking with artisans and traditional dancers. After repeated invitations from a few dancers in the Vanguardia Indígena (Indigenous Vanguard) I recognized that appearing in the upcoming show was very important to them. A gap between what I thought worthy of attention and what was meaningful to my K'iche' consultants persisted. As part of an ongoing effort to adjust focus and broaden my perspective, I decided to join the trip.*

Although Guatemala is a small country, the journey from the K'iche' highlands to the port city of Puerto Barrios on the Caribbean coast is long, involving a number of striking transitions. Cool mountain air gives way to moist tropical heat. Pine forest (which always reminds me of my wife's childhood home on the Cumberland Plateau) is replaced by flora more consistent with popular expectations for a Central American country. The cultural transitions are evidenced primarily in women's clothing. Outfits that include (or are exclusively of) handwoven material expressing Maya identities, aesthetics, and cosmology give way to manufactured clothing that makes Guatemalan women indistinguishable from women of any other place around the Caribbean. Experiencing these shifts in climate and culture over the course of a daylong bus trip helped me better understand the fundamental bi-ethnicity of Guatemala. Attending the cultural revue revealed some of how interethnic relations are negotiated.

At "Chitinimit ('from the hometown') '95" culture was constructed and presented through dance. The Vanguardia Indígena began their journey in a community where they were in the ethnic majority (in excess of 95 percent of the population). They were now to represent all of the highlands and the Maya in general in a nonindigenous (or Ladino) town in the nonindigenous part of the country. A local group of Ladino dancers constructed a version of Guatemalan national identity that was heavily influenced by the ideology of mestizaje *(hybrid national culture derived from Spanish and Maya roots). Garifuna dancers presented their Afro-indigenous culture in song and dance as well. These two visiting groups, K'iche' and Garifuna, constructed identity through dance representations of their own culture. The Ladino hosts built a notion of identity from varied sources, some their own, others intentionally borrowed from indigenous life.*

As the program unfolded, Garifuna performances were much of what I expected—Afro-Caribbean music and colorful flowing costumes. Loosely matching outfits combined pants and skirts of similar red and blue plaids with white blouses and skirts. Woman in straw hats with frayed edges performed a kind of round dance while men provided vocal and rhythmic accompaniment on what appeared to be handcrafted maracas and drums.

The K'iche' performance was similar to what I had experienced before. A courtship-wedding dance was enacted. Women wore handwoven blouses and skirts that they might wear for an actual rite of passage or other special event. Although women in Toto are now apt to wear clothing from a variety of Maya towns, for the performance they chose matching dress in the style that once marked women specifically as Totonicapense. Men dressed in cofradía *(church confraternity) suits whose fabrication I had observed. Calf-length black pants combined with red capes and black waist-length jackets, all brightly embroidered. In sum, the group marked their indigeneity through garb, reconstructed and specialized, but of their own community. To those not familiar with Toto, the men's outfits in particular must have looked unique and perhaps exotic. To those who know the community, the clothing constructed an image that was uniquely Totonicapense.*

In addition to the courtship and wedding dance (a standard of folkloric dancing) the Vanguardia presented bits of particular traditional dances, including the Dance of the Deer. Interestingly, regalia from traditional dance was employed and traditional dance was embodied within folkloric performance—a sort of dance within a dance. Certain accommodations had to be made (in addition to presenting only short excerpts of hours-long dramas). Recorded music replaced live performance on the drum and reed flute. Women participated as masked dancers side by side with men. I began to realize that such adjustments allowed meaningful cultural performance under the control of the people themselves to reach a much wider audience. I would later learn that Mexican folkloric dance creator Amalia Hernández had garnered first renown and eventually criticism for her appropriation of the Yaqui version of the Deer Dance. Here, as they are apt to do, Maya performers inverted context. They appropriated folkloric dance and made it accommodate their regalia and form.

Despite the ability (derived from field experience) to see how the K'iche' forms had been adapted to the venue, it was the performance of the local nonindigenous dance group that was most challenging to watch. Typical of folkloric dance, it referenced Indianness. Specifically, it presented a standardized set of symbols to construct the colonial Indian. Well-practiced performers deployed dress common to the representations of indigenous Others in folkloric dance. Men wore bright white shirts and calf-length pants with red sashes and straw hats. Women wore well-coordinated traje (indigenous dress) of matching patterns. Dances enacted ideal images of life in an Indian village. There were courting, women with their textiles, and a folk Catholic ceremony.

"Matching but manufactured" describes the material and performance. The clothing of neither the men nor the women referenced any town in particular but rather a generalized notion of Indianness, much as the feather bonnet has come to symbolize all Native people north of the Rio Grande. Where the Vanguardia Indígena drew on a combination of current practices and past traditions to assert a multilayered (Maya-K'iche'-Totonicapense) culture and identity, the nonindigenous folk group referenced a one-dimensional conception of Indianness. The carefully matched garb and precisely executed steps demonstrated obvious middle-class privilege; dancers had the cash to buy props and costumes and the time to train and practice extensively. Their performance was professional and polished, but Ladinos dancing as Indians in the presence of actual K'iche' Maya were uncomfortable. Why were such representations necessary, I wondered?[1] Like any group, non-Maya Guatemalans work to construct identities that are satisfying and this often involves referencing the past. As part of a practice also common to culture created by settler societies, the past invoked to create a meaningful sense of Guatemalan was an indigenous one. The performance laid claim to a Maya heritage through stereotyped images of Indians. However, enacted in the presence of actual Mayas, it also referenced the reality of inequality and political strife in the present. This event came immediately to mind when I later read Philip Deloria's Playing Indian (1998). Of varied U.S. efforts to create unique identities from Native cultures, Deloria notes a pattern of cognitive dissonance when the imagined Indian and an actual indigenous person come into proximity.

2.1. Tradition and Folklore. Dressed in traditional dance regalia, a member of Totonicapán's Vanguardia Indígena receives an award for participation at Chitinimit '95. The Guatemalan flag and a prop representing a Classic period stele stand in the background. (Photograph by author.)

At the end of the show, the Vanguardia Indígena was presented an award in appreciation of their participation. As the emcee lauded their contribution to the program, a leader of the group stood by. Pride was evident in his posture and expression. They had worked hard to assert an image of Mayaness of their own making and had set it alongside a notion of Indians meticulously constructed by ethnic Others. In nearly every sense the Vanguardia had created something that seemed much more authentic than their Ladino counterparts could deploy. It was ironic. In Toto, I had seen folkloric dance as inauthentic and here it was a triumph of authenticity. On that day I continued to struggle to unpack my biases about folkloric dance and also reconsidered what is meant by "authentic." An idea that in certain respects was appealing suddenly seemed capricious. Within the same country, the same performance had seemed inauthentic in one context and authentic in another.

If secular ritual is social behavior in which abstract multivalent key symbols are elaborated and exchanged, creating strong moods and motivations in people, the obvious question is, what are these symbols about? The answer has both general and specific dimensions; the latter I will explore in the context of the particular dance genres. While I will examine specific content later, there are some themes that transcend representational dance. Perhaps the most salient but most diffuse concept is authenticity. It is constructed in representational dance and sought by its audiences.

In a world of frequent transnational movement of culture, the authenticity of a particular cultural behavior or cultural artifact is subject to regular judgment and contestation. As societies undergo regular and often rapid changes, authenticity, as it symbolizes stability and truth, is in high demand. In market terms, it is both scarce and valued. Not surprisingly, the authenticity of a commercial production, such as folkloric dances presented by traveling professional companies, is crucial. To be labeled "inauthentic" limits access to important venues and has negative implications for the financial viability of a troupe (Shay 2006:49). Authenticity has implications beyond the market for less material though crucial issues of identity and meaning. For many performers the stakes are less monetary and more existential. Ethnic identities and the symbols used to represent them require an air of authenticity if they are to be satisfying. Judgment of authenticity, then, has political bases and repercussions as well as market ones.

It is when the performers and audiences differ in culture and in power that the politics of authenticity comes to the forefront. Presentation of indigenous culture in performance or material culture is where assessment of authenticity has direct policy implications. States are bound and obligated in their treatment of their indigenous groups by combinations of treaty, constitution, and international standards. While states regularly violate their legal duties to indigenous groups, they nonetheless have incentives to bureaucratically define "indigenous" and to limit (or at least control) the number of people who can claim such status (Niezen 2003:160–164). Authenticity derived from varied markers such as blood quantum, language, economic practice, dress, and so forth is employed by states to define indigenous identity. However, states also respond to pressure from constituent groups. Although indigenous people are often politically marginalized, they have been active in asserting and contesting authenticity and the policies based on authenticity. Accordingly, the intersection of symbols of identity and real economic and political power is where authenticity dwells. But what exactly is authentic? In this chapter I examine authenticity: its definition, its use by social actors, and its characteristics revealed from a social science perspective. I also discuss how we might approach and deal with authenticity.

Defining authenticity requires examination of denotative meaning and its use by social actors. According to the tenth edition of *Webster's Collegiate Dictionary*, something authentic is "2a: worthy of acceptance or belief as conforming to or based on fact . . . b: conforming to an original so as to reproduce essential features . . . c: made or done the same way as an original . . . 3: not false or imitation: real, actual . . . 5: true to one's own personality, spirit, or character." When applied to cultural practices, the conceptual components of authenticity described above carry varied loadings. Perhaps most interestingly, cultural outsiders are often quite confident in judging authenticity even when quite unfamiliar with the particulars of the practice in question. Each generation is prone to bemoaning, triumphing in, or romanticizing the end of authenticity, apparently ignorant that the last generation took a similar position. All of this reflects a set of presumptions about the way culture and technology vary and that authenticity is somehow a generalizable concept, applicable across cultures. In this sense it is a popular or "folk" theory about culture and change.

In this popular usage, an authentic practice is traditional and unchanging. Tradition itself is difficult to define but entails, at the very least, invention in a remote past. We may label something we invent "a new tradition," but the authenticity of a tradition derives from its rooting in the past, and the deeper in the past, the better. The less visible evidence of change is, the more authentic the tradition.

Webster's definition also includes "not false . . . real, actual . . . true." Not surprisingly, truth and purity are key elements of authenticity as employed by social actors. The authentic "truth" here is unsullied dedication to tradition free of outside culture. Not only should a practice show little sign of change over time, but it should be free of contamination by the influence of

Others. At the individual level (in societies that stress individualism) artistic expression is deemed authentic when it reflects the personality and experiences of the performer, which she speaks in her own voice. Extended to the collective, an authentic shared tradition is one derived by the people themselves. This notion of purity penetrates beyond the action or object that is supposed to present a tradition uninfluenced by outside forces (especially those of "Western" origin). Objects, in particular, should be made of pure materials and made by traditional tools and processes. In terms of dances presented by indigenous people, steps, music, and vestments (by the ideals of authenticity often imposed by outsiders) should be original to the people and their ancestors. Traditional songs played on handmade instruments are pure and authentic. Electric amplification, the use of power tools to make the instrument, and instruments that originated outside the group introduce a degree of impurity in the eyes of some consumers of authenticity.

Perhaps one of the most paradoxical dimensions of authenticity is a tendency in performers and audiences to find or locate authenticity in Others and then attempt to appropriate it as their own. In some of the forms examined in this book, dancers and audiences seem to live comfortably with the apparent contradiction that they can create meaningful identities for themselves by dressing and dancing as Others. Beyond performance, though, are some difficult politics. When the Other does not seem as authentic as we would like him to be, is he no longer an Other? What if the Other conceptualizes her authenticity in ways that diverge significantly from the way we imagine it?

To address these questions requires that we step back and attempt to understand authenticity as a cultural practice. Unfortunately, however, anthropology has performed less than adequately when dealing with authenticity. Too often we have claimed or accepted the role of authoritative judge of authenticity, embracing elements of folk theory.[2] Perhaps as much as anything, the field's concept of culture has dealt, at times, poorly with change, tending toward essentialization of a set of characteristics that define a particular group and its culture. Listing essential traits that make a given people who they are was a common anthropological practice and one that assumes authority over something that most social groups feel is theirs to determine. Connected to early models of culture that saw change as an end to a people's authentic distinctiveness has been uncritical acceptance of the notion that authenticity has an objective basis. In other words, we have occasionally applied a conception of authenticity rooted in particular societies to others as if it were universal. In the process, we have been less than complete in the examination of our own motivation and cravings for authenticity. All of this leads to a basic question: what are we to do with authenticity?

The first step involves critically examining the concept, particularly the versions that are authored by our own societies. In the end, as defined by *Webster's* and enacted by its seekers, authenticity is not possible. First, the notion of unchanging tradition is fraught with problems; any tradition was at some point an innovation. Cultures are not static objects but dynamic processes, and all cultures and the practices that they inform change, sometimes slowly, sometimes rapidly. We are better suited by understanding "tradition as a process in which people find meaning in the present through referring to the past" (Eber and Tanski 2002:36). As such, authenticity is relative to social and cultural contexts. Just as the world is filled with culturally distinct peoples, so it is marked by authenticities. The expectation of unchanging tradition in Others reflects the culture and needs of the seekers of authenticity as much as anything.

Second, the notion of pure truth is also not suited to realization. At the individual level, any words that one speaks are bound to language that is shared, fundamentally social in its creation and circulation. Indeed, the notions of authenticity produced by industrialized large-scale societies reflect the concepts of personhood that have tended to develop in such societies. We believe in pure authenticity because we also believe that individuals are products of their own will. We stress individual agency rather than the cultural, social, political, and economic forces that constrain and influence individual choice. As such, we enter the discussion of authenticity with notions about the construction of behavior that are not supported by the close examination of human culture and society. Just as no individual is purely of her own making, all cultural practices are the product of intersections of various influences, some homegrown, others imported or borrowed. In the end, when subjected to a rigid, purist conception of authenticity, no individual or collective practice is authentic.

Although there are obvious gaps between the ideals of authenticity and social reality, it is still important to social actors. Accordingly, social science has an obligation to address it. In doing so, our focus must be on accurate description and thoughtful analysis of the construction of authenticity, its inherent inequalities, and its fundamental subjectivity. Kay Warren and Jean Jackson (2002) deal with the authenticity conundrum by working at detailed consideration of the *construction and deployment of authenticity*. They seek "no absolute standard of authenticity" but consider "authenticators . . . and the production and construction of authenticity" (2002:10). Employing such an approach to indigenous activism and its responses reveals that authenticity has a double-edged quality. An indigenous leader is effective if he or she references culture that is authentic in the eyes of potential allies in the audience. However, the content must be understandable by the audience as well; it often must be expressed in a nonindigenous language or through complex communication technology. Combination of material and behavioral culture of diverse origins (although common to all human societies) is exploited by those opposed to indigenous cultural and political goals. By using Spanish, an indigenous leader may be labeled no longer indigenous (Graham 2002:184). So authenticity can be a weapon for or against those who deploy it in political discourse.

Considering the contestation of authenticity reveals inherent inequalities that are expressed in how it is judged and who gets to judge it. In particular, those who enjoy positions of privilege in the global era also enjoy the privilege of judging authenticity. As a result, our treatment of authenticity must take into account how it reflects inequality of power and distributes consequences rather unevenly. Examining the inequalities of authenticity means recognizing that it is a product of the linked processes of industrialization and colonial expansion.

European expansion brought Europeans into contact with peoples profoundly distinct from their previous experience. Industrialization brought fundamental changes, including the depersonalization of production and anonymous urban life. The cultures of Others encountered through colonialism seemed exotic and were imagined to be unchanging. Moreover, from these colonized peoples, core economies extracted resources and gained markets. Additionally, some intellectuals within the core colonial powers (including anthropologists) saw in the cultures of the colonized a means to counter the alienating changes present in their own societies. Various folk and crafts movements that developed in core countries reflect the need for personal, human objects and relations in the context of impersonal and rapidly changing societies.

Exploring the colonial roots of authenticity is only part of the solution. As Warren and Jackson acknowledge (2002:8–10), reevaluation of authenticity is part and parcel of a general reevaluation of the concept of culture. Accordingly, we must recognize and be clear that culture changes and that this change is not something that is necessarily mourned and certainly not romanticized. Indeed, appreciation that all culture changes is well established in anthropology. Nevertheless, in the public mind change is often still equated with the end or loss of culture, reflecting cognitive difficulty with death and ambivalence about how rapidly modern societies change. However, it is death that is static and life that changes, and, as such, a static cultural practice is dead. Living forms are dynamic, responding and adapting to changes in economy, environment, technology, political structures, and so forth. That antiquated models of culture persist in the public mind is one sign of a need for better engagement of general audiences by anthropology. However, affirming that cultures change is only the beginning. We must examine and describe how culture changes as well. Our job is to help unpack the assumption that outward changes mean wholesale change.

Specifically (and perhaps paradoxically), culture changes in a way that often expresses continuity. While it seems obvious that a change in some dimension of behavioral or material culture does not correspond perfectly with cultural knowledge that informs the actual act or object, popular models of culture tend not to recognize this complexity. Under the purist notion of authenticity, outward change is the same as the cognitive or ideational structures that inform it. As Edward Fischer (1999) has argued about Highland Maya culture in particular, behavioral and material culture can change substantially but be informed by underlying ideational forms that are more stable. Such a model allows us to address and describe change while also recognizing continuity between present and past. Of course, this pattern of change and continuity applies beyond the highlands. Very few contemporary U.S. citizens are the yeoman farmers that Jefferson imagined. Yet notions of freedom and individual self-reliance persist as salient (even if sometimes conflicted) mainstream values.

In the end, the approach to authenticity advocated here asks us to embrace its fundamental subjectivity and recognize that social actors hold varying notions of authenticity. As such, we endeavor to address it from the perspective of the insider. Accordingly, if a performance, a ritual, or a festival is meaningful and satisfying to its social actors, it is authentic. However, difficulties emerge when one conception of authenticity is applied to a cultural Other as if it were an objective phenomenon. In such cases, paraphrasing Graham (2002:188), authenticity is "a folk theory about the folk."[3] Its standards of preconceived purity, truth, and essential culture are not subject to empirical evidence, making it, like race, a folk theory. Moreover, it is applied to Others who are viewed as primitive, backward, rural, exotic, or the like—that is, "the folk."

How people construct and contest authenticity is fascinating in and of itself but also reveals diverse responses to common challenges of life in an era of simultaneous global interconnectedness and gross global inequality. Performance of culture in representational dance becomes an act that reflects the dynamic processes of continuity and change among material, behavioral, and ideational culture. In it, performers assert control of their identities (and occasionally the identity of Others). They also construct what is authentic in both specific and general senses. This is our tradition and this is how it is done. It is how we authentically incorporate change while expressing connection to the past. The question remains: why is representational dance a common tool to assert authentic culture and identity?

The answer lies in the similarity and interdependence between authenticity and ethnicity. A viable ethnic identity needs distinctive authentic symbols, and authenticity often is founded on the cultural practices of a particular ethnic group. Both authenticity and ethnicity are abstract and contested concepts that require a ritual-like performance to create and circulate meaningful, multipurpose, and durable symbols. Also similar to ethnicity, authenticity has roots in the past, and both reference and enact myths to create and extend key unifying symbols. As I explored above, dance is expressive through multiple channels and generates a powerful impression; it is well suited to asserting control of the cultural images and identity. The commonality in this diversity of forms is their enactment in glocalities of cross-cultural encounters and growing economic inequality.

In this and the previous chapter I have explored tools and concepts that apply to and manifest in four genres of representational dance. The discussion occasionally has referenced particular forms covered in this book but has remained general and theoretical. In my specific treatments of traditional, folkloric, powwow, and Indian mascot dancing, I will explore how common challenges of the global era impact differing social statuses. These discussions endeavor to demonstrate how in particular cultural traditions, varied histories are enacted in settings marked by unequal power and generate a diversity of contemporary dance forms. Audiences and performers, in varying ways, embody and respond to that folk theory of the folk: authenticity.

In Part Two, I explore K'iche' Maya traditional dance. We will find dancing that is at once representational and dramatic and that combines elements of secular and sacred ritual. Although often performed for audiences that are largely indigenous, traditional dance from its birth in early colonialism has always been subject to observation by powerful outside Others. It evinces that quality essential to the continuance of the culture of the colonized: adaptability. Traditional K'iche' dance asserts indigenous Maya culture and contests the nature of identity. It does so in a way that obscures its more confrontational messages through the use of symbols that are multilayered and difficult for outsiders to read.

The next dance form covered, Native American powwow, manifests interesting similarities to and divergences from K'iche' traditional dance. Both forms have roots in a period of colonization in which Native dancing was suppressed and channeled into forms acceptable to colonial authorities. In both cases indigenous dancers employed a variety of means to obscure meanings through change in form that resulted in dances acceptable to their respective colonizers. Traditional K'iche' and powwow diverge in some of the particular symbols that they deploy (but also draw on similar cosmologies). They also reference differing layers of ethnic identity. Powwow constructs identification with both particular Native nations and the pan-ethnic political category of Native American. Traditional K'iche' dancing tends to focus on local identity more than pan-Maya political identity, although in other forms, including *baile folklórico*, K'iche' dancers construct broader identities of Maya and indigenous for globalized audiences.

I next consider folkloric dance, where Shay's concept of parallel traditions is most evident. I address folkloric dance as constructed by immigrant troupes in the United States and by K'iche' dancer-activists in Guatemala. This flexible and portable form is employed to assert and contest identity by actors from positions of varied political power and social privilege. Its use by K'iche' dancers to combat negative stereotypes and influence the perception of potential allies is similar to the work of powwows that target white audiences. Immigrant folkloric dancers work to construct connections to the cultures of their homelands while also building political cooperation within the American-made category of Latino. Folkloric dances reflect a particular version of national identity that walks a conceptual tightrope, asserting national unity while referencing peoples and cultures marginalized by nation-states.

Following folkloric dance, I address the phenomenon of Indian sports mascots in U.S. society. I will focus on perhaps the most salient dancing Indian mascot, Chief Illiniwek of the University of Illinois. "The Chief" constructs an imagined Indian dance that claims origin in powwow dancing. However, the character and his performance are deplored by indigenous activists but vigorously defended by many students and alumni. In the struggle over this dancing chief much is revealed about the nature of contested representations of indigenous culture.

I conclude with a discussion of what these varied forms of dance tell us about the nature of identity in the global era. Not only are the particulars of indigenous, national, or pan-ethnic culture contested in dance, but the very nature of identity itself is subject to varied perspectives. Additionally, I will comment on the implications of the continuance of cultural diversity constructed in representational dance. If globalization acts to homogenize culture, it finds a good many people who seem disinclined to homogenization. Representational dance is but one of many forms of discourse and performance that assert particular ethnicities and work to show how said ethnic identities are unique. It does so in an era marked by global wealth inequality.

NOTES

1. I should note that not all non-Maya Guatemalans find these kinds of performances appealing or even necessary.

2. See descriptions of recent such missteps in Graham (2002) and Little (2004: 261–262).

3. Graham (2002:188) argues that "[t]he concept of authenticity is a colonial folk category that emerges out of contact imperialism and was circulating in notions of the 'folk' in Europe by the late eighteenth and early nineteenth centuries."

Part Two

K'iche' Maya Traditional Dance

Three

Conquest, Colonialism, and Continuity

It is January, the height of the dry season in the western highlands of Guatemala. After a dust-filled, half-hour trip from the Pan-American Highway, we have arrived. Our destination is Tacajalve, a satellite community of San Francisco el Alto, Department of Totonicapán. A K'iche' Maya community in a department that is over 95 percent indigenous, Tacajalve is consumed by feria *(fair or festival). An otherwise quiet rural town is frenetic with activity in celebration of the community's patron saint.*

I have gained a greater appreciation of the idea of crowd by experiencing the mass of humanity that overtakes communities during fairs. Like a river that seasonally runs over its banks, the fair crowd makes a community almost unrecognizable. In constricted parts of the center, or at intersections of streets, independent movement is nearly impossible.

Vendors hawk everything from traditional fair foods like peanuts and roscas *(a circular, lightly sweetened hard bread) to everyday products including soap. Faces of some of the vendors are familiar from other ferias, part of the mobile community that moves from festival to festival. In addition to migratory vendors, families from surrounding hamlets come to enjoy the fair. Furthermore, community members who work on coastal* fincas *(plantations) return for the fair, bringing lengths of fresh raw sugarcane, which are cut, chewed, and sucked. People from neighboring communities also visit. On this occasion, an anthropologist from the States and a couple of friends from San Miguel Totonicapán are a few more drops in the sea of humanity.*

If the fair is understood in terms of Maya textiles, it is the peak of an alternating pattern. It is the height of activity in strong contrast to periods less busy. It also represents peaks of alcohol consumption and possible social transgressions. In the alternating pattern, feria *is the zenith of sound. Human voices are accompanied and often drowned out by amplified marimba bands.*

I have come here to see the Dance of the Conquest (el Baile de la Conquista or La Conquista for short). More a play than a dance, La Conquista depicts the events surrounding the invasion of the K'iche' Maya territory by the Spanish led by Pedro de Alvarado in 1524. La Conquista, among other traditional dances, is most often presented during feria*. It takes some work to find and get to the area where the performance is taking place. When we do arrive, the dance, as usual, seems slightly anachronistic. The unamplified handcarved drum (*tun*) and shawm flute (*chirimía*) that provide musical accompaniment for the dance are barely audible; the handcarved masks and handmade velvet suits worn by the dancers have a baroque quality; the dance steps themselves seem antiquated. At first glance, the dance simply cannot compare with the flash and sound of other* feria *events.*

*The first time I saw the dance performed it was almost impenetrable. Although I had read various accounts of the Dance of the Conquest, in performance it was hard to discern the characters and the significance of their actions. The play does have a written script; however, the performers recite lines that are virtually inaudible (and entirely unintelligible). The din of the rest of the fair overwhelms words already muffled by wooden masks, I remember writing in my fieldnotes after the first time I saw the dance performed. Even though I understood the basic story, I found watching the entire dance challenging. "After much anticipation [I] got to see the Conquest. It started fairly early and lasted all day [from] 10–6 more or less. The pace was almost too much for me. I can't imagine [watching] it if I didn't already know the story. [The dance] didn't garner much attention until [the] confrontations between Alvarado and Tecum and then [a] large crowd [gathered]." By this day, however, I had been working with mask-makers (*mascareros*) and vestment makers (*moreros*) for some time and had learned how to identify characters and the significance of much of their actions. As it turns out, the written and spoken script only tells part of the story.*

At a certain point, as I had been doing frequently, I wondered why the dancers dance. Their performance is not central to the fair and is sometimes given low priority by fair organizers. Viewers come and go. The story seems remote, telling of events that took place nearly 500 years ago. In fact, forces such as globalization, programs of assimilation often enforced with violence, and the high cost of costume rental have led to a decrease in performance. Yet, despite all the contravening forces, the dance continues, off and on in some communities and more consistently in others.

The explanation of why the dancers perform lies in the meaning of the dance. Typical concrete motivations such as prestige or material benefit do not apply. Certainly the struggle of K'iche' ancestors against Spanish invaders is meaningful to contemporary dance participants. The dance contains layers of meaning, history, and commentary on current cultural struggle and social arrangements. It contrasts with other fair events in which multinational products have penetrated the most local of markets. Dance performance is not a product of the "global village." Although tourists are sometimes encouraged to watch, it is not a show put on for tourists. Rather, the Dance of the Conquest is an organic part of Maya culture and society.[1]

3.1. Crowd at Feria. *A normally open church plaza is filled with people and booths as the parade initiating the fair of San Cristóbal Totonicapán passes, July 2007. (Photograph by author.)*

K'iche' Maya traditional dance is the first specific genre of dance explored in this book. An overriding characteristic of K'iche' traditional dance is its multivalence. That is, it carries multiple layers of meaning, some available only to some parts of the audience. That a form of dance would have this capacity is not surprising. In the present case, a rich stock of Mesoamerican symbols and concepts, the necessities of survival under formal Spanish colonialism, and the challenges of life within the contemporary Guatemalan state shape a genre of dance particularly complex in meaning. I make decoding and understanding this multivalence the main undertaking of this and the following chapter.

Presently, I address traditional dance in terms of its commentary on unequal ethnic relations and how it presents cultural continuity. These dimensions of traditional dance reflect stark necessities of colonial and neocolonial relations. In the following chapter I explore how traditional dance contests the myths and notions of nation and national identity.

My treatment of K'iche' Maya traditional dance is based on ethnographic fieldwork conducted during an apprenticeship to a Guatemalan *morería* (a traditional dance regalia shop). From July 1994 to September 1995, I worked closely with experienced artisans and co-apprentice novices at the Morería Nima' K'iche' in Totonicapán. I also had regular contact with dancers (as they were clients of the *morería*) and observed several performances of the Dance of the Conquest and other traditional dances. I supplement data from my apprenticeship with participant observation during shorter visits to the *morería* in 1997 and 2005 and from 2007 through 2010. During fieldwork in the summers of 2007, 2008, and 2010 I was able to observe one of the principal traditional dances, the Dance of the Conquest, performed in San Cristóbal Totonicapán and Momostenango.

FEATURES OF TRADITIONAL DANCE

There are a wide variety of traditional dances, including the Dance of the Conquest, the Dance of the Moors and Christians, and the Dance of the Mexicans. Some, such as the Moors and Christians and the Conquest, have origins in the colonial period and were imported from Spain and modified in Mesoamerica. Others, most notably the Dance of the Mexicans, have fairly recent, postcolonial origins. Still others, for example the Rabinal Achí, the Dance of the Monkeys, and the Dance of the Deer, have aboriginal Mesoamerican roots. Traditional dances are marked by some common characteristics. In general, they are presented in public outdoor spaces. Performers are not formally trained actors or dancers and do not earn a living from traditional dance. In fact, participation in traditional dance incurs considerable expense for performers, who typically have little disposable cash income. Nearly every traditional dance requires masks and special clothing. Vestments run the gamut from slightly modified everyday clothing to intricately decorated velvet capes, chest pieces, and pants. Masks, almost universal in traditional dance, vary from directly representational to fairly abstract. Many traditional dances are dramatic; they tell stories with a narrative structure, including lines spoken by performers. Choreographed movement is incorporated into presentations but is supportive of storytelling, and these forms are often called dance-dramas.

In addition to blurring the line between dance and narrative play, performance of traditional dance can be as much ritual as theater. Preparation for performance often involves sexual abstinence, fasting, and ritual treatment of dance paraphernalia, particularly the masks. In fact, masks are viewed and treated as powerful objects. Many have spirits, and masks of especially significant figures are said to invoke the spirit of the figure they represent. They are something more than mere props in service to drama.

Traditional dances are most often performed during the *feria* (fair) in honor of the patron saint of the local community. (One is described in the opening section of this chapter.) A combination of processions, music, dance, and commerce, the annual *feria* changes the life and space of a town for about two weeks around the feast day of the town's namesake. Streets fill with vendors' booths, and open plazas host music stages and dance arenas. The *feria* is cacophonous and crowded, the collective social event of the year. Although the *feria* features common activities and common traditional dances from town to town, in many ways it is a celebration of the local community, a primary locus of identification for many Highland Maya.

The outward characteristics of present-day traditional dance have origins mainly in the colonial era. The context of performance is a festival introduced by the Catholic Church and the masks have a certain baroque style. Indeed, the importation of European-style dramatic dancing was colonial in purpose as well as in style and era. On the European side of the Atlantic, the Church employed the Dance of the Moors and Christians to dramatize the ascendancy of the Crown and Church in their effort to re-Christianize reconquered southern Spain. As the official transcript of Spanish colonization of Mesoamerica emphasized the extension of Christendom, similar tools of conversion would be employed in New Spain. Indeed, versions of the Dance of the Moors and Christians were presented in central Mexico as early as 1538 (Montoya 1970:15). Max Harris, in discussing central Mexican forms, notes that representation of the conquest through dance "draws on both European and indigenous sources" (2000:19).

These European forms were grafted onto existing dances, as K'iche' traditional dance has recent and local as well as ancient and distant aboriginal sources. Indigenous written documents from the early colonial period, most famously the *Anales de los Kaqchikeles*, indicate that narrative and themed dance was an important feature of the pre-Columbian Highland Maya social landscape (Montoya 1970:21–24; Carmack 1981:61). Additionally, the *Popul Wuj*, the creation and origin story of the K'iche', also frequently refers to dancing. The *Popul Wuj* is the original sacred book to many Highland Maya and is better known and more widely read than other indigenous-authored texts. In the thirteenth chapter of part two, the hero twins set about to deceive the death lords of the underworld. Disguised, the twins, Hunahpú and Xbalanqué, "performed the dance of the *puhuy* [owl or churn-owl], the dance of the *cux* [weasel], the dance of the *iboy* [armadillo], and they also danced the *xtzul* [centipede] and the *chitic* [that walks on stilts]" (Goetz and Morley 1950:156, brackets and italics in original). The number of different dances listed here indicates a fully developed genre of themed dance among the Highland Maya. Furthermore, even though the version of the *Popul Wuj* that survives was recorded after the conquest, the important place dance has in the document certainly has origins before the Spanish invasion.

Moreover, there is abundant evidence of widespread ritual dancing from earlier periods and other Maya regions. Freidel, Schele, and Parker (1993:258) and Grube (1992) discuss the glyph representing the verb "to dance," found in Classic period (AD 250 to 900) writing. Freidel, Schele, and Parker (1993:236) also describe depictions of masked dancing in the murals of Bonampak' that date to AD 790. Images of dancing appear widely on Classic period pottery, including the famous polychrome vase from Altar de Sacrificios that depicts "six *wayob* dancing in fantastic scenes of pageant" (Freidel, Schele, and Parker 1993:265). Most important to the present discussion, these images of dancing (among many others) manifest a clear connection between the ordinary and human realm and the sacred and supernatural. They are rituals in which fundamental aspects of social life, cultural patterns, and religious beliefs are symbolized (Freidel, Schele, and Parker 1993:265). Accordingly, traditional dance has roots that extend to the colonial period and to late and earlier pre-Hispanic eras. The breadth of these roots reaches across Mesoamerica and Spain during the reconquest.

Connecting K'iche' Maya traditional dance to the broader discussion of dance offered in Part One places it squarely in the class of "in the field" dance that Shay (2002:13–37) describes. It is self-taught, performed in indigenous communities by indigenous dancers. Beyond this label, traditional dance skirts and straddles categories. It is occasionally the source for theatricalized forms (particularly the folkloric dances that I explore in Part Four). However, as Shay notes, this is not to say that one form is more authentic than the other or that one replaces the other (2006:9–14). Indeed, traditional dance is paralleled by other dancing within and without K'iche' communities. Moreover, traditional dances, generally speaking, are representational dances. They tell stories and make a distinction between performer and audience. Folks attend a traditional dance to see it, to be entertained, to have fun, but not to actually dance. Nonetheless, because of frequent reference to the sacred, they are not strictly secular theatrical performances either.

ETHNICITY IN TRADITIONAL DANCE

The subject of my doctoral dissertation research was the Guatemalan Dance of the Conquest, and I entered the field with the intention of decoding the meanings of the masks, costumes, and props made by artisans and used by traditional dancers. My interest in identity, conflict, and resistance and the previous scholarship on traditional dance had me focused on how the Dance of the Conquest expressed ethnicity and ethnic conflict. Accordingly, when I left to begin my apprenticeship, the focus of my investigation was how masks and costumes employed in the play were used to express ethnicity. That is, I took the dance as a secular ritual about identity.

This research approach grew out of certain realities, literature review, and general trends within the field of anthropology. Guatemala is a country noted for profound inequality and persistent ethnic conflict. Such salient realities certainly influence traditional dance and most of Maya belief and practice. Pre-fieldwork preparation also revealed a strong current of themes of ethnicity and ethnic conflict in Highland Maya traditional dance-dramas. Although I began my investigation of ethnicity in traditional dance by considering the Dance of the Conquest, it became readily apparent that ethnic relations is a theme common across many traditional dances.

In the ideology promulgated by elites of particularly unequal societies, ethnic inequality is denied or explained by cultural inferiority. Scott argues that in public performances (such as traditional dances) both elites and subordinates must seem to be within the parameters of what he identifies as the "official transcript" (1990:138–139). To communicate potentially subversive ideas in public presentations, Scott discerns two basic techniques employed by people in politically weak positions: "those that disguise the message and those that disguise the messenger" (1990:139). In terms of its commentary and practical advice concerning interethnic relations, key traditional dances disguise both message and messenger. Before discussing ethnicity in the Dance of the Conquest, I address it in two popular dances, one fairly new and one very old.

Ethnicity in El Baile de los Mexicanos

The Dance of the Mexicans (El Baile de los Mexicanos) is among the most popular dance-dramas performed in K'iche' communities. Said to originate in visits to Mexico by migratory agricultural workers (or in the experiences of Mayas fleeing the violence of the early 1980s), Los Mexicanos is a farmworkers' story. A boisterous comical affair, the dance-drama is set on a large Mexican plantation during the feast of the Virgin of Guadalupe. A wealthy plantation *patrón* has sponsored a festival for the benefit of his workers, who seldom have contact with women. The main event of the party (and of the dance) is a bull-ride. The worker who stays mounted longest gets to dance with the daughter of the *patrón*. Dark-skinned, long-nosed masks and outlandish sombreros identify the workers. The daughter (La Margarita), danced by a man, features a long dress and a mask that, while not as dark as the workers, is not white either. The *patrón* wears a white-skinned mask with a white beard and mustache. His mask is reminiscent of elite patriarchs and vaguely evocative of the images of historic figures on Guatemalan currency. The story, and particularly the improvised horseplay during performance, suggest sexuality, the amorous intentions of plantation workers toward the Margarita.

The Dance of the Mexicans carries potentially dangerous messages about class, ethnicity, and sexuality. Although not as common at present, travel to lowland plantations to perform agricultural labor is a part of shared and personal memory among Highland Mayas. Indeed, some of the most radical politics of the Guatemalan civil war grew out of the dreadful experiences of migratory farmworkers. To enact directly the Guatemalan plantation and portray its unequal ethnic relations is unwise at best. The clowning and the overt suggestion of sexual relations between poor agricultural laborers and the daughter of a wealthy landowner also enter risky territory. Some space to discuss these dangerous topics is afforded by dislocation in space of the setting of the dance. This is about Mexico and Mexicans, not Mayas and landowning elites. As such, it taps into nationalist rivalry; making fun of Mexicans highlights the Guatemalan identity of the dancers and offers a background for their class and ethnic identities. To emphasize that this buffoonery and sexual transgression are not about Guatemalan plantations or Guatemalan landholding families, Mexican flags are incorporated into the costumes and sometimes paraded around the arena and carried in *feria* processions. The most overt discourse constructs a story about outlandish Mexicans. A second discourse is available (and deniable). It addresses social inequality through ribald humor.

Ethnicity in El Baile de los Venados

Ethnic commentary extends beyond newer dances to ones that have origins in the pre-Columbian past. Chepe, a *morero* (vestment maker / business operator), chose the deer dancer's cape as one of my first lessons as an apprentice. He knew that my research topic was the Dance of the Conquest but pulled out a deer *capa* and explained that a well-executed deer cape was the pride of the *morero*. We discussed the Dance of the Deer itself. I learned that it has pre-Columbian roots. It is a dance that recalls the ritual asking of permission before killing an animal. Asking permission is essential to maintain an appropriate balance between human beings and nature. Chepe also noted, as he would occasionally, that the deer was extinct in the contemporary Guatemalan highlands. The Spanish killed them all and denuded the mountains of the trees that once made up the deer's forest habitat. Additionally, conversations with other K'iche' Mayas about the Dance of the Deer regularly involve commentary about the deer's virtual extinction at the hands of the Spanish.

Because it has obvious implications for the present, the story of the destruction of the deer's habitat disguises the message and messenger. In their discourse on Spanish environmental abuse, dance specialists dislocate ethnic commentary in time. We are, after all, discussing the events of several centuries past. Moreover, because state ideology concerning independence emphasizes Spanish colonial excess, a jab at their ecological practices can easily be read as nationalist. A degree of uncertainty pervades the discourse, offering the speaker protection. Such commentary may align the speaker with Creole elites and the Guatemalan state they founded (and against the peninsular Spanish authorities). It may also find commonality between Ladinos and Spaniards, thus presenting an Other against which contemporary Maya respect and alliance with nature can be contrasted.

Ethnicity in el Baile de la Conquista

The Dance of the Conquest (or La Conquista) relates the story of the 1524 military defeat and religious conversion of the K'iche' Maya and is sometimes identified as the national dance of Guatemala. Spanish clergy introduced peninsular-style dance-drama as a means to instruct the converted, and the Dance of the Conquest, in one sense, must be understood as a tool of colonialism. However, it has become something else, organized and performed by Mayas largely for Mayas.

The main Maya cast of the Dance of the Conquest comprises military, civilian, and religious characters. Military commander Tekun Umam[2] is assisted by a loyal first lieutenant in Witzitzil Tzunun. Three to five *caciques* round out the K'iche' army. Tekun Umam receives counsel from Ajitz, a diviner, magician, and unbending foe of the Spanish. Rey K'iche' is the Maya civilian political leader. The Spanish are led by Pedro de Alvarado, who is accompanied by a group of fairly indistinguishable Spaniards.

La Conquista typically begins with a scene depicting an idyllic pre-Columbian existence. When news of the fall of the Aztec empire reaches the K'iche' capital, Rey K'iche' promptly delegates Tekun Umam to head the Maya military forces. The K'iche' political leader then becomes largely inactive for the rest of the story. Before battle is joined, both sides prepare for combat and probe their enemy. The Spanish solicit surrender, which is angrily rejected by Tekun Umam. The play reaches its climax when the armies engage one another in earnest and Tekun Umam is killed by Pedro de Alvarado. The Maya then end military resistance, and Rey K'iche' relinquishes political autonomy and accepts religious conversion on behalf of his people. The play closes as Maya and Spanish march together in peace and harmony. Although the goal of religious officials who introduced the play was to solidify adherence to Christian belief and practice, this scene of conversion is short, anticlimactic, and generally ignored by the audience.

The Dance of the Conquest, as a story of violent conflict between Mayas and Spaniards, offers context for a sophisticated discussion of ethic relations. It presents a range of strategies for dealing with powerful Others, varying from martyrdom to collaboration. Most predominant in the dance is the story of Tekun Umam. Despite prognostic dreaming and priestly divination that predict his death in battle, Tekun Umam (in a dark, angry mask) enters battle and embraces his destiny. He is an ideal martyr. Witzitzil Tzunun (second in command) and lesser Maya *caciques* resist the Spanish violently until hope for victory is lost, living to fight (perhaps) another day. The K'iche' king (in a white mask) is rather passive to events, remaining at the side of the arena, peripheral to the action for almost the entire play. He deals with the Spanish by avoidance until he must accept their dominance.

A character whose mask, costume, and action in the play vary from performance to performance, Jikake (sometimes Monacho) collaborates with the Spanish.[3] In some performances, wearing a white-skinned mask, he rather enthusiastically helps the enemy.[4] Challenging the official ideology that makes Tekun Umam a symbol of military service to the Guatemalan state, one consultant identified Maya participation in the army with Jikake, that is, with the traitor rather than with the hero. Identification with the aggressor is a tactic of at least individual survival. In other productions, his assistance is ambivalent, gained through bribery and coercion. He both complies and resists, reminiscent of the combination of overt compliance with foot-dragging, feigned ignorance, and other elusive forms of noncompliance that Scott identifies as "weapons of the weak" (1985). Accordingly, the play is a bit of self-commentary and an articulation of various tactics of interethnic relations of unequal power.

In discussing Maya defeat, dancers and artisans also emphasize the dishonorable conduct of the Spanish in battle, particularly their advantages in weapons technology. Although firearms are not portrayed in the play, consultants frequently point out that Spanish employed guns against the Maya warriors, who lacked such weapons. These notions are also presented in the props employed in the play. The Spaniards are equipped with realistic metal swords. The Maya characters carry small wooden bows and arrows or sticks. Tekun Umam carries a small baton that, although explicitly identified as *macaná*, does little to evoke the destructive power of a heavy obsidian-studded club. The diminutive size of the Maya weapons and their lack of functional details make them more abstract symbols than representational props. In comparison with the realistic swords of the Spaniards, the mostly symbolic weapons of the Maya seem ineffectual (Figure 3.2). Whereas the official transcripts emphasize the Spanish as bearers of beneficial technology, here Old World technology is a symbol of efficient destruction and shameful behavior.

Offstage commentary on the context and history of the conquest and the colonialism that followed is rather counter-hegemonic as well. Despite the official message of Christian peace and harmony presented in the final scene of the dance, an elder mask-maker notes that the Spanish soon made slaves of the Maya and treated them with utmost cruelty. They were forced to work in rivers and mines to extract precious metals. Noncompliance with Spanish plans for mining brought harsh punishment: *estos pobres . . . les asaltaron con el asote que es arma mortal* ("those poor people they assaulted them with a cat-o'-nine-tails, which is a mortal weapon").[5] At one level, the play—in its performance and in the discussions it fosters—is a powerful commentary on the treatment of the Maya at the hands of the Spanish as an invading army and as a colonizing people. Although infrequently discussed overtly, the connection between the conquest and colonial periods and current social, political, and economic arrangements is obvious.

Indeed, economic exploitation is strongly emphasized in offstage commentary, revealing, for example, a hidden layer of meaning in a common prop (Figure 3.2). What seem to be tambourine-like musical instruments carried by the Maya characters are said to represent the silver and gold that the Spanish came to exploit. In fact, material wealth as a motive of the Spanish invasion is a common theme of discourse in discussions of the dance away from its performance.

The Dance of the Conquest addresses ethnic inequality but obscures message and messenger. First, it disguises the message by its dislocation in time. Overtly, it is a story about events that transpired 500 years ago. The struggle, nominally, is between a former colonial power and a people who no longer exist. Its performance is easily read as quaint Indian culture. Any reading suggesting commentary on current realities is as easily denied. The messengers are disguised most directly by their masks and costumes and to a lesser extent by the fact that performers' actions are "within character." The direct and violent resistance of the Maya against the Spanish is part of the story and not a call for Indian violence against Ladinos.

In dealing with the powerful Other, direct resistance is but one approach. In dislocating this presentation in time, dancers and audience have deniability at their disposal. Moreover, the play does, after all, present the official transcript of Maya conquest. Scott hypothesizes that just such an approach is common to subordinate groups: "subordinate groups have typically learned,

3.2. Wealth and Weapon. K'iche' Maya cacique *Witzitzil Tzunun carries a* plato *in his right hand and a bow and arrow in his left, Momostenango, July 2008. (Photograph by author.)*

in situations short of those rare all-or-nothing struggles, to clothe their resistance and defiance in ritualisms of subordination that serve both to disguise their purposes and to provide them with a ready route of retreat that may soften the consequences of a possible failure" (1990:96).

Traditional dance, therefore, reflects a common strategy of hiding message and messenger. However, traditional dance also conveys content beyond ethnicity, sometimes hiding its messages in code that is also culture.

TRADITIONAL DANCE AND CULTURAL CONTINUITY

I entered my field study of traditional dance with a framework that stressed ethnic inequality but also emphasized culture as changing and ephemeral. Anthropology of the early and mid-twentieth century had developed concepts of culture that were static and essentialist. These models accommodated dynamic social reality poorly, often equating change with destruction and under-investigating how people accommodate large social forces beyond their control. In response, late twentieth-century anthropology developed a model of culture that stressed its construction in fleeting moments of social discourse. Culture became neither static nor inflexible, but it also lost a sense of depth. As a result, evidence of culturally distinctive connections between the past and present have tended to be underestimated in recent anthropology.

Much as Edward Fischer describes in "Cultural Logic and Maya Identity: Rethinking Constructivism and Essentialism" (1999), interactions with consultants presented me with data that were not well accommodated by either static models of culture or overly fluid ones. While my questions were concerned with politics and ethnicity, my consultants' responses and discourse pointed in other directions. I came to realize that traditional dances, beyond ethnicity, express certain common themes, including the reciprocal relationship among human, spiritual, and natural realms and indigenous cosmology, worldview, and religion. As a result, feedback from dance specialists helped me to develop a better sense of the context of my research and to discern particularly Maya and Mesoamerican themes expressed in performance.

In "Continuities, Imputed and Inferred" (2004), Richard G. Fox argues that such continuity of belief and practice merits attention as a primary subject of investigation. Fox urges scholars to move beyond representing contemporary Maya cultures as products of colonialism or globalization and to make subjects of investigation belief and practice that persist and transcend such forces. Moving continuity to the foreground of research is a most fruitful way to consider the varied meanings in K'iche' traditional dance. This approach understands change as patterned by worldview, cosmology, values, beliefs, and other shared cognitive structures. In other words, culture's expression and transmission in momentary social interactions marked by ethnic inequality do not preclude an underlying ethos that connects the present with the past. However, emphasizing continuity does not imply that human belief and practice are unchanging. It does, though, recognize that change varies in its pace and does not occur in a purely random fashion. Moreover, by avoiding the assumption that the culture of an indigenous group reflects only their colonial experience or their contemporary poverty, indigenous agency becomes implicit in the investigation of continuity.

The following sections explore continuity of Maya and Mesoamerican culture in traditional dance. I first consider the continuity of culture expressed in the Dance of the Deer and the Dance of the Monkeys. I then turn to the Dance of the Conquest and explore how the play enacts continuities in ritual, cosmology, and belief. These dances presents Maya understandings of the relationship between human beings and the supernatural, the orientation of the world, and how the world came to be the way it is. In doing so, some make repeated overt and covert references to the *Popul Wuj*, revealing a distinctly Mesoamerican worldview. In short, I contend that traditional dance has become a reservoir of uniquely Maya conceptions, or "the essential continuity of underlying cultural forms" (Fischer 1999:476).

Continuity in the Dance of the Deer

As I described above, the Dance of the Deer holds a special place in the stock of the *morería*. This reflects the general importance of the deer in Highland Maya culture. The deer has its own day (Kej) in the Maya ritual calendar and was a game animal of central importance to Mesoamerican peoples. In referencing a pre-Columbian hunting rite dedicated to an animal of some cultural significance, the dance anchors current K'iche' values to the past in two ways. First, the play emphasizes proper ritual conduct and asking permission. The hunters seek elder characters to make an offering to the spirit-owner of the deer. In this ritual of offering, human beings ask permission to kill and that a corporeal deer appear and surrender to the hunters. This practice reflects the importance of reciprocity between human beings and the spiritual dimension. Indeed the Highland Maya storytelling corpus is full of tales in which those who properly ask permission and make offerings are rewarded and those who do not are punished. The Dance of the Deer enacts one version of this narrative.

Additionally, cooperation and sharing are a primary theme of the dance. The deer is pursued by hunters and their dogs as well as wild predators, including lion and tiger (or jaguar and ocelot). In the end, through cooperation, the deer is captured and all share and enjoy its meat. Where proper ritual is practiced through asking permission of the deer's spirit, harmonious relations among people and between people and nature are effected through exchange of labor and the product of labor. Reflecting an indigenous Mesoamerican worldview, these dimensions (social, spiritual, and natural) are mutually maintained through reciprocity. This exchange takes form in sharing among the corporeal and in offerings given by the corporeal to the spiritual. The Dance of the Deer, then, realizes contemporary K'iche' values rooted in a Mesoamerican worldview of considerable temporal depth.

Continuity in the Dance of the Monkeys

The Dance of the Monkeys is an enactment of a scene from the *Popul Wuj*. Costumed dancers whirling around suspended ropes recall the episode in the fifth chapter of the K'iche' sacred book. Although they play a crucial role in the story and in making the world ready for human beings, the hero twins are initially subordinate to their boastful older brothers. In this episode, they trick their older brothers into climbing a very tall tree in the forest and convert them into monkeys. The older monkey-brothers are summoned back from the forest by the flute and drum playing of the hero twins. Upon their return, the older monkey-brothers begin to dance and become the patrons of art and music (Goetz and Morley 1950:128–129). Typical of mythology, this story fits into a larger story of the origin of the world and humankind and reinforces important values. The humble hero twins vanquish their privileged brothers, and music and art gain primordial sanction. The enactment of the story in dance communicates these messages effectively and fosters the continuity of Maya worldview.

THE DANCE OF THE CONQUEST, RELIGION, AND CONTINUITY

From this point, I shift to consideration of the Dance of the Conquest in detail and exclusively. First, I focus on La Conquista because it is a primary traditional dance. It may not be performed as frequently as the Dance of the Mexicans, but it is considered more important. Second, considering that the Dance of the Conquest is an institution introduced specifically to disrupt religious continuity suggests something about how continuities occur. Third, the Dance of the Conquest is unique in the depth to which it works on the three main themes I explore here. In addition to dealing with unequal ethnic relations, it shares with the Dance of the Deer and the Dance of the Monkeys an articulation of Maya cosmology and worldview, which I will explore momentarily. However, its appellation as the national dance of Guatemala is unique. As such, La Conquista combines, as no other traditional dance space, commentary on social inequality, elaboration of cultural continuity, and contestation of national identity.

Presently, I examine the multivalence in the Dance of the Conquest, focusing on religion in this chapter and national identity in the next. The dance expresses a continuity of religious belief and practice, but it also contests nationality. As such, La Conquista cannot be understood strictly as a product of colonial or neocolonial relations. That is to say, it is about more than military defeat, religious conversion, and the politics of unequal ethnic relations. It includes references to cosmology and mythology of pre-Columbian origin while also contesting the basis of national identity of the present.

The Dance of the Conquest is a manifestation of a general pattern of dual discourse in which continuity is constructed among various Maya groups. Outwardly, formal performance acknowledges the political and religious dominance of the Other. Inwardly, representations are invested with meanings of clear Mesoamerican origin. Smith (1990:3), among others, has noted that a relatively small number of Spanish colonial officials and colonists came to reside in the Guatemalan highlands. A large population formally under the control of a small number of Spanish officials necessitated a compromise between Maya communities and individuals on one side and the colonial order on the other. As long as Mayas appeared to be converted and conquered (particularly in the presence of non-Mayas), they could expect a fair degree of local political and cultural autonomy. When we understand it in these terms, we begin to shift the emphasis away from colonial power and toward Maya agency. Moreover, embedded continuities cannot be missed, revealing themselves as we concentrate on indigenous actors.

In a variety of ways the Dance of the Conquest articulates K'iche' and Mesoamerican religious concepts. It enacts and considers mythology, cosmology, and ritual. From the opening scenes, the dance expresses Mesoamerican cosmology as dancers traverse the arena, tracing a cross within a square, a common articulation of the four cardinal directions to center. On the ritual front, Ajitz and his diminutive twin conduct non-Christian divination that proves an accurate prediction of events later in the play.

Moreover, three of its principal characters reference deities of pre-Columbian origin. The K'iche' leader Tekun Umam, in offstage discourse and onstage iconography, references the K'iche' version of Quetzalcoatl. Witzitzil Tzunun (second in command) alludes to the Aztec patron Huitzilopochtli. Ajitz (warrior-priest) is connected to three pre-Columbian deities. Ajitz is referred to as K'oxool and Tzitzimit,[6] divinities associated with millennial destruction-creation events. Additionally, Ajitz is accompanied by a dwarf twin. This figure and the anthropomorphic scepter carried by Ajitz share the name of the K'iche' patron deity Tojil. Enactment of these figures implies a particularly

Mesoamerican framing of political and religious change. It is appropriate that these figures would appear in a play about profound political and religious shifts.[7] Accordingly, some suggestions about how such transformations are understood from Maya and broader Mesoamerican traditions are in order.

That one group would dominate another was not an entirely new concept for the Maya peoples when Pedro de Alvarado invaded the highlands. The pre-Columbian history of Mesoamerica is characterized by cycles of political centralization and decentralization. Periods of domination by core city-states are followed by eras in which power is diffused among a greater number of smaller polities. Particularly during periods of centralization, most communities paid a portion of excess production in tribute to powerful core city-states. Often, such shifts in the landscape of political power were justified in terms of mythology. The rise of the Aztec patron deity Huitzilopochtli was connected with Aztec ascendancy in the Valley of Mexico (Taube 1993:49–50). Thus the beginning of a new era, that of Aztec dominance, is marked by the incorporation of a new, specifically Aztec deity into the pantheon. The sections of the *Popul Wuj* that connect K'iche' adoption of Tojil and other divinities with their ascendancy make a similar claim of a mythological basis for political change (D. Tedlock 1996:47–52).

This is not to say that the Spanish colonialism was nothing new. Rather, native Mesoamericans had a frame of reference through which they could understand the meaning of military defeat and political and economic subjugation. While having an existing model to interpret events was useful for peoples militarily defeated by the Spanish, the model was not necessarily held by the conqueror. Under the Mesoamerican system, tribute payment accompanied a good deal of local political autonomy. It is not unreasonable to think that defeat at the hands of Europeans would result in a similar outcome. Whatever extra-community power a given city-state enjoyed would be ceded to the new outsiders, and communities already dominated would expect to shift payment and allegiance to a different group of outsiders. It soon became apparent, however, that Spanish colonial demands of tribute and subservience would be much heavier and would bring about profound social and demographic dislocation.

In addition to a framework for understanding political shifts as religious shifts, K'iche' dancers and dance audiences draw on Mesoamerican notions of how religion itself changes. Within what we might call Mesoamerican theology is a strong implication that religious truth is changeable. The granting and quick withdrawal of powers to see far in time and space described in the *Popul Wuj* articulate a view that sees religious truth as emergent (D. Tedlock 1996:148). Our human imperfection makes us incapable of seeing all that is and of completely understanding the divine order of the world. Innovation,

3.3. Ajitz and Dwarf Twin. Iconic axe in right hand and Tojil figure in left, Ajitz (also known as Keq K'oxool and Tzitzimit) performs during the 2008 performance of the Dance of the Conquest in Momostenango. The K'iche' warrior-priest is trailed by his diminutive twin, sometimes also referred to as Tojil. Both are outfitted in distinctive red regalia. (Photograph by author.)

3.4. Witzitzil Tzunun. The second-in-command of the K'iche' Maya forces leads other caciques *at the 2007 performance of the Dance of the Conquest in San Cristóbal Totonicapán. The distinctive mask indicates a connection to the Aztec patron Huitzilopochtli ("hummingbird to the left"). It features a hummingbird above the forehead, and the feather array surrounding the face references rays of the sun. In addition to the similarities in the first part of the figure's name,* tz'unun *is K'iche' for "hummingbird." (Photograph by author.)*

whether from another Mesoamerican society or from Europe, can be accommodated in a way that does not undermine existing beliefs. Previous ways of thinking were not wrong; we were simply not able to see and understand this newly revealed dimension. Contemporary daykeepers struggle to see beyond the veil of everyday experience to the unseen order. They do so through a system of beliefs that occasionally incorporates both aboriginal and Christian concepts and rituals. In other words, for daykeepers and many other Mayas,

Christian truth is added to existing truth. They are not inherently incompatible but instead mutually accommodated.

While there seems to be some agreement that religious and political changes happen together, European and Mesoamerican understandings of the specific implication of such changes are at odds. The Spanish certainly carried a foreign notion of conversion; the Truth of a particular system of belief is asserted to be supreme and largely unalterable. As was the case of the Crusades, the reconquest, the Inquisition, and the missionization of colonized peoples, European ideology of religious change tends more toward replacement of one set of beliefs and practices with another (self-ascribed) superior form. However, the Spanish colonial order's emphasis on social/ethnic hierarchy and extraction of material wealth undermined its lofty goals of a Christian Kingdom of God in the New World. In addition to ideological contradictions, it failed institutionally. Ultimately, Spain provided few clergy relative to the number of *indígenas* to be converted, and consequently, indigenous Highland Maya would have a degree of control over much of the indoctrination.

The final scenes of the play reflect the notion that Spanish military victory does not lead to the religious changes envisioned by the Spanish religious institution. Ajitz does not appear during the scene in which the K'iche' king accepts conversion on behalf of his people. Consultants are clear that the red-masked character survives the battle, escapes to the mountains, and continues indigenous religious ways, converting not from Maya to Christian but from human to spirit. The underlying cultural forms of the Maya groups subjugated under such circumstances persist. The Dance of the Conquest, in addition to expressing continuity of religious belief and practice, provides a model of political change that challenges the Spanish conception of conquest. By implication, this alternate version of conquest calls into question not only the colonial order but the states forged out of colonialism.

In this chapter I have explored the colonial dimensions of K'iche' Maya traditional dance. I began with the role of conquest in forming contemporary dance from pre-Columbian roots. In addressing ethnicity, traditional dance comments on unequal ethnic relations (a predominant product of colonialism) but also models a range of strategies for dealing with the powerful ethnic Other. It does so in a way that blunts its message through dislocation of events in time and space. Traditional dance also obscures its content by encoding it in multivalent and culturally specific symbols. In this way, traditional dance effects cultural continuity while protecting performers from reprisal by various authorities.

Just as K'iche' traditional dance has evolved in particularly Maya ways, so has the broader Guatemalan society changed in response to shifting macrosocial forces. The end of the Cold War and intensifying globalization have changed the landscape of Guatemalan identity. Not only is open, positive self-identification as indigenous possible, but what it means to be Guatemalan (indigenous or not) is subject to change. Where religious continuity in the play challenges the official history of conquest, manipulation of symbols of the contemporary state challenges the ideology of the nationalism. This I explore in the following chapter.

NOTES

1. I employed this vignette to introduce my doctoral dissertation.

2. The name Tekun Umam is variously written and translated. Tedlock translates the leader's name as "black butterfly" (1993:104). Otzoy (1999) employs Tekum Umam for Maya versions of the figure, reflecting both accurate orthography and Maya colonial manuscripts. When discussing the appropriated version of the Maya leader, she uses Tecun Uman. I employ Tekun Umam, as it is the preferred pronunciation among the mask-makers, regalia shop managers, and dancers who taught me. Consultants are uncertain about its exact meaning, but many agree that the final /n/ of the first name is best made part of the second. *Numaam* glosses as "my grandfather" or "my respected elder." Consultants are less clear about the meaning of *teku*, often noting that the meaning of the name is open to interpretation. Judith Maxwell (personal correspondence, 2000) suggests the Nahuatl title term //tekw-//. The resulting translation would be along the lines of "my king, my respected elder."

3. It should be noted that this character is explicitly identified as non-K'iche', non-highland, and sometimes called "Lacandón."

4. In summer 2008 a *morero* noted that some groups rent two masks for the character. A dark-skin mask is replaced with a fair-skin mask once Jikake begins to assist the Spanish.

5. Interview with Don Bonifacio Son Elías, August 1995.

6. Unprompted, a young man attending a July 2008 performance of the dance in Momostenango informed me that the red-masked character was known as Tzitzimit. He continued, reporting that the actual spirit represented in the dance resided on the edge of town and was regularly observed by Momostecos.

7. For more detail regarding references to pre-Columbian religion, see Krystal 2008.

Four

The Dance of the Conquest and Contested National Identity

After scaling the stairs of a pyramid temple, the famed warrior Tekun Umam kneels before the K'iche' king. Not long ago news reached K'uumarkaaj, the K'iche' capital, that the great Aztec empire had fallen to the Spanish. Deeply troubled by this turn of events, the K'iche' king has ordered the meeting to delegate military command to Tekun Umam. Able fellow warrior and second-in-command Witzitzil Tzunun is beside Tekun Umam when he receives the symbol of his command, a staff carrying the cerulean and white flag of the contemporary state of Guatemala. It is a critical moment both in the life of Tekun Umam and in this version of the most salient Guatemalan national origin story.

After bidding appropriately respectful farewell to their political leader, the K'iche' warriors descend the stairs of the temple, leave K'uumarkaaj, and set about preparing for battle. They assemble an army and consult Ajitz, the Maya priest-warrior-scout. Meanwhile, Pedro de Alvarado and his army are on the march, intending to conquer and convert the K'iche'. In a few hours the Maya and Spanish will meet in battle, their respective leaders confronting one another in a struggle to the death. Tekun Umam will fight valiantly but will be defeated and killed by Alvarado. Witzitzil Tzunun, recognizing the significance of the loss of Tekun Umam and a good many other Maya soldiers, will call for the cessation of battle. The K'iche' king,[1] resigned to his fate since he learned of the fall of Tenochtitlán at the beginning of the play, now accepts conversion on behalf of his people at its end.

Three platforms have been erected to represent Maya pyramid temples. Typical of drama, enjoying the performance requires a fair amount of willing suspension of disbelief. Wooden platforms become stone temples, great distances are implied by criss-crossing the dance area, wooden masks make corn farmers into heroes and invaders. However, these necessary compromises of space and material are not what draw my attention when Tekun Umam accepts his assignment. My eye, conditioned by a commodified, linear concept of time, is drawn to Tekun's staff. Although the play is set in the sixteenth century, the K'iche' captain carries the flag representing a state that will not exist until the nineteenth century. It is one of the many ways that performers and audiences present and discuss multiple layers of meaning in the Dance of the Conquest. The apparent incongruity of the flag reflects a particularly Maya telling of history in which similar events in distinct eras are represented as recurrences of one another (Gossen 2004:144–145). That the martyr to Maya political and religious autonomy carries the symbol of a state that has pursued policies aimed at erasing Maya cultural distinctiveness also highlights the contested nature of national identity and its conflicted and overlapping loyalties. However, it would be a serious misreading to suggest that the dancers and audience lack consciousness and are embracing the dominant ideology.[2] Moreover, there are certain difficulties in reading the flag as only a national symbol. Its crest, after all, predominantly features a quetzal bird. If anyone in the audience is unaware that the quetzal is Tekun Umam's fate-sharing spirit twin, or nawal, *the presence of images of the bird on his mask and at the top of his crown implies a significant relationship. In a certain respect, dancing Tekun Umam is an example of what Gossen identifies as "encyclopedic moments" that "bring together the disparate essences of person, community, and cosmos to celebrate the totality of these essences" (2004:144).*

In this chapter I consider the story of Tekun Umam and his regalia as the source and subject of discourse about nationalism and identity. So far I have explored the multivalent nature of traditional dance, particularly the Dance of the Conquest. I argued that for performers and audiences the dance provides models for interethnic relations and also acts as a storehouse of particularly Maya iconography and mythology. Here, I turn my attention to Tekun Umam and his appropriation by the Guatemalan state. I will consider how the state and ethnic Others have attempted to use Tekun Umam and the story of the conquest in ritual and myth of identification. As it has been the commonly taught (Wilhelm 1994) and publicly shared history of Guatemala, I begin with the official, state-sponsored story of the conquest. I follow with the unofficial and K'iche story concerning Spanish invasion and Maya resistance as

4.1. *A Hero's Story.* Above: *Tekun Umam kneels before the K'iche' king and accepts command of the military resistance to Spanish invasion. Witzitzil Tzunun* (back to camera) *and two K'iche' princesses observe (Patachaj, March 1995).* Right: *Tekun is in command, carrying the flag of the state of Guatemala; Witzitzil Tzunun follows (San Cristóbal, Totonicapán, July 2007).* Below: *Tekun* (left), macaná *painted in Guatemalan national colors, confronts Pedro de Alvarado, staff wrapped in the Spanish flag (Tacajalve, January 1995). Note the quetzal bird at the top of Tekun's crown in each image. (All photographs by author.)*

presented in dance performance and offstage discussions. In exploring the unofficial account, I first outline how it rejects indigenous acquiescence (or lack of agency), and second how it presents symbols and ideas of Mesoamerican origin.[3]

TEKUN UMAM AND THE CONQUEST AS AN OFFICIAL STORY

The Dance of the Conquest, introduced by Spanish clergy for the purpose of converting Native populations to the Christian faith, must be understood in part as an official narrative of the Church. It provides a key scenario, elaborating a narrative that scripts conversion to Christianity. Similarly, as mid-twentieth-century elites appropriated Tekun Umam (Otzoy 1999:30) as a national hero, the resulting story of the conquest, designed to serve nationalism, must be understood as an "official transcript" (Scott 1990) of the state. The Spanish mission of extending a pure Christian faith generated particular notions of conversion. Pure conversion sought by the Spanish diverged sharply from the Mesoamerican tendency to adapt and change belief and practice as ideas, symbols, and practices circulated among various peoples and polities. The version of nationalism that has enjoyed official Guatemalan predominance is rooted in these Spanish notions of conversion. It assumes that cultural homogeneity is a prerequisite of national unity. This take on nationalism is likewise discordant with Maya notions of place and identity. Therefore, before getting into the official story of Tekun Umam, some comment on nationalism and the nation-state is necessary.

Inspired by the evocatively titled *Imagined Communities: Reflections on the Origin and Spread of Nationalism* by Benedict Anderson (1983), numerous scholars have explored the abstract, remote nature of identification with the nation-state. While such issues of nationalism certainly pertain in Guatemala, I rely more on the later work of Ronald Niezen (2003) as it focuses on the implications that nation-state formation and administration have for indigenous peoples. The predominant conception of the nation-state—and its assumed correspondence between nation (as a group of people sharing a common history, language, culture, etc.) and state as a bureaucratic, geographically defined political entity—has had tragic consequences for the world's indigenous populations. States and their politically dominant subsectors hold strongly to the notion that nation and state correspond, and the persistence of indigenous culture and community is often the most striking evidence to the contrary. The consequent state policies and state actions tend toward marginalization (pretending that state and nation do correspond), assimilation (trying to make state and nation correspond by erasing cultural distinctiveness), or genocide (cleansing the state of cultural distinctiveness through mass murder) (Niezen

2003:53–57). These policies often have unintended consequences and elicit the opposite effect. Among its survivors, state brutality does little to foster attachment to existing formulations of nation-state identity (Niezen 2003:86–93). Moreover, the primary loyalty and identification that the nation-state demands of its citizens threaten the strong, affective ties to concrete communities and places found among many indigenous peoples (Niezen 2003:215). Face-to-face, kinship-embedded community is more satisfying than "imagined," abstract community. Concordantly, ritual attention to local sacred spaces is often more meaningful than de-territorialized spirituality.

These general difficulties of state and identity have their specific manifestation in the nation-building projects of Guatemala and its myth of foundation in conquest. While Tekun Umam is a figure in the Dance of the Conquest dating to 1872 at the latest (Bode 1961:251), his incorporation into the official ideology of the state is not until the mid-twentieth century. Otzoy situates the official adoption of Tekun Umam in two historical contexts. At the state level, "Tecun Uman's name emerged when the country entered into crisis during the process of its nation-building in the aftermath of the 1944 capitalist revolution" (Otzoy 1999:30). Beyond Guatemala, mid-century Latin American (predominantly Mexican) *indigenista* policies made Tekun Umam an obvious symbol for the official state transcript. This *indigenista* approach emphasized a national unity that would be accomplished by assimilating indigenous people into a "national culture" that was predominantly mestizo with "some Indian elements" (Otzoy 1999:30). As a result, the adoption of Tekun Umam reflects a perceived need for unity in a time of societal transition at a moment when images of Indians of the past were thought ideal symbols for national cultures. As a consequence of this nationalist appropriation of Tekun Umam, his name and likeness have appeared in public statuary, on currency, as the name of a city,[4] and in a plethora of brand names and advertising campaigns (Figure 4.2). In 1960, congress decreed Tekun Umam the "national hero of Guatemala" and designated February 20 a "day of homage to Tecun Uman" (Otzoy 1999:82). *Monumento a Tecun Uman* (Castañeda 1965) recounts the planning, design, and construction of the main monument dedicated to Tekun Umam in the capital and is full of idealistic musings on patriotism and nationalism. The leader of Maya resistance is presented as a "martyr" to patriotism, a "hero" who died defending nationality (Castañeda 1965:6).

These efforts to make Tekun Umam a hero of the state and a martyr to nationalism have had results that diverge from their original patriotic impulses. Otzoy argues that the presence of Tekun Umam as a national hero makes undeniable (if voiceless) the presence of Mayas in contemporary Guatemalan society. Additionally, she contends that the appropriation of Tekun Umam must be seen as part of a failed attempt to create a unified national identity (Otzoy 1999:36).

4.2. The Tecun Uman Typing School. San Lucas Tolimán, 2007. (Photograph by author.)

Despite (or perhaps because of) this failure, the official story of the conquest reaches a level of mythology and has enjoyed widespread saliency. Kay Warren (1998:134) discusses "the national obsession" with the myth, noting that its official transcript, "published by cultural elites, foreign scholars, and (interestingly enough) the Guatemalan military [has] reappeared in school texts, newspaper articles, and advertisements." Wilhelm (1994:181) describes elements of the national elementary education curriculum of the mid-1990s. The instruction concerning nationalism contains "romanticized images of pride in the pre-Columbian Maya culture and in the *historic bravery of the Maya resistance to Spanish rule* . . . promotion of positive images of the Spanish as bearers of 'civilization' to the indigenous population . . . [and] . . . *only limited mention of any historic or continuing Maya influence* in the development of Guatemalan national culture" (Wilhelm 1994:181, emphasis added).

The emphasis on cultural homogeneity at the core of traditional nationalism has its particular forms in contemporary Guatemala. The assimilationist "*mestizaje*" identified by Hale (2006:51) or "hispanization" described by Warren (1998:137) is a central theme of the official transcript of the conquest. Indeed, the official goal of Spanish colonialism was the extension of religious homogeneity. The Dance of the Conquest was introduced to effect this goal. The final scenes, in which the Maya are militarily defeated and the K'iche' king accepts Christianity and Spanish political rule, imply nothing of a blending of two traditions into new cultural and social forms. Rather, the vision of peace and harmony proffered rests on Maya acquiescence to legitimate (won in battle) and superior (by virtue of European origin) spiritual, social, and political orders. There are strong parallels between these official Church messages in the dance and official state versions of the conquest and Tekun Umam. Put to use as a story of national unity, conversion to Christianity becomes assimilation to the "national culture" and acceptance of Spanish colonial rule becomes acquiescence to the power of the centralized state. The Church asserts a story that affirms the triumph of Christianity. The state finds in the story a moment of ethnogenesis, a mythological basis for its ideology of identity. Accordingly, as official transcript, the story of the conquest argues for a common element of modern nationalism: ethnic homogeneity.

Indeed, officially sanctioned celebrations of Tecun Uman Day have been loaded with public acts of national identification that emphasize unity and loyalty to the state. The national anthem is sung, the flag saluted, speeches given, and so forth (Otzoy 1999:85–88). While official commemorations at the statue of Tekun Umam in the capital have greatly diminished in recent years (Otzoy 1999:90), state officials, including members of congress, continue to promote the importance of Tekun Umam as a symbol of national unity (Otzoy 1999:122–123). Given its predominance in the Guatemalan state, the military (not surprisingly) has also appropriated Tekun Umam as an important symbol. For its institutional purposes of training and indoctrination, Tekun Umam becomes the ideal soldier. Within public celebrations of Tekun Umam, the military enthusiastically uses him as both an institutional and a state symbol. Otzoy describes a pamphlet produced by the military for the 1996 celebration of Tecun Uman Day in Guatemala City. It concisely (if somewhat bluntly) asserts the official state and institutional transcripts:

> For all Guatemalans, the figure of our courageous warrior TECUN UMAN should represent: (a) a lesson in patriotism; (b) an example of authentic nationalism; (c) a symbol of national identity; (d) an example of the defense of freedom, foundation for national unity; (e) champion of sovereignty; (f) the honor and courage of the Guatemalan soldier; (g) principle of dignity for the Guatemalan Army. (Otzoy 1999:133)

Despite the earnestness of the dream of national unity (and the willingness to use force to make it real), the official positions, as articulated here and above, are loaded with ambiguity and contradiction. What is the subject of Tekun Umam's patriotism and whose sovereignty does he champion? Is nationalism "authentic" because it references an indigenous person? What is the place of contemporary Maya in the national identity he symbolizes?

In *Playing Indian* (1998) Philip Deloria discerns a common pattern in the appropriation of indigenous culture to create authentic, non-European, American (U.S.) identity. From the Boston Tea Party to New Age spirituality, white identification with Native American cultures becomes consistently problematic when those playing Indian come into direct contact with actual, living indigenous people. Lakota, Menominee, or Oneida individuals and communities are too complex to be understood through the lens of the imagined vanishing noble savage. Although the United States and Guatemala are distinct along a wide array of parameters, this pattern of appropriation of Indianness and the resultant conceptual discordance applies to the Guatemalan adoption of Tekun Umam as a hero of the state. The official assertions of unity, patriotism, and so forth, given the context of conflict in which the state has readily employed violence against its own citizens, reveal only one disjuncture of ideology and experience for many Guatemalans.

The telling and retelling of the official story of the conquest have led to a national hero that, while easily referenced as a symbol, remains elusive in meaning. Otzoy identifies a degree of ambivalence that transcends class and ethnic lines, noting a paucity of "people (Mayas and Ladinos) that either understand and accept or directly reject Tecun Uman. In contradistinction, there are more people that either disregard it or are frankly indifferent" (1999:22). Deloria's observation concerning the cognitive disjuncture that occurs when actual corporeal indigenous people are read through ideologies of imaginary Indians reflects a common challenge of telling stories about ourselves. As I explored in Part One, creating a compelling narrative sometimes requires that we ignore certain past acts and present realities. For the Guatemalan national origin story, continued vigorous Maya resistance after the fall of Maya capitals such as K'uumarkaaj and Iximche is forgotten.[5] However, the contemporary presence of millions of Mayas is not so easily ignored. One way to deal with this gap between official transcript and demographic reality is to deny or diminish the connection between contemporary Maya and their pre-Columbian ancestors. Otzoy describes how those invested in distinguishing Maya from Indian reject overwhelming evidence of cultural and linguistic continuity in favor of "any type of pseudo-scientific argument to deny the Maya ancestral roots of the Mayas" (1999:162). It is not surprising, then, that a key part of the official transcript of Guatemalan nationalism is the distinction made between contemporary Indians and ancient Maya.

Deloria (1998:184–185) notes that despite the cognitive difficulties of identification with imaginary Indianness in the presence of actual Native Americans, whites continue to play Indian. In fact, the inherent contradictions are what make appropriation of images of indigenous culture "compelling" (Deloria 1998:185). The ideology of the noble savage is a fundamental motif of colonial conceptualization of indigeneity that embraces just such a contradiction. It imagines free, independent, noble Indians that are at the same time primitive, occasionally violent, and in need of colonization. In the official transcripts of Guatemalan national identity and nationalism, the noble-savage motif appears in the distinction of ancient Maya (noble) from contemporary Indians (savage).

Jakaltek Maya anthropologist Victor Montejo, in "Maya Identity and Interethnic Relations" (2005), identifies the separation made between the ancient Maya and contemporary Indians as the foundation of historic and contemporary anti-Maya racism. The ancient Maya are made symbols of nationalism, revered for their accomplishments in mathematics, calendrics, architecture, and so forth. Indians, on the other hand, are "backwards beings condemned to disappear or assimilate" (2005:1). In terms of the official transcript of the conquest, those Indians of the present who insist on being Indians are rejecting the peaceful assimilation won in battle and duly and legitimately agreed to by the K'iche' king. It is not far from this disjuncture of story and reality to discourses that view contemporary Mayas as obstacles to progress, the cause of the state's image of weakness, disunity, and backwardness.

The moment in the official conquest story that most enacts the separation of Maya from Guatemalan Indians is the death of Tekun Umam. This event is tied to other colonial mythology. One of the most pervasive elements of conquest myths across the Americas is the notion that indigenous peoples initially ascribed divine status to the European Other. In the official story of the conquest, this element is expressed in the battlefield conduct of Tekun Umam. It is said that the Maya leader mistook Pedro de Alvarado and his horse for one two-headed being (Otzoy 1999:71; Warren 1998:155). Believing that one decapitation would destroy the whole body, Tekun Umam cut off the head of the horse. This, of course, did not kill Alvarado and the hapless Indian was subsequently dispatched by the conqueror. However, Otzoy reveals that only through a selective reading of the documentary evidence is such a conclusion possible (1999:71). Moreover, this mythologized moment of peculiar indigenous misperception has strong negative implications for the image of Tekun Umam and of Mayas in general. The state-sponsored story presents Indian worldview as incompatible with the world brought by Alvarado. A reason for Spanish victory is proffered that both asserts and confirms Indian stupidity and backwardness.

So far I have argued that the death of Tekun Umam (by the official transcript) ends legitimate resistance to the Spanish colonial order, begins appropriate acquiescence to the Christian spiritual order, confirms Indian inferiority, and, by implication, identifies reluctance to assimilate to a non-Maya Guatemalan identity as illegitimate and backward. However, beyond these facets of a particularly Guatemalan version of state nationalism, Tekun Umam's death reflects a common element of the ideology of conquest and colonialism. In a certain respect this separation of the primitive, backward Indians of the present and the cultured, ingenious Maya of the past is the Guatemalan version of what Renato Rosaldo (1989:68–87) has identified as "imperialist nostalgia." Exploring narratives of colonial officials, missionaries, and anthropologists, Rosaldo identifies a common tendency for the colonizer to remember with nostalgia, even venerate, what he has destroyed (or at least contributed in changing profoundly). There is evidence suggesting that reverence of the destroyed Indian started almost immediately upon the death of Tekun Umam. According to the *Título de la Casa Ixcuin-Nahaib, Señora de Otzoya* (Recinos 1984:89–90), after his death, Tekun Umam

> appeared covered with quetzal feathers and very beautiful plumes . . . And immediately, the Adelantado [Alvarado] called to all his soldiers to come and see the beauty of the quetzal Indian. Then the Adelantado told his soldier that he had never seen another Indian as gallant and noble and covered with such beautiful quetzal feathers, in Mexico, nor in Tlaxcala, nor in any of the towns that he had conquered.[6] (translated by Burkhart and Gasco 1996:151)

While it is difficult to discern exactly whose reverence for the dead Tekun Umam is expressed in the passage authored by indigenous Maya (Otzoy 1999:67), the nostalgic worship of Tekun Umam eventually becomes part of official transcripts.[7] Below, I explore how the meaning of the death of Tekun Umam is layered with other occasionally counter-hegemonic meanings in the hidden transcript of the Dance of the Conquest. However, given the amount of nationalist veneration of Tekun Umam in his death, it is a crucial symbolic moment in the official transcript. One heroic Maya leader is converted from living to dead and the whole of the surviving population from Maya to Indian (or assimilated Ladinos). It is, as Otzoy observes, a categorization offering only marginality, "a space in which the Mayas are present in the form of death, without any real participation, without political inclusion" (1999:153).

If we read the story of the conquest as official transcript, it communicates several ideas fundamental to Guatemalan nationalism (and some common to nationalism in general). The Maya are made ancient, their descendants made Indians. Cultural homogeneity of the state is presented as a blending that results in a culture that is nominally hybrid but is fundamentally non-Maya. Independence from Spain is justified, made heroic. Somewhat ironically, a battle to preserve K'iche' Maya political autonomy has come to symbolize various non-Maya causes. Whether remembering Creole liberation from Spain, expressing dismay at English control of Belize (Castañeda 1965:6), or fighting Communists, Guatemalan elites have seen themselves in Tekun Umam.

A MAYA VERSION OF EVENTS: TEKUN UMAM RESISTS THE INVASION

Hope for military victory is now lost. After succeeding in killing his mount but not Alvarado himself, Tekun Umam lies dead. Although his nawal *is not directly portrayed in the play, most of the audience, Ladinos and Mayas alike, know that at the moment of death of the K'iche' leader his* nawal *quetzal bird also dies. The actors-dancers portraying the other Maya characters gather around and, while depicting the concern of soldiers for a fallen leader, they surreptitiously replace the flush, angry mask of the vital, living Tekun Umam with the ashen and bloodied mask of the dead leader. One of the most striking items in the inventory of the* morería, *the death mask lacks the painted glass eyes that give traditional dance masks an impressive, lifelike gaze. The lines of expression, furled brow, and other markers of anger and resistance are also absent.*

The small Ajitz, having offered himself as a pillow to comfort Tekun Umam in death, remains lying prone under the leader's head. Witzitzil Tzunun, having secured a cease-fire, holds Tekun's crown and Guatemalan flag and staff and readies himself to report to the K'iche' king (Figure 4.3). However, the audience is already fading away. They seem as uninterested as they were rapt at the moment when Tekun Umam and Pedro de Alvarado charged at one another with utmost malice. The crowd is quite thin when the K'iche' king accepts Spanish political rule and the Christian faith. Those who remain (and are not already aware) might notice that Ajitz, the character most dedicated to Maya spirituality, is absent when others are converted. By the time the king and the surviving Maya characters march in apparent harmony with Alvarado and the Spanish soldiers, there will be virtually no audience (Figure 4.4). Meanwhile, most still present seem to be dancers' wives and other kin, who now pay more attention to the task of gathering children and packing up food and other supplies that they brought in support of the performance. I would not have to work hard to convince myself that I am the only member of the audience who finds anything of the onstage action as worthy of more than a passing glance. I contemplate briefly the clergy who saw in the dance a chance to extend true faith to "their Indians." What must be one of the most important elements of the Church's official narrative is effectively ignored by the audience. Could it be that while Tekun Umam died and the Maya suffered a military defeat, the idea that political and religious harmony then followed is rejected?

Then again, it is late in the day, the performance has gone on for several hours, and seats on the bus home are certainly dwindling.

Above, I argue that the death of Tekun Umam is a critical moment in the official transcript of the conquest. His death is central in the hidden and offstage discourse as well. Dancers and artisans stridently contest one of the key elements of climatic death in the official transcript. The Maya leader did not think that Alvarado and horse were a single, two-headed beast. By decapitating the horse, Tekun hoped to negate the considerable advantage cavalry has over infantry. He was not a foolish Indian awed by the godlike Spanish, but an intelligent warrior adapting to unanticipated circumstances.

Although the death of Tekun Umam is taken as a gallant act that seems to confirm the valor of the Spanish through the worthiness of their opponents, to dance insiders the martyrdom is more Christlike. Once, while I was sitting with teachers and a community elder, talk turned to the similarities between Jesus Christ and Tekun Umam. Both figures suffered and sacrificed so that their people would survive and persist. Christ suffered for sinners and Tekun Umam for the Maya (*"la raza maya"*). The similarities continue, as a teacher related to me on a later occasion. Just as Christ appeared as a spirit after his death, so did and does Tekun Umam. A person who burns *poom* (incense) with strong faith might see him. Such a comparison indicates the reverence for the sacrifice of Tekun Umam and his prominence in K'iche' culture. Or, put another way, elements of official doctrine are recontextualized and adapted to unofficial purposes.

The death of Tekun Umam is extended to contemporary violence as well. Linda Green (1994:235) notes how the story of the conquest and the death of Tekun Umam are frequently used to help make sense of the violence of the counterinsurgency. One consultant, referring to recent state-directed violence, remarked, "It was the same as when they killed Tecum Uman" (Green 1994:235).

The prominence of Tekun Umam through his mask is felt in other traditional dances in ways that invert the official conquest story. Performers of the Dance of the Moors and the Christians also rent costumes from the *morería* where I apprenticed. The mask of Rey Carlos, the leader of the Spanish, is identical to the Tekun Umam mask except that it is painted to have white skin. The masks share the same important characteristics, including a uniformly angry countenance and a bifurcated quetzal bird above the brow. This is best understood in terms of the parallel roles of the characters and somewhat turns the world upside down. Both figures combat foreign invaders of different religions. Tekun Umam struggles against the Spanish invaders of

4.3. The Death of Tekun Umam. Witzitzil Tzunun looks down on a dead Tekun Umam. Tzunun is in the process of assuming command. He has Tekun's crown (identified by the small stuffed quetzal bird) and staff with the contemporary Guatemalan flag. (Photograph by author.)

4.4. The Play Ends. Rey K'iche' (center with flag) leads a Maya cacique, *Witzitzil Tzunun, and Pedro de Alvarado* (left to right). *The Maya leader has accepted Spanish political control and Christianity, San Cristóbal Totonicapán, July 1995. Note the diminished audience in the background compared with Figure 4.3. (Both photographs by author.)*

the K'iche' homeland. Rey Carlos, in a repainted Tekun Umam mask, fights to expel the Moors from Spain, inverting the usual parallels (particularly as understood by the Spanish) between the reconquest of Spain and the conquest of the New World. In at least one community in the highlands, an indigenous understanding of the similarities between the reconquest and the conquest includes an equivalence of the Maya with the Spanish. Just as Tekun Umam, officially an obstacle to Christianity, is understood by dancers and artisans as Christlike, so he becomes Spanish-like. This highly oblique reference from one play to another implies a strident heterodoxy. The Dance of the Moors and the Christians, by associating the Maya with the Spanish, potentially connects the Moors to Ladinos. That Rey Carlos succeeds in expelling the Moors from Spain after hundreds of years of Muslim control has striking implications.

So far I have explored ways in which Tekun Umam is used to counter the ideology of the state, through cultural artifacts, in multivalent performance, and as subject of offstage discourse. I have focused on the politics of ethnicity and inegalitarian social and economic realities. However, beyond these overtly political issues, Tekun Umam (as well as Ajitz) carries another layer of meaning, one that emphasizes what Fischer identifies as "underlying cultural forms" (1999:476).

TEKUN UMAM AND CULTURAL CONTINUITY

Opening the door to the regalia shop reveals a mixture of the odors of mildew, sewing-machine oil, and sweat setting in clothing. Once my eyes adjust to the low light, I find it in its typical state. Masks, scraps of all sorts of fabric, pieces of costumes, and all manner of sewing implements lie about the room. This arrangement, I know from spending some time as a helper in the shop, reflects various projects under way more than it does a state of disorder. Although most things sit where they were put down when the previous day's work was completed, a few masks are grouped together, facing us and the door through which we have just passed. Staring at us in the peculiar way of glass-eyed masks, they frame a conspicuous scrap of paper. It is a note written in the voices of Tekun Umam and Witzitzil Tzunun. As the shop manager reads, his face forms a smile, and he begins to laugh aloud. Tekun and Tzunun, it seems, have lodged a complaint about their rigorous rental schedule. They are tired and need rest. We all have a good laugh. We deduce that one of the other apprentices and a good friend must have left the note.

After we enjoy the note for a while, our teacher tells us that to the dancers, the idea that Tekun and Tzunun would speak through the masks is not that strange. They are powerful objects to be treated with care and respect. A few stories are exchanged concerning the power of masks, costumbres, *and spirits invoked*[8] *in performance of La Conquista. As I curiously listen, I find that my conception of masks representing various degrees of resistance, models for cross-ethnic interaction, does not completely describe their significance. The relationship to Maya religious belief and practice is another layer of meaning that must be addressed. I remind myself once again that culture and meaning are polysemous and that my models about masks in the Dance of the Conquest must address this newly discovered multivalence.*[9]

As I explored above, elements of dance performance and paraphernalia not directly related to the politics of ethnicity revealed themselves to me only after months of fieldwork. My difficulty in discerning these elements reflects an important characteristic of hidden transcripts. Scott observes that

> cultural expression by virtue of its *polyvalent symbolism and metaphor* lends itself to disguise. By the subtle use of codes one can insinuate into a ritual, a pattern of dress, a song, a story, meanings that are accessible to one intended audience and opaque to another audience the actors wish to exclude. Alternatively, the excluded (and in this case, powerful) audience

> may grasp the seditious message in the performance but find it difficult to react because that sedition is clothed in terms that also can lay claim to a perfectly innocent construction. (1990:158, emphasis added)

Such polysemous symbolic complexes are, of course, part and parcel of the cultural distinctiveness of a given people. In effect, one way the dance hides its subversive message is through the use of what it seeks to preserve: the continuity of its unique system of symbols and worldviews. The code is also the goal.

Just as the play is loaded with Mesoamerican religious symbols, so does Tekun Umam offer material for cultural continuity. Although the story of the spirit-twin relationship between Tekun Umam and the quetzal bird is available to all Guatemalans, it cannot be dismissed as significant only in the official transcript. In fact, Gossen (1996:313) suggests "the concept of individual co-essences" as one of the core elements of Mesoamerican spirituality. Its inclusion in the official transcript and its availability to an ethnically plural audience legitimize some presence of Maya culture in the dance. The literal transformation of Tekun Umam into a quetzal bird emphasized in the official story (Otzoy 1999:69–70) seems rather romanticized and has parallels to the unity-of-man-and-horse element of the story. When told by the powerful, the transformation of Tekun Umam into a bird speaks of an Indian past that is incompatible with present reality. On the other hand, by presenting it officially as part of the end of Maya cultural distinctiveness, it may shield those elements described below that are more counter-hegemonic. Moreover, an important spiritual relationship between human and avian can be manifested without the material conversion of Tekun Umam to quetzal.

As I mentioned above, the quetzal is repeatedly referenced in the paraphernalia of Tekun Umam. It appears bifurcated on his mask, in the form of a small stuffed animal on the top of his crown, and even in the crest of the flag of Guatemala he carries into battle. Other references are more oblique. The connection to his quetzal *nawal* is reiterated in the predominance of the color green in the costume of Tekun Umam. Performers select elements of their costume (chest piece, pants, and cape) from a general stock. Actor-dancers playing Tekun Umam prefer items dominated by green. Moving further away from the officially sanctioned presence of Maya symbology in the dance, the green of Tekun Umam is loaded with other meanings. It denotes a more general intimate connection to nature, inverting the negative assignment of culture to Ladinos and nature to Mayas. It is also read as a color of life force and vitality. Its association with center in Maya color-direction cosmology cannot be ignored.

Offstage commentary on the death of Tekun Umam, as I mention above, sometimes references Christ. Occasionally, these discussions venture into what happens to the Maya leader after his death, and the fate of his earthly remains is also a topic of the play's offstage discourse. Although consultants are quite aware that Tekun Umam was a native son of Totonicapán, where he was laid to rest is not certain. Instead of being entombed in a known location, Tekun Umam is said to have disappeared, converted into a spirit.

The performance of ritual by contemporary daykeepers, reports of spirit apparitions in the present, and the disappearance of the body of Tekun Umam in the past are all associated with caves. This cluster of space, ritual, and divinity has a certain Mesoamerican character to it. According to an elder consultant referencing explicitly the *Popul Wuj*, as part of turning into a spirit, Tekun Umam (along with Witzitzil Tzunun) hid, crouched down in a cave, and turned to stone. Part Four of the *Popul Wuj* involves the first dawn of the current world. The original human beings await the sun accompanied by four supernatural patrons, who have provided, most notably, fire and demand payment of sacrifice in return. In the dark, cold, damp predawn, the sun rises, drying and warming the earth. In the process, a variety of natural and supernatural creatures turn to stone, including the patron deities (D. Tedlock 1996:161). The relationship between human beings and their divine patrons does not end with the dawning of the new era. The corporeal have an ongoing obligation to ritually name and feed the spiritual (D. Tedlock 1996:163). In the hidden transcript, Tekun Umam undergoes a similar transformation. At the beginning of the Hispanic era, his living form is petrified and converted to spirit that subsequently is named and honored in ritual. In *Time and the Highland Maya*, Barbara Tedlock (1992:154–155) notes that K'iche' divination rituals begin with a prayer asking for permission. "In the name of the *Father Tecum Umam* and King Quiché Mountain [spirit], C'oxol Mountain [spirit], Tzitzimit Mountain [spirit], the first mountain [spirit] I ask for one blessing, one favor" (B. Tedlock 1992:154, emphasis added). So the hero of K'iche' military resistance (along with two other characters of the Dance of the Conquest) becomes a divinity that one must address in proper execution of ritual.[10]

Beyond his association with world-changing transitions, some dancers connect Tekun Umam directly to the K'iche' version of Quetzalcoatl, Q'ukumatz. This god that combines avian and serpentine elements is "[o]ne of the great gods of ancient Mesoamerica" (Miller and Taube 1993:141). The multiple references to the quetzal bird in the mask and costume are layered with additional meanings. Moreover, with less direct symbolism, consultants make the same link to the K'iche' king. The association of both characters with Q'ukumatz has a certain logic. The figure is said to have taken on different forms at different times. Indeed, a man who has danced the part of Tekun Umam several times describes the various forms of Q'ukumatz. In different forms, Q'ukumatz was a woman, a man, and a feathered serpent.

> *Q'ukumatz era un dios que se formaba en tres símbolos, tres personas. Siete lunas se convertía en hombre, siete dias en mujer, y siete lunas se convertía en serpiente; a veces se llama Q'ukumatz.*[11]
>
> (Q'ukumatz was a god that was formed from three symbols, three persons. Seven moons he became a man, seven days a woman, and seven moons a serpent; at times he's called Q'ukumatz.)

Another consultant suggests an explanation of the fair-skinned mask of the K'iche king; Quetzalcoatl, in one manifestation, is said to be white.

In this reading, Tekun Umam and the various forms of Q'ukumatz are represented as not layered on one character but spread over two figures. Tekun Umam (with his dark, determined mask) and the K'iche' king (with his pale, worried mask) can be interpreted as the opposing forces within one god or figure, one Q'ukumatz. Tekun expresses resistance, masculinity, and warrior aspects. The K'iche' king presents passivity, femininity, and the prophet predicting (or at least resigned to) the demise of his followers. That Tekun Umam and Rey K'iche' may be different manifestations of the same figure came up during a K'iche' language lesson when my teacher emphasized that Tekun Umam himself is often identified as the K'iche' king.[12]

The reference to Q'ukumatz and the manner in which Tekun Umam and Witzitzil Tzunun are converted into spirits infuse the dance with particularly Mesoamerican millenarian overtones. In fact, Garret Cook (2000:119, 139–140) outlines just such a reading of La Conquista in Momostenango, emphasizing the identification of Pedro de Alvarado with the Aztec sun god Tonatiuh. Cook (2000:139) describes Tonatiuh / Alvarado as "the personifier of the new order . . . the new sun." Tekun Umam becomes "a personifier of pre-sunrise liminality" (Cook 2000:119). As such, the struggle is between the new sun seeking to impose a new order and those of the previous era attempting to destroy the new sun. In this reading, what outwardly appears to be a struggle between Spanish and Maya adversaries becomes a contest between deities. Accordingly, the dance again references the story of the dawn of the present era found in the *Popul Wuj* (Cook 2000:119). Momostecos express varied interpretations of the meaning of the dance (Cook 2000:119). Some describe Tekun Umam as a dictator who remains in office too long and must be forcibly removed (Cook 2000:136). Accordingly, Tekun becomes the false, boastful sun (Cook 2000:140). Others imply that Tekun will be reborn, replacing a false Tonatiuh / Alvarado sun. In particular, that Alvarado assumes the role of the sun without self-sacrifice and rebirth presents inconsistency with Mesoamerican millenarian stories (Cook 2000:119). Such an interpretation leaves open the possible "rebirth of Tecum . . . as the yet unrealized transformative sunrise" (Cook 2000:140). Indeed, resurrection is implied in the repeated links that Totonicapense consultants make between Tekun Umam and Jesus Christ.

In addition to Tekun Umam and the K'iche' king, as I explored earlier, Ajitz (the soldier-priest) and Witzitzil Tzunun (second-in-command to Tekun Umam) reference pre-Columbian deities with millenarian implications. These coded and offstage discourses present a particularly Maya view of change, one that has adapted to deal with the shifts brought on by Spanish invasion and colonization and the Guatemalan state. Various characters are both historical figures, bound to a certain moment, and supernatural beings that transcend world-altering transitions. In the official story, political subjugation, religious conversion, and cultural assimilation are asserted. In the K'iche' version, the defeated are not vanquished but converted into spirits who are venerated and honored as part of religious traditions that are adapted but not replacements of the old. The play does not deny the presence of powerful outsiders. Nor does it suggest the end of Maya culture as a consequence of such forces. Rather it presents ways to accommodate the two; it adapts Mesoamerican mythology to understand change and the adaptations it necessitates.

The dance presents elements fundamental to a uniquely Mesoamerican worldview. However, Cook (2000:119) points out that there are various ways that consultants understand the coded meanings of the Dance of the Conquest. In other words, the hidden transcript is not uncontested. Nonetheless, in the names, actions, and iconography of key characters in the play, there are available counter-hegemonic views of the Spanish invasion and the changes it brought. Specifically, the play challenges the notion that to be Guatemalan is to be assimilated and non-Maya. In a sense, the coded ideas and symbols are part and parcel of the struggle to maintain Maya cultural distinctiveness. Consistent with more overt indigenous activism, it is not easy to classify offstage discourse of the dance as either exclusively political or exclusively cultural. It presents both modes of dealing with powerful ethnic Others (political strategies) that allow cultural continuity and the content necessary for cultural continuity (cultural goals). It also provides culturally salient material for the construction of post–Cold War conceptions of national identity. Guatemalans have an official national hero who is Maya. His counter-appropriation in the context of ongoing Maya cultural revitalization seems troubling to the state and its political elite.

TEKUN UMAM AND REINVENTING NATIONALISM

The walk from the hotel to "the obelisk" is manageable. It is long but direct and does not involve moving from one zone to another, a transition that in the past has gotten me lost in this, the largest and capital, city of Guatemala. The hotel staff has been helpful, providing directions that I am able to visibly confirm using a large detailed map posted on the wall of the lobby. It figures (and turns out) to be about a twenty-minute walk.

Along the way, I reflect on earlier visits to the capital and on my fieldwork in general. Some twelve years earlier, K'iche' artisanal masters in Totonicapán introduced me to Tekun Umam, a principal character in the Dance of the Conquest, a figure of history and a member of the spiritual pantheon. Now I make my way along a wide boulevard to encounter Tekun Umam in official statuary of the state.

Otzoy (1999:90) describes how the obelisk—a statue of Tekun Umam as official hero of the Guatemalan state and once the central object in secular rituals of state and nationalism—was obscured by the construction of a cloverleaf exchange between the two main thoroughfares that meet at the plaza. The plaza that once focused the eye down long, wide boulevards is now barely visible. In fact, only after crossing a circular traffic ramp and walking down a path am I able to see the statue. The plaza itself, bounded by bridging, ramps, roadways, and the always cold, dark space under highways, is profoundly vacant. A couple passes through, and a legless man sits with his back to the statue. I take a number of photos as I approach the statue. I expect to find a nostalgic inscription on the plaque affixed to the statue's massive concrete base. Instead of memorializing the national hero of Guatemala, the note remembers the building of the transport infrastructure that now surrounds and hides the plaza. The only person commemorated is former mayor and eventual president Oscar Berger. After taking a few more photographs, I leave the plaza to approach and view it from another direction. From some angles, the head and spear of Tekun Umam are visible above the bridge deck with its passing vehicles. I cross the plaza again and head back to the hotel.

As is often the case in fieldwork, by accident I find another space of interest. The National Museum of Archaeology and Ethnology is convenient to my route. After turning off the main boulevard and walking about a block along a tall, inviolable metal fence, I pass through a gate to enter a space that evokes Walter Little's (2004:64–88) description of tourism in a transnational border zone. The entrances of an archaeology and ethnology museum and an art museum face an open area where tourist buses, tourists, guides, and security guards mingle. Flanking the entry to the archaeology and ethnology museum are two more statues. Tekun Umam is represented by one, and drawing me again back to the community of my first fieldwork, the other is a likeness of Atanasio Tzul. Both figures are claimed by Totonicapenses as native sons. Tekun Umam led K'iche' resistance to the Spanish invasion of 1524. Tzul led a rebellion against the Spanish colonial order in 1820, briefly reigning as king of a breakaway K'iche' polity. In the official history of the state, Tekun Umam is the national hero, and Atanasio Tzul, the initiator of the drive for independence from Spain. Both statues reference "authentic" Maya culture. Tzul, in colonial Indian garb, displays corn. Tekun Umam is adorned with stylized hieroglyphs. Both also reference violence. Tekun Umam predominantly wields an axe. Tzul has at his feet a basket containing the severed head of a Spaniard.

The obelisk of Tekun Umam is barely visible to anyone; the museum statues, visible mostly to tourists. The spaces and the orientation of and representations in the statues are all marked by great ambivalence. National pride in the Maya past is evident, but obscured. Toward both figures there is a sense of both adoration and fear, emotional closeness and ethnic distance. This informal masking of official iconography reveals uncertainty in an era of political transformation.

4.5. The Obelisk. Tekun Umam in statue overlooks an empty plaza encircled by a road ramp, December 2006. (Photograph by author.)

Publicly questioning official ideology has been a dangerous endeavor in Guatemala. However, various factors, including the end of the Cold War and the 1996 Peace Accords, have led to a Guatemalan society somewhat more tolerant of open discussion. In short, what I have presented as the official story of the conquest is now more available for public contestation. Kay Warren (1998:154–156) describes an ongoing discussion among Maya intellectuals concerning the meaning of the Spanish invasion and the story of the conquest. Otzoy (1999:163–164) describes discourses of varying degrees of openness that are reconsidering the meaning of Tekun Umam and the story of the conquest from a variety of perspectives. Ronald Wilhelm (1994) describes the efforts by elementary education teachers working through PRONEBI (Programo Nacional de Educación Bilingüe Bicultural, the national state-sponsored bilingual education program) to create counter-hegemonic classroom activities concerning the significance of the conquest. The conquest or invasion is but one area of the official ideology of state and nation that Maya intellectuals have criticized (Cojtí Cuxil 1996; Montejo 2005; Raxche' 1996; Sam Colop 1996; Warren 1998).

As official ideology comes under more public contestation, material for new conceptions of state, nation, and identity are needed. Scott (1990:183–201) notes that making public the hidden transcript does not represent an entirely new mode of thought, as ideologies that challenge power are sometimes described. Rather, what was once transmitted secretly is now discussed openly. Accordingly, we are mistaken to think that sharing hidden transcripts is nothing more than the grumblings of the illiterate masses. They embody vital ideational foundations for survival of subordinate groups, and given the appropriate setting, hidden transcripts can become the ideology of social movements that change societies. In this vein it is interesting to note that the rejection of the official transcript argued by Maya intellectuals parallels discourse offered by the hidden layers of the dance. Enrique Sam Colop argues that the Maya did not see the Spanish as godlike (1996:108). La Conquista insiders and Maya cultural activists both reject the notion that Tekun Umam perceived Alvarado and horse as a two-headed supernatural monster. As Mayas involved in cultural revitalization repudiate the official story of the conquest and its "virtual erasure of indigenous peoples as historical agents" (Warren 1998:134), so the dance's hidden transcript describes continued resistance of various forms and suggests paths to change and continuity.

The Dance of the Conquest not only codes counter-hegemonic strategies and ideas, but also is an ideal storehouse of meanings and symbols, the nuts and bolts of the belief and practice Maya cultural activists seek to preserve and revitalize. It references pre-Columbian divinities and cosmological order and asserts a notion of political and religious transition in which the local may be altered but is not destroyed. It reflects the Maya goal of local autonomy and self-determination common from colonization to the present. The contemporary struggle for local autonomy (even when "local" means Maya within the Mexican or Guatemalan state) noted by Nash (2004) represents a continuity of strategy to effect continuity of culture. That is, Maya insist and have insisted that change happens within meaningful parameters. Through this lens, it matters not whether the dominant outsider takes the form of Spanish colonialism, with its baggage of religious purity, or contemporary states, with their conflation of modernity and assimilation.

Not only are Maya symbols and worldview expressed in the dance, but national symbols are deployed as well. That Tekun Umam carries the flag of Guatemala more than shields the counter-hegemonic messages of the play. It says that Mayas are both patriotic Guatemalans and proud bearers of a millennial cultural tradition. This is not to say that Guatemala should become a Maya state. Montejo echoes other Maya intellectuals and argues for an inclusive and plural Guatemala that respects the cultural and human rights of all, noting pragmatically that "we cannot say that we are all mestizos or that we are all Maya" (2005:8). Indeed, Niezen (2003:198–200) notes that the accommodation of cultural pluralism within states enjoys a largely successful record of peace and stability. Yet, many states still seem to favor policies and ideologies that stress cultural homogeneity. Moreover, the "unity" that motivates and justifies policies aimed at erasing cultural diversity is best achieved by embracing pluralism. "Within nation-states, the paradox that openness and pluralism create unity is confirmed with a consistency that makes the frequency of intolerance and ethnic violence confounding and frustrating" (Niezen 2003:199).

Overcoming this unhappy record of state policy includes reconceiving nationalism in a way that accommodates pluralist realities. For Guatemala this process means reexamining the story of the Spanish invasion. As such, the Dance of the Conquest, with its multivalence, can be the source for a meaningful review of nationhood and identity. It presents multiple ways to be Maya and multiple ways to be Guatemalan. It constructs, presents, and shares some of the core symbols and concepts of Maya cosmology and mythology in living cultural practice. It presupposes cultural pluralism rather than cultural homogeneity. Just as Zapatistas make prideful claims on their Mexicanness (Gossen 2004), so do K'iche' traditional dancers lay stakes to their Guatemalanness.

Indeed, Irma Otzoy argues for counter-appropriation of Tekun Umam. Echoing this relationship between hidden transcripts and agendas of open social movements, Otzoy envisions a rewriting of the conquest story in which "Maya intellectuals could learn from the rural Mayas. Ironically, as evidenced in the Conquest Dance, neither they nor their history have been totally conquered" (1999:164). The iconography and action of Tekun Umam in the Dance of the Conquest provide various means to challenge the presuppositions of traditional nationalism; his status as a national hero gives him saliency and weight. His incorporation into the Maya pantheon rejects the notion that Guatemala is or can be culturally homogeneous. The persistence of Mayas in both corporeal and spirit forms effects real and ideational cultural diversity. It should be clear by now that efforts to make a culturally homogeneous Guatemala through assimilation or elimination of Maya cultures and communities have failed. Moreover such efforts have done extensive damage to the prospect of Guatemalan unity and prosperity and to the state's international reputation. Cultural pluralism is not the problem; attempting to erase it is.

Representational dance is an extraordinary means of constructing identity. However, it also can be an excellent means of communicating complex multilayered symbols and concepts that are the foundation of a people's unique cultural heritage. In the preceding two chapters, I have explored how K'iche' Maya traditional dance affords performers a means to express their unique cultural knowledge and identity. These expressions, while certainly shaped by the realities of colonialism and persistent social, political, and economic inequality, in traditional dances also realize, in concrete acts and objects, continuity between past and present. Traditional dance is, then, both process and product of indigenous Maya survival.

In Part Three, I shift my attention to a form of Native dance in the United States. As I will explore in more detail, indigenous dancers in Guatemala and in the United States have worked within the constraints of power. In both cases, indigenous-performed representational dance has become a way to express cultural distinctiveness while also accommodating the expectations of powerful Others. In both cases, changing circumstances have allowed greater freedom of expression in recent years. Connected to indigenous groups worldwide, Maya and Native American groups are in the midst of cultural revitalization. Dance seems to be a part of indigenous representations to Others, although under varied political circumstances, for some time to come.

NOTES

1. While the dance-drama El Baile de la Conquista identifies many characters by specific name, the K'iche' political leader is known by the generic Rey K'iche' ("K'iche' king"). Who exactly delegates Tekun Umam as military leader is not clear in the dance.

2. Otzoy (1999:5, 21) agrees.

3. My description of the meanings shared among dancers, artisans, and other insiders in the audience is largely based on my fieldwork as an apprentice and more recent observations of performance of the dance. Analysis of the official transcript of Tekun Umam in the larger Guatemalan society is based on my field data as well as the work of other scholars, particularly *Tekun Umam: From Nationalism to Maya Resistance* by Irma Otzoy (1999).

4. The change of the community's name from Ayutla did not come without protest by some of its residents (Otzoy 1999:83–84).

5. Such resistance has become recovered memory among Maya involved in cultural revitalization (Warren 1998:155).

6. Rosaldo briefly explores the connection between imperialist nostalgia and the mythology of the "hunter hero" (1989:72), and the tone of the passage is evocative of the relationship between hunter and felled prey.

7. Grandin identifies a "cult [of Tekun Umam that] developed among Quetzalteco Ladino intellectuals" in the early twentieth century (2000:289). Here, interest in Tekun Umam certainly reflects the regional autonomy that had been expressed politically in the form of the breakaway Republic of the Highlands (1838–1840). In this case, the

martyr to K'iche' liberty becomes the hero of anti-centralism (and by implication anti-state nationalism).

8. Scott (1990:141–142) notes that spirit possession is an ideal context for outward expression of counter-official discourse. If the shaman may publicly pronounce known (if not openly discussed) transgressions to effect social control, might a possessed subordinate criticize elites?

9. This vignette is adapted from my doctoral dissertation. I was fortunate to work with consultants who sensed the gaps in my understanding and who often took advantage of such "teachable moments."

10. The incorporation of Tekun Umam into the pantheon is not limited to the K'iche'. A ritual that I observed in December 2005 in the Kaqchikel community of San Lucas Tolimán began similarly with the supplication of Tekun Umam.

11. This quote came from an impromptu interview with the guide/groundskeeper at K'uumarkaaj in August 1995.

12. The *Popul Wuj* notes that Tojil "is the same as the god of the Mexican people, who is named Yolcuat and *Quitzalcuat*" (D. Tedlock 1996:162, emphasis added). The feathered serpent, then, is referenced, sometimes directly and sometimes rather indirectly, by three characters in the dance.

Part Three

Native American Powwow

Five

Origin, Change, and Continuity in Powwow

Tulsa in August is certainly always hot, and this weekend in August is particularly so. The weather competes with sporting events for headlines and space in the local paper. However, it is neither the weather nor sports that has brought me to Oklahoma. I am here to attend the thirtieth annual Intertribal Indian Club of Tulsa (IICOT) Powwow of Champions. Before this IICOT powwow, I have attended powwows only in the upper Midwest, which draw dancers and audiences primarily from Ojibwe, Potawatomi, Ho-Chunk, and Menominee communities. It is to complement my experiences with Woodland powwows that I have made myself a part of the audience in the Tulsa Expo Square for this most noted Southern Plains contest powwow.

Expo Center is a cavernous fieldhouse-like structure, affording large, open floor space well suited for a variety of uses. Although predominantly gray and starkly functional, it is air-conditioned and well lit. The space, aside from the pitch of the roof, is rectilinear; squares and rectangles predominate in the shape of walls, windows, and floor and their orientation to one another. Its length is split into two areas sharing the same roof, separated by a break in the level of the floor. The lower level is employed for the IICOT powwow and, visible and audible to all, the upper level hosts a carnival. IICOT organizers make the most of the functionality of the space and overcome its less appealing aesthetic qualities.

After entering and purchasing a ticket, I make my way to the dance arena, which is bordered by a few rows of benches and folding chairs arranged in an octagon. The orientation of the floor seating forms a transition between the squared lines of the building and the circular dance space. Dancers and their families and other supporters hold the benches and chairs in this area. Personal items (Pendleton blankets, bustles placed carefully to keep their eagle feathers from touching the ground) adorn many of the seats. In addition to softening the corners of the Expo Square, the floor-seating area adds color and texture to the space. The west end is anchored by a row of seats for the current, former, and visiting princesses. Elevated to afford a clear view of the entire arena are tables for announcers and officials of the sponsoring organization. The orientation of the powwow arena can be read according to the space of a Plains tipi, with the place of the host on the side opposite the door (Gelo 1999:46).

Immediately behind the floor seating on all but the host side is a walkway that separates the general audience from dancers and their supporters. Portable grandstands, for the general audience, have been placed behind this walkway on two sides. On the remaining side of the arena are vendors of crafts and foods and representatives of educational institutions and social service groups, all ordered into neat rows and aisles. A stroll through this area provides a chance to buy blankets, jewelry, t-shirts, videos, and so forth. It also provides a chance to learn about health and social issues. The view across the dance floor toward the rows of booths is dominated by a large backlighted sign advertising "Indian Tacos." The tacos feature a mixture of chili and cheese served on fry bread, the key component that makes the taco "Indian." A product of the need to survive on government-ration flour during the early reservation period, fry bread has become a necessary part of powwows and a symbol of intertribal tradition.

Overall, I am reminded of the American Indian Center's annual powwow at the University of Illinois, Chicago. There, as here, the powwow seating arrangement circles and softens the lines of hard, angular utilitarian spaces. Also common to both are expansive areas of neatly ordered rows of booths. However, here the dancing that follows, while similar, has a distinctive Southern Plains flavor.

Because of its location, size, and reputation, I anticipate that the IICOT powwow will be something new to me. My expectations to see something different are met almost immediately upon my arrival. Before the grand entry, we are treated to a session of gourd dancing. Women in shawls, and men with long red and gold stoles and feather fans in their left hands, shake rattles consisting of cans mounted on the ends of long shafts with their right hands. All begin by facing the drum circle at the center of the arena. While the women maintain their position relative to the drummers, the men work their way toward the center at varied rates, periodically bowing heads and shoulders in unison. Between intervals of music and movement toward the center, men occasionally walk in a path concentric to the drum. All is done to a low-tempo rhythm. At times, there are breaks in the music, and the dancers respond with a hushed kind of whooping. Occasionally, a blanket is carried through the arena and donations are collected, mostly from members of the group.

The rattles, I read in the IICOT program, represent percussive instruments made of gourd and rawhide that were widely used in aboriginal times. The program further informs me that the Gourd Dance, like much of powwow, is given to honor Native veterans and emphasizes "grace and dignity." Although not a central or competitive powwow dance, gourd dancing followed a path to the present similar to that of other forms. Born of dances performed by warrior societies, it was suppressed by government officials, underwent a mid-twentieth-century revival, and spread among various Native nations, exhibiting both intertribal (or shared standard) features and practices specific to particular groups (Howard 1976). However, where other powwow dances are widespread beyond the Southern Plains, gourd dancing remains largely a regional phenomenon.

Gourd dancing's place at the very beginning of the typical powwow program makes it somewhat marginal to the rest of the dancing, and not many other dancers or spectators are in attendance. However, it seems to have a transformative effect, converting everyday utilitarian space into something less mundane, perhaps sacred. Observing the dancers' deliberate movements and absorbing the repetitive rhythms of the music create a clear sense of transition. Its solemn, cyclic pattern is a soothing contrast to the disorienting pace and space of modern life. In their methodical progress around the drum and toward the center, dancers give the impression of imposing, through persistent concentrated effort, a circle on the rectangular space. The floor of the Tulsa Expo Square made ready, dancing, honoring, and socializing can now begin.

Powwow is an event as much as it is a genre of dance. Indeed, Daniel Gelo defines powwow as "a festival of dancing and dance contests, feasting, gift giving, camping, and other social activities" (1999:40). With its intense socializing, food, and calendric (often annual) scheduling, powwow is a bit like the Guatemalan indigenous *feria*, but with dance more central. Also like *feria*, powwow has cultural, economic, and political dimensions. Dancers in both events face the challenges that come with being indigenous in a society dominated by nonindigenous Others. Histories of genocide and ethnocide must continue to be overcome, and the twin pillars of indigenous survival—common culture and experience and the social solidarity born from them—are constructed at powwow and *feria*. Powwow perhaps sets itself apart by its simultaneous construction of both local concrete identity and culture and of the more abstract pan-ethnic category of Native American. *Feria* concentrates much more exclusively on the local community, in space and identity.

Although the work of self-representation and the politics of cultural survival are crucial, powwow is also fun. It is an engaging, enjoyable event, a

5.1. Circle within Square. Tulsa Expo Square is configured for the 2007 Powwow of Champions. (Photograph by author.)

chance to catch up with extended kin and old friends. The ubiquitous emcee fills lulls in dancing with humorous stories and jokes. Even in dance competition, enthusiastic handshakes and laughter are shared among opponents more often than bitter rivalry and protested results. There are music, dancing, joking, raffles, and special treats that all add to a festive atmosphere. Because powwow is so much fun, it excels at promoting mutual support, positive image, and political alliance. At the same time, however, this fun does not mean that powwow is frivolous. There is space for clowning and laughter but also respect and reverence.

Part Three departs from the previous in method and sources. Fieldwork does continue to play an important role. I attended about a dozen powwows primarily in the upper Midwest (all no more than a day trip from Chicago) as well as the IICOT Powwow of Champions in Tulsa. However, I rely less on primary fieldwork and more on the published work of other scholars. I also employ electronic ethnography on a wide variety of websites dedicated to powwow. Additionally, I rely on event programs available at powwows that I have attended. In short, my approach to powwow in the field has been as an audience member. As I will explore in more detail below, powwow contests the Indian of the white imagination. It often declares "everyone welcome" in its advertising, and field research has emphasized what powwow says to spectators. Indeed, Thiesz identifies powwow as "quintessential *public* American Indian cultural expression" (2005:86, emphasis added). It is an act of self-representation in a symbolic domain crowded with stereotypes of Native people.

So what then makes a powwow a powwow? In a general sense it is a set of dances and the context of their performance. Given the profound cultural diversity of Native North America, the existence of an event performed across a variety of indigenous nations is counterintuitive. In fact, Robes Kipp identifies powwow dancing as one of the preset notions of how Indians are preconceived by whites. Along with the war bonnet, powwow is one of the features of "Indian culture" in the mainstream imagination (2001:33). Noted powwow authority Clyde Ellis, citing Gloria Alese Young (1981), argues that at one level powwow constructs "Indianness," what Alese Young identifies as a "supertribal level of identity based on a set of previously established stereotypes" (2005:11). However, Ellis (2005), Gelo (1999), and other contemporary powwow scholars contend also that powwow is the means to express local, specific tribal identities.

As such, a common theme explored in my treatment of powwow is the ongoing coexistence of diversity and commonality among Native nations of North America. In terms of powwow, this means considering a form that manifests certain broad themes and practices, many of which originated on the Great Plains. However, it also means that within a common framework, the realization of a specific powwow reflects a particular culture and group of people who share it.

It may help to think of powwow as a kind of common language among Native nations, a collection of dialects with enough common structure and vocabulary to allow for cross-cultural (or "intertribal," in the words of powwow enthusiasts) understanding. Common features of the grammar indicate connection among dialects of the language, but their divergence suggests that varied speech communities adapt general structures to their specific needs and tastes. Dialects are mutually intelligible, but speakers are able to understand and express themselves most ably in their mother dialect.

To unpack this set of dialects of dance, this chapter covers the origin and evolution of powwow with emphasis on its aboriginal roots and postwar development. In the next chapter, I discuss the structure and characteristics of powwow in the contemporary period (which, I argue, begins with the collapse of the Soviet Union). Subsequently, I consider powwow in terms of recent scholarship on indigenous politics, that is, as "self-representation" that asserts multiplicity of identity.

ORIGINS AND DEVELOPMENT

Both Plains and Woodland powwows derive from a similar pattern of change and continuity, of response to colonization and ethnocidal policies, of economic adaptation to inadequate reservation resources and the vagaries of wage labor. I begin with a discussion of aboriginal dance and then briefly cover its response to colonization during the nineteenth century. I then explore the emergence of powwow dancing in the context of twentieth-century U.S. society. I conclude this chapter with a discussion of the Cold War and post–Cold War political and cultural climate.

Often performed for the ethnically mixed audiences characteristic of globalization, contemporary powwow is fundamentally a representational dance. However, powwow also has roots in dance of the precolonial past. As is likely the case for all human societies, the peoples of Native North America put varied dance traditions to social and sacred purposes. In other words, cultural and social diversity among aboriginal Native nations generated a diversity of dancing. Within the diversity/commonality tension of current powwow, these varied cultural roots are expressed sometimes subtly, sometimes overtly.

Red Lake Ojibwe artist and historian Robert DesJarlait (1997:117) traces Anishinaabé dance to the primordial past. Evocative of the form of dancing familiar to powwow-goers today, the original man, "who could not walk or crawl, took his first two steps with his right foot, one harsh, one soft, on Mother Earth." Moving from first human beings to aboriginal ancestors, DesJarlait notes a connection between dance and economy. A key pre-European context for dancing among the Anishinaabé was the Niimiwin, seasonal festivals of trade and socializing among neighboring groups. The Niimiwin featured social dancing of communal orientation accompanied by hand drums. Revealing a pattern reminiscent of contemporary intercultural representations, where the image of the community is in play, participants dressed in their finest vestments for Niimiwin (DesJarlait 1997:117–118).

Intergroup trade festivals were a common feature of North American aboriginal economies and were likely the occasion for dancing across the continent. Raiding and other forms of low-intensity, intergroup violence were also likely features of the aboriginal political landscape. It was on the Great Plains, however, that warfare and dancing were connected in a way that would strongly influence the evolution of powwow. Here developed a dance tradition concerned with the celebration of good fortune and bravery in war. Reflecting its presence among a variety of Native nations, these warrior-dance societies came to be identified as Helushka, Heylushka, Hethushka, and Hedushka (among others). Hethushka is both a society of warriors, dancers, and singer-drummers and a genre of dance itself, having origins in Omaha and Ponca warrior societies of the 1600s. Hethushka membership was marked by "warrior regalia, including roaches, scalps of opponents, and feather belts or bustles," and the performance of songs particular to the group (DesJarlait 1997:118). At the beginning of the nineteenth century, Hethushka regalia developed into a form familiar to powwow-goers of today: "eagle feathers replaced crow feathers, and braided sweetgrass replaced scalps." Over the course of the nineteenth century, Hethushka traditions spread beyond the Plains (DesJarlait 1997:118–119).

The Hethushka is most associated with the development of Plains powwow dancing, but it was also central in the evolution of dance of the Siouan-speaking Ho-Chunk of what is now southern Wisconsin and northern Illinois. Arndt (2005:55) identifies the Ho-Chunk Heylushka dance as the origin of what, by the early twentieth century, was identified as "war dance" and presented to white audiences. The linguistic relationship of Ho-Chunk to Ponca and Omaha (all part of the Siouan language family) may have aided the incorporation and development of Hethushka/Heylushka into Ho-Chunk society.

As a result, by the early nineteenth century, various aboriginal traditions on the Plains and in the Woodlands came together, forming social structures and motivations for Native dance. Two key characteristics of powwow were in place: honoring military accomplishment and festive intertribal gatherings with political and economic functions. Both have roots in the period before European invasion, and both evolved in response to European presence on the continent. Conflict on the Plains intensified as groups pushed by European incursions into the east migrated west. The incorporation of the horse further invigorated existent raiding traditions, enhancing mobility of raiders and providing a valuable asset (the horse) through which to express wealth and prestige. The aboriginal trade festivals described by DesJarlait expanded to accommodate additional trade goods of European origin and reflected a growing need to cooperate among Native nations as they dealt with, first, the imperial aspirations of European powers and, second, the expansion of the new settler state.

The Plains and the upper Midwest at the turn of the eighteenth to nineteenth century witnessed the new United States beginning to exercise direct political control and provide extensive entry for settlers. To address the "Indian problem," the new republic instituted a policy first aimed at removing Native people from the landscape. At times this meant simply overwhelming Native groups with settlers who frequently exerted semi-organized and largely condoned violence. Sometimes more formal military force was applied. In a pattern common to indigenous histories, the end of violent conflict was interpreted differently by state and imperial powers than by Native peoples.

Dance was employed in at least one moment of interpolity negotiation following conflict. Arndt (2005:50) notes that in 1828 a Ho-Chunk diplomatic mission to Washington, D.C., executed a "war dance" near the White House. The year before, the Winnebago War had brought the Ho-Chunk into direct violent conflict with the United States. However, neither the settler society nor its government shared the hope that Native nations would retain the political and cultural autonomy the Ho-Chunk sought. Policy and popular opinion sought to greatly curtail Native presence on the landscape.

Once eradicated, confined to reservations, or otherwise deterritorialized, Native people were subjected to policies that sought to erase their cultural distinctiveness. However, beginning with the Indian Reorganization Act of 1934, policy oscillated between Native self-government and imposed assimilation. Dance continued, responding to pressures of policy and economy, first as a means of cultural survival and later as self-representation (Arndt 2005; Ellis 2005; Nesper 2003).

Popular American entertainment forms—including fairs, rodeo, the traveling Wild West show, and early ethnic tourism—provided context and structure for Native dancing (Arndt 2005:51; Ellis 2005:14, Nabokov 1999:261; Nesper 2003:448–450). Results of these influences coalesced into what we recognize today as powwow with the need to welcome home and reincorporate Native veterans of World War II (Ellis 2005:8). Songs and dances that had celebrated returning warriors now honored Native soldiers. Although fascism was defeated, Native dancers faced an ethnically stratified U.S. society. Moreover, anxiety about Communism drove animosity toward cultural diversity. Indeed the end of World War II and the beginning of the Cold War are proximate events that require additional attention if we are to understand contemporary powwow as representational dance.

GEOPOLITICAL BACKGROUND OF CONTEMPORARY POWWOW

Federal policy that under the "Indian new deal" of 1934 had emphasized self-determination shifted back toward assimilation during the Cold War. Dancing, as it had earlier, conformed enough with the expectations of white audiences to avoid censure. Indeed, Nesper (2003:458–459) argues that the construction of "authentic fake" Indian performance reflected an exchange between white audiences and Native performers. Whites had their position of social superiority reinforced as Native people clowned and enacted an Indianness that conformed to mainstream stereotypes. Dancers and other indigenous performers were, in Deloria's terms, "imitating non-Indian imitations of Indians" (1998:123). In the process, Nesper (2003:459) contends, Native communities gained the tacit recognition that they were products of distinct histories and cultures. Authentic faking secured permission to express diversity, even as official policy identified such expressions as potentially Communist.

The end of the Cold War in the early 1990s diminished the force behind the label "Communist." Expression of distinctive cultural identities, while irksome and existentially threatening to many whites, no longer readily suggests the Soviet menace. Post–Cold War powwow dancing, then, is representational dance in which Native people work more freely to construct or influence Indianness. This is not to say that power differentials no longer matter. Indigenous dancers still must contend with whites who seek in Native people certain preconceived notions of authenticity. As Deloria (1998:159–173) points out, the counterculture of the 1960s, the New Age, and other mainstream movements and styles inspired by postmodernism continue to frame Native people in flat stereotypical terms. Contemporary multiculturalism may be more sympathetic to cultural diversity, but when it defines the channels of expression, it comes into conflict with Native goals for robust collective political autonomy (Niezen 2003:218).

Nonetheless, powwow dancers in the early twenty-first century enjoy a greater degree of latitude in how they represent Native cultures to outsiders. At present, the notions that Native dancing should be restricted or that it is Communist hold little saliency. However, the dominating society, in a variety of ways, continues to claim the privilege to define Native identity and culture. So powwow dancing works on the common indigenous obstacle of being defined by outside Others. Where dancing earlier struggled to keep forms alive, it now struggles to assert continuity of Native culture and to control the definition and image of Indianness in the mainstream imagination.

Nesper (2003:464) notes that the construction of "authentic fake" Indianness contributed to the revitalization of rituals and eventually morphed into award-winning educational facilities among various Native nations of Wisconsin. Powwow has undergone a similar course of development. Moving beyond imitations of the imaginary Indian, powwow often takes on an overtly educational tone. That is, it frequently works consciously to express particular Native culture and to shift the conception of Indianness for the better.

In powwow, as in K'iche' traditional dance, we find a dance form with pre-Columbian roots adapted to the realities of invasion and colonization. Threads of continuity are found in both dance forms. Contemporary powwow, as we will see in the next chapter, continues to adapt to macro-social forces in local and culturally distinct ways. A form solidified during the Cold War of the twentieth century, powwow in the twenty-first must continue adapting to needs and challenges, old and new.

Six

Characteristics, Functions, and Meanings in Contemporary Powwow

Contemporary powwow largely under Native control is the context for both construction of image and identity and the work of maintaining social cohesion. Fowler (2005:68), echoing Gelo's definition, emphasizes the importance of reciprocity and sociality in her discussion of the general characteristics of powwow. However, in addition to "social cooperation" and "emotional bonding," Fowler notes "struggles over leadership" and "challenges to the status quo" (2005:68). In short, powwow provides the context for the basic political and social functions of a human community: maintenance of social connections, resolution of disputes, and determination of group action.

Powwow also works on questions of identity; it defines members of communities as well as what it means to be a Native person in general. This cognitive work, not surprisingly, deals in the connection between past and present. As Fowler describes, powwow provides a venue for public "expression of modern identities, values," and "interpretations of the past" (2005:68). As I argued in the first chapter, dance is a human activity particularly well suited to expression of cultural continuity and change. A skillful dancer can simultaneously express tradition and innovation. The larger festival of powwow dancing itself, then, is where folks "try to establish identity and introduce change"

(Fowler 2005:68). Dance works on political as well as cultural continuity and change.

Beyond internal social and political functions, contemporary powwow expresses a commonality among Native nations. It negotiates continuity and change for the local group while also working to control and alter the ideology of the generic Indian. In the process of enacting dimensions of general Indianness, powwow provides cognitive and social space for intertribal connection and cooperation. Continuing the metaphor of powwow as a kind of lingua franca among Native nations, this chapter explores the activities characteristic of powwow and their meanings.

According to Ellis and Lassiter, "most powwows have a grand entry, most begin and end with prayers and memorial songs, and Fancy dancers in Oklahoma look a lot like Fancy dancers in California" (2005:vii). In addition to the grand entry and powwow dances, other typical features include a master of ceremonies (emcee) who narrates and entertains, music provided by ensembles of musicians who play one large drum and sing, a variety of forms of exchange among participants, the honoring of veterans and others who serve, and a mixture of sacred and secular elements. This set of common features promotes both particular indigenous identities rooted in specific histories and cultures and more general Native American political identity.

GRAND ENTRY

Grand entry begins the powwow and originated as a practice in rodeos and Wild West shows of the mid- to late nineteenth century. Essentially, it is a parade in which various types of powwow participants process into and through the dance space. Just as dance orders individuals in space, so a parade or procession is formalized group behavior that presents, through the deliberate placement of bodies in space, ideas about social organization. Accordingly, it is at grand entry that the various elements of the powwow come together. As with all events taking place in the arena, coordination of various individuals is conducted by the emcee, who typically asks the host drum to perform an entry song. Leading the way are eagle-feather staffs and flags of various entities borne by Native veterans. Some dress in powwow regalia, while others wear military uniforms.

After the flags and banners come the head dancers, followed by invited dignitaries, honorees, some of the organizers, current princesses, visiting and former princesses (sometimes referred to collectively as "royalty"), and other individuals who have been identified for recognition. In different ways they are recognized for manifesting or supporting Native culture. Typically the longest part of the grand entry, the dancers enter the arena, organized by dance categories and age. When all are present in the arena, veterans are honored in speech and song. Next the flags and staffs are retired (secured in a rack located in a predominant position in the arena), accompanied by an appropriate flag song. Grand entry typically ends with a prayer often given by a respected elder and many times offered in the local indigenous language (with or without translation). Grand entry, then, is a secular ritual (with some sacred elements) that articulates individuals in a variety of ways to the event that is powwow. It orders and sorts things, providing a physical enactment of the social structure that informs the events that follow. If powwow were a jazz piece, grand entry would be the opening statement, the musicians playing themes together that they will revisit individually throughout the performance.

THE MASTER OF CEREMONIES

The central position of the master of ceremonies (emcee) is one of the first indications that powwow is fundamentally representational dance. Indeed, common website advice offered to powwow newcomers is to "listen to the emcee and follow his instructions" when in doubt. The presence of an audible narrator at Native social and political gatherings is nothing new. Gelo (1999:42) argues that the emcee of the Southern Plains is rooted in an aboriginal social complex that places a high value on oratory. Public-speaking practices developed in the settler society had a role as well. Carnival barkers, rodeo announcers, and other nineteenth- and twentieth-century public-address traditions also influenced the development of the powwow emcee (Gelo 1999:43). By the early twentieth century, we find Native announcers whose role is to orient non-Native spectators. Arndt (2005:52) notes that by 1908 the Ho-Chunk Black River Falls powwow included a "manager of ceremonies" who informed whites in the audience about the dancing. Once again, aboriginal practices and values combine with practices of the larger U.S. society to form what is now a key feature of powwow.

Occupying a table overlooking the arena from its west side and equipped with a public address system, the emcee initiates grand entry, dancing, giveaways, and other events through his calls for needed participants at appropriate times; relays directions and information from the organizers; selects types of songs and their duration; provides entertainment during breaks in the action; and explains to outsiders (who could include Native people of other nations) the meaning of events that they witness (Gelo 1999:41–42).

Humor is central to the emcee's discourse, but it is more than a kind of Native stand-up comedy routine. This "patter," as Gelo (1999) identifies it, is woven with political commentary. It also works to define identities among

Native nations and between Native American indigenous and nonindigenous. Often jokes and stories are about how whites (of various backgrounds) and Indians are different. Whites present may be subject to gentle ribbing (Axtmann 2001:8; Gelo 1999:52). Tourists and anthropologists, as a category of regular visiting outsiders, are also recurring characters in humorous discourse (Gelo 1999:53). The kidding is directed inward as well. Common themes of jokes about ethnic self include poverty, "the Indian car," lack of education and consequent unfamiliarity with technological innovations, and romantic liaisons in the powwow campground (Gelo 1999:50–53).

Beyond working the Native-white ethnic border, jokes frequently address how one Native group is different from another. At one Midwest powwow where a Zuni man was dancing, the emcee riddled the audience.

> RIDDLE: "What's a mile long and five feet tall?"
> ANSWER: "A Zuni grand entry."

The joke played on the Zuni reputation for short physical stature and also their intensive participation in dance traditions. It was enjoyed thoroughly by all, including the visitor from the Southwest.

Gelo roots powwow humor in the importance of joking in "social control and status delineation" among Plains societies (1999:54). We observed such use of humor at powwows large and small in the upper Midwest. Moreover, humor is a common cultural institution that promotes the mental health and survival of indigenous peoples in the United States and beyond.

In addition to humor, a common discursive device of the emcee is the phrase "this is our way" or the like (Gelo 1999:48). For example, while attending a Menominee contest powwow, we received clear instructions regarding the orientation of our bodies during prayer. The discourse stressed how in some traditions people stand, in others they kneel, and in still others they sit during prayer. Moreover, a good person respects the culture of the community that he/she visits. The culture of other places included that of other Native nations as well as of the larger white-dominated society. We had a chance to reflect on our own practices while learning something about Menominee practice, all in a context of mutual respect.

Gelo (1999:49) describes how the emcee's use and discussion of time reflects "our way" as well. Often there is a tension between written (or otherwise announced) schedules and actual events in the powwow arena. Emcees occasionally quip about "Indian time," but there is more to powwow time than jokes about tardy Natives and white people who measure their hunger by the hour on a clock (as in a common joke described by Nabokov [1999:70]). The emcee must negotiate a balance between the autonomous clock of the larger dominating society and powwow norms that stress wide participation and prioritize social interaction. In short, powwow time is event-oriented. For example, the duration of grand entry and subsequent contest dancing depends primarily on the number of dancers who register to participate (Axtmann 2001:8). Moreover, speech giving, honoring, prayers, and so forth are not subjected to strict regulation by the clock. While the emcee will work hard to keep things close to the schedule—many attendees have to travel and be back at work—the clock is not fully autonomous and events unfold largely by their own accord. Powwow, then, challenges the mainstream culture of time, prioritizing the proper and satisfactory conclusion of the current activity over the abstraction of a schedule. As is the case with satisfying ritual (secular or sacred), time is manipulated in a way that gives participants a sense of a clear break with mundane, everyday experience. The ordinary is often governed by the culture of the nonindigenous Other, and the extraordinary by the culture of the Native self.

These sorts of public, shared affirmations of cultural distinctiveness define identity and build social solidarity. Moreover, articulating "our way" and then having people follow it firmly establishes that the event and its procedures are under Native control (Gelo 1999:49). At root, sovereignty (or collective political autonomy) lies in the ability of a people to define rules of proper conduct and apply them to a particular space. Powwow, by clearly defining "our way" and articulating individuals to these group norms, enacts one dimension of sovereignty.

It is in narrating events in the arena that the emcee really makes powwow a representational event. Jokes and kidding help define Native identity by contrasting it with white identity, but they also define identities among Native nations by a similar process of humorous comparison. The process of defining and realizing "our way" states custom, generates solidarity, and enacts shared political power. However, beyond identity, the running discourse makes accessible and comprehensible events not otherwise clear to outsiders. The dancers and musicians, of course, know what to do almost all the time. Family members and aficionados also need little explanation. Spectators, however, could find themselves confused or lost without guidance from the emcee.

An analogy may illustrate the point. Imagine someone attending a ritual in an unfamiliar faith community. The congregants know what to do, when to stand, kneel, and sit, and when and with what to respond. The newcomer has his outside status marked the first time he misses a cue. His understanding of what and why is also limited. Imagine now a commentator with a microphone telling outsiders what to do and when to do it and providing a remedial interpretation of events. The service becomes less about affirming faith and order to insiders (although this certainly continues to happen) and more about educating outsiders. The emcee is just this sort of cultural guide. His predominant role at powwow thus marks the event as one that no doubt builds solidarity among certain participants but also strives to include and inform outsiders.

POWWOW DANCES

Outside the arena, Tulsa is in the midst of a heat wave that, along with the Pro Golfer's Association championship tournament, has garnered national coverage. Inside, on the lower level of Expo Center, the Intertribal Indian Club of Tulsa (IICOT) Powwow of Champions is in its second and principal day (Saturday). Compared with the heat and the golf tournament, the powwow is barely a blip on the radar screens of local and national media. Some social realities are confounding to the social scientist. Powwow has everything a golf tournament has. It is competitive and certainly more athletic than golf. In both events, audience members are spectators and occasional participants, although not at the level of the competitors. The IICOT powwow, in addition to presenting individual athletic competition, features drumming, singing, and dress that is far more engaging than the staid attire of golf. Despite a degree of invisibility in the official media, for powwow followers and participants, the Powwow of Champions is well-known.

I have come to have high expectations for Saturday evening at powwow and am not disappointed. Drumming, singing, and dancing have been excellent. The first round of intertribal dancing has a palpable sociality. Dancers talk with one another as they circle the arena. Some stop briefly to shake hands with a friend in the first rows of the audience. In this phase of powwow all ages and forms are invited to dance. Where the grand entry that preceded it had clearly ordered dancers and dances, intertribal dancing collapses categories and emphasizes connection and commonality among old and young, male and female, fancy and traditional dancers. It is a moment to consider the array of dances and expressive possibilities available to dancers. After all, the quintessential feature of a powwow is the presentation of powwow dances.

If representational dance is the unparalleled expression of ethnic identity, as Shay (2006) contends, powwow styles and outfits manifest a notion of ethnicity that allows for a great deal of individual expression. For both men and women, dancing powwow affords an array of choices, first in style, then in composition of the outfit, and finally in actual performance. How a dancer selects a style and creates an outfit reflects choice, talent or calling, and kin. All ages participate in powwow dancing and the influence of parents and elders on young people is clear. This is not to say that young dancers are slaves to tradition. Not all sons of Grass dancers become Grass dancers, and each dance form and its regalia leave room for the individual to express tradition in his or her own way. All of this results in a living performance genre that exists in

6.1. Intertribal Dancing. American Indian Center Powwow, University of Illinois, Chicago, November 2006. (Photograph by author.)

the space between general and local, change and continuity, individual and group.

The dances encountered at a typical powwow include some local forms that may not be encountered at powwows hosted by other Native nations. For example, Smoke dancing, which I explore in the next chapter, is a tradition of Iroquoian origin and is not typically performed outside of the Six Nations homeland. It is, however, presented at the annual Oneida powwow in Wisconsin. Beyond these local dances, there are forms that are found at powwows across regions. These are, to varying extents, consistent from powwow to powwow, forming a transcultural or intertribal means of expression. The basic categories (Traditional/Straight Dance, Grass Dance, Jingle Dress Dance, and Fancy Dance) explored in the following paragraphs are common to powwows hosted in a wide variety of Native communities. These dances express and sort themselves by some basic, dualistic themes: warring/hunting and healing/creation, male and female, and modern and traditional.

Men choose (most commonly, with important regional and tribal differences) among Straight/Traditional, Grass, and Fancy Dance. Straight and Traditional Dances stress hunting or warring and have common origin in the Omaha Dance of the late nineteenth century. The Omaha dance (also known as Crow or Grass Dance) appeared among the Omaha, Ponca, Kaw,

Kiowa, and Pawnee peoples, becoming central to the warrior associations of the Southern Plains peoples (Ellis 2005:15). As the Omaha dance developed, it incorporated elements of the Midewiwin (Drum or Dream Dance) as well as revitalistic influences from the Ghost Dance religion. Plains dancers would come to identify this dance as "Straight Dance" (Ellis 2005:15).

The Omaha dance, with innovative large drums, was readily adopted beyond the Southern Plains, migrating north and then east toward the Great Lakes (DesJarlait 1997:119). Among Anishinaabé, the arrival of the Omaha dance meant that large dance drums, surrounded by groups of musicians, replaced small hand drums. As a result, greater participation in dances became possible. As it was adopted and adapted, Omaha/Straight dance became "Traditional Dance" to Woodland powwow dancers (DesJarlait 1997:119).

In both Straight and Traditional Dances, performers crouch to evoke following a trail. In both, a dancer occasionally raises an arm as if parrying attacks. Traditional/Straight Dance outfits tend toward natural and dark colors. Traditional Dance regalia features one feather bustle. Straight Dance lacks a feather bustle (Figure 6.2).

Featuring a faster tempo and a distinct, heavily tasseled outfit absent feather bustles, "Grass Dance" emerged on the Northern Plains of the late 1880s or early 1890s (DesJarlait 1997:119). Grass Dance (Figure 6.3), although the interpretations vary, emphasizes healing, protection, and spirit power.[1] Its step is sometimes said to imitate a disabled dancer who could not dance other forms but whose vision (which involved swaying grass) led to curative knowledge and ability. In this interpretation, "grass" refers to braids of sweetgrass—a plant renowned for its healing properties—worn by aboriginal dancers. Grass Dance may also refer to the act of pressing down vegetation to prepare a campsite and the associated ritual acts to protect its inhabitants (Axtmann 2001:10).

Contemporary regalia emphasizes a multitude of long, flowing tassels and a wide range of colors and materials deployed to depict grass. Distinctive elements in the headpiece include devices designed to spin or rock pairs of feathers (Axtmann 2001:10–11). Dancing expresses balance, as each step to one side must be repeated to the other (Axtmann 2001:12).

In the late nineteenth century, Kiowa and Comanche dancers created a new form of regalia, which incorporated more feather bustles and color-coordinated elements, including "dyed long johns" (Ellis 2005:16). The dance executed while wearing these elaborate outfits became known as "Fancy Dance." Contemporary Fancy Dance (Figure 6.4) allows the greatest degree of individual expression; one IICOT emcee explained that the dancer "can do whatever he likes as long as it is on the beat." It is highly athletic and, in many ways, a youthful dance. It is the most modern form and the one that is most

6.2. Male Traditional Dance. Note the single feather bustle, head roach, and muted tones. In the background is an array of flags, Menominee Nation Contest Powwow, August 2006. (Photograph by author.)

6.3. Young Grass Dancers. American Indian Center Powwow, November 2006, University of Illinois, Chicago. (Photograph by author.)

consistent from powwow to powwow, regardless of region. Fancy Dance regalia is elaborate, deploying two feather bustles. An elaborate headdress with moving parts creates additional visual cohesion with the rhythm of the music. Colors are bright, frequently fluorescent. It is a dance that, although anchored by the other forms and by the drum, is about change and adaptation. It posits a way to be indigenous while embracing selected dimensions of modernity. In short, it is both modern and traditional, a sure sign that powwow is a living, expressive art.

For women there are choices in style as well. As is the case with the male dances, female dance forms include traditional and modern and also healing-themed dances. Traditional Shawl, sometimes divided into cloth or buckskin categories (particularly in the Southern Plains), emphasizes control, balance, and dignity (Figure 6.5). Dancers seem to glide through the arena, their bodies largely still. A tasseled blanket over one arm sways with the beat of the music, and a fan of eagle feathers is held in the other hand. Outfits feature

6.4. Male Fancy Dancers. Note the female Fancy Shawl dancer in upper left corner of the image, Oneida Contest Powwow, July 2007. (Photograph by author.)

long dresses and shawls adorned with long tassels, appliqués, and beadwork. Leggings and moccasins are common to buckskin outfits in particular. A chest piece often with intricate decorations hangs from neck to below the waist. Shawls often make reference to symbols and styles particular to the dancer's Native nation. Traditional Shawl outfits are fairly muted in color, although (as with men's outfits) red, black, yellow, and white are often found together, either directly in the form of spirit wheels or as major components of outfits. Here there are interesting connections to the Mesoamerican cosmology, which employs the same four colors to identify cardinal directions, and K'iche' Maya performance, which occasionally realizes the cardinal points and their colors in dance.

6.5. Traditional Shawl Dancers. IICOT Powwow of Champions, 2007. (Photograph by author.)

Whereas men's styles offer Grass Dance as a healing-themed dance, women may select Jingle Dress Dance. It was around the turn of the twentieth century that this distinctly female dance emerged. By the 1920s, Jingle Dress dancing spread from its birthplace to the Northern Plains. After waning performance during the 1960s, the form has enjoyed a resurgence (Axtmann 2001:16). It has become a staple of Southern Plains powwows as well (IICOT 2007). As such, Jingle Dress Dance makes the repertoire of powwow dances truly intertribal in source, complementing Plains-originated dances with an Anishinaabé-derived tradition.

The Jingle Dress outfit features numerous cone-shaped metal jingles originally made from rolled tobacco-tin lids. With the movement of the dancer, the jingles strike one another, making the outfit into a high, metallic percussive instrument that complements the low tones of the large dance drum (Figure 6.6). The dress and dance reference a healing vision in which four women appeared in colored, jingling dresses, with instructions about the dance and its music (Amik n.d.). In some versions of the story the recipient himself was sick. In others, his daughter was gravely ill (Amik n.d.). When the vision was realized, the sight of glittering, jingling female dancers resulted in a miraculous recovery. To the present, dancers speak of the curative power of dancing Jingle Dress (Sexsmith 2003).

6.6. Final Round of the Jingle Dress Competition. Note the woman in Traditional shawl acting as judge in the upper right of the image, American Indian Center Powwow, Chicago, 2006. (Photograph by author.)

As noted earlier, men's Fancy dancing dates to the late nineteenth century. The 2006 American Indian Center powwow program dates women's Fancy Shawl Dance to the 1960s, when "[w]omen were looking for a new style of dance similar to the men's fancy dance" (AIC 2006). Indeed, according to the emcee at the 2007 Cherokee Days Powwow, women's Fancy Shawl began "when women's lib. hit the reservation." Lloyd, Perlstein, Podlasek, and Spencer date the dance to the early twentieth century, as part of a broader change in women's clothing (2004:83). Whatever the date and context of origin, the existence of a highly athletic dance with brightly colored regalia for

6.7. Fancy Shawl Dancers. IICOT Powwow of Champions, August 2007. (Photograph by author.)

women strikes a gender balance among powwow forms. Fancy Shawl dancing and regalia are evocative of the butterfly. Dancers extend their arms, opening and displaying brightly colored shawls. Quick and athletic hops and graceful spins are predominant movements (Figure 6.7). As is the case with men's Fancy Dance, Fancy Shawl—through the drum, the basic form of the outfit, and its themes—is anchored in tradition. Bright colors and athletic expression make Fancy Shawl a form that collapses "traditional" and "modern," choosing both instead of one or the other.

As a whole, these common powwow dances afford individuals a variety of expressive outlets that reflect some of the fundamental issues of being human. Gender is constructed. Men's traditional dances include predominantly themes of war and hunting. Female traditional forms counter the unrestraint of warring with dancing that is restrained and balanced.[2] This can be read as an expression of complementary gender roles. Women's roles in procreation and nurturing are stressed and opposed to men's roles in the destruction of war and in the killing of animals to provide sustenance. However, although female and male roles are defined in powwow dances, there are parallel opportunities for expression for men and women (Figures 6.4 and 6.8). A notion of distinct but complementary gender emerges. There are healing-themed dances for both men (Grass Dance) and women (Jingle Dress) that

6.8. Gender in Dance Styles. Powwow affords a variety of complementary male and female dance forms, American Indian Center Powwow, November 2006. (Photograph by author.)

access life-giving spirit power (Axtmann 2001:16). Moreover, traditional and healing forms complement and define (and are complemented and defined by) modern fancy forms. So in this set of dances, performers and audience work on fundamental problems, such as the nature of male and female, the relationship between death / destruction and procreation / healing, and the tension between modern / change and tradition / continuity. That these dances are presented across a wide variety of Native nations of diverse history and culture adds dimensions of politics and political identity. Powwow dancing also works on the accommodation of local culture expressed in concrete social relations with the abstract pan-ethnic identity that, while less concrete, is a means to political voice and power.

Dancers, particularly at contest powwows, are sorted not only by gender but by age as well. Categories such as tiny tot, junior, adult, and golden age further participation (and competition) and allow dancing to express additional ideas about social structure. Young children are introduced to and taught dancing through the tiny tot category and develop skills and social connections through child and adolescent categories. In adulthood, dance and social leaders (Fowler 2005) emerge. Golden age dancers become models of lifelong commitment and enjoy the prestige afforded elders. So powwow is not only about certain dualities but also about the life cycle, that human universal that helps us sort and assign roles based on age. Human societies define how the course from birth to death is to be categorized and what roles are to be assigned at each stage. Powwow dancing provides a flexible structure through which stages can be defined, contested, and expressed. In one respect, powwow is an ideal space for such discourse. Not only does it overtly express stages but it also, by traversing the dance arena in a clockwise direction, traces the path of the sun and symbolizes one's journey through life.

DRUMMING

An event is not a powwow without dancing, and a powwow dance is incomplete without its distinctive large dance drum. When referred to as "our grandfather" (AIC 2006), the drum (or drums) at the center[3] of the dance arena is evocative of the stones at the center of the sweatlodge often conceptualized as ancestors. The drum's beat is evocative of that of the human heart (Gelo 1999:47) and becomes a symbol of life-giving essential force as well as an anchor of the present to the past.

The manner in which the drum is played allows for contemplation of social relations. For example, compare and contrast powwow drumming to forms common in mainstream popular music. A pop drummer plays alone, surrounded by various percussive instruments. Whereas mainstream popular-music drumming emphasizes the individual and specialization, powwow drumming stresses communal production of music. Powwow drummers surround one large drum and play and sing together. Some lines are sung by soloists, and senior drummers typically lead within the group and head drum groups lead other groups. This coordination is geared to the difficult business of expressing the connection of the past to present through tradition. Young drummers will become senior drummers through a process of tutelage. So powwow drumming collectively expresses and values social connection; individuals are articulated to the common task of expressing tradition and identity. As such, performance articulates individual expression around communal material culture.

Powwow drumming also expresses ideas about gender, although differently in Woodland and Plains powwows. According to DesJarlait (1997:124), women generally do not drum or sing at Woodland powwows. My field observations correspond, with some exceptions. Plains powwows offer a different division of labor. Men drum and sing while typically seated; women sing while typically standing concentric to the drum and behind the men. The vocal range made available by such an arrangement allows for striking harmonies and moving call-and-response phrasing. Plains music more directly expresses male-female complementarity. Both approaches stress social solidarity by coordinating individuals in space and in action. The music produced emphasizes playing and singing *together* on a common drum.

EXCHANGE

Economic exchange is pervasive in these events of dancing and drumming. Indeed, Gelo (1999:40) includes exchange in his definition of powwow and Fowler (2005:68) stresses the importance of giving. In short, material culture and resources (including money) flow among participants in a variety of ways. Some powwow exchanges fall squarely into the category of generalized reciprocity. They are informal and circulate items without the use of money. Other exchanges are more formalized. Most are in one way or another "giveaways"; resources are collected from the group, accumulated, and then dispersed to an individual or small group. Powwow participants among the Ho-Chunk recognize giveaways, including the free meals provided to performers as part of the "Heylushka way," anchoring the tradition in the aboriginal past (Arndt 2005:57). Gelo notes that Southern Plains powwow emcees frequently refer to the generosity manifested by giveaway as part of "our way" (1999:48), distinguishing it from the concentration of wealth common in the mainstream. Sometimes, as Ellis and Lassiter (2005:viii) describe, a powwow's main function is to collect resources for an individual in need. This sort of powwow is similar to strategies of mutual aid and support employed by the impoverished African Americans described by Carol Stack (1974).

Powwows that I have attended, from small to large, feature games of chance that are also giveaways. A fifty-fifty raffle helps the powwow's organizers defray costs or supports a community organization while benefiting some lucky member of the audience. A deck of cards—with the purchaser receiving half a torn card, the other half thrown in a hat—often serves as the lottery tickets. These giveaways do not aim to support some individual in specific need but can help members of the audience (who are not necessarily in immediate economic crisis but may be short of cash) while raising funds for the powwow or community or both.

Other giveaways are designed to recognize and reward people for their accomplishments. For example, powwow is the ideal place to collect money for and announce winners of scholarships. However, the most common award giveaway is for excellence in dancing and drumming at contest powwows. Money collected from admission tickets, rents from vendors, and contributions from sponsors (including tribal enterprises) are accumulated and distributed to winners in the wide variety of categories generated by the intersection of style, age, and gender. Performances are carefully scrutinized, using elaborate scoring protocols. Although it strikes some as materialistic (DesJarlait

1997:125), these awards widen participation, encourage dancers to travel and connect with Native people of other tribes, and motivate dedication to dance. I argued earlier that performance at aboriginal trade festivals represents an early connection between economic exchange and dancing. Colonization and modernity have furthered this link in powwow. The various modes of giveaway discussed here address needs common to indigenous people in the twenty-first century. Informal giveaways provide mutual assistance among families and individuals who must deal with persistent economic discrimination and marginalization. Moreover, prize-money giveaways make the work of cultural continuity and positive self-representation financially viable in a world where wage labor makes time equal money.

HONORING

A less tangible, more social form of exchange is also common to powwow: the public pronouncement of individual accomplishment in service to culture and community. We might think of honoring at powwow as a gift of social prestige from the group to the individual in recognition of proper, valued behavior. The regard or positive social esteem of the community is directed toward individuals of various types, most notably veterans but also young people, dignitaries, and community leaders. Indeed, honoring may be the most important part of powwow, recognizing people within and outside local communities with words, acts, and formal social status. Honoring establishes a relationship between giver and receiver that functions to establish and maintain identities, one of the primary functions of powwow (Fowler 2005:68).

Throughout its development, powwow has recognized the accomplishments of warriors, and its current form was profoundly shaped by the return of Native soldiers from World War II. From the beginning of a powwow, veterans and active-duty soldiers are central to events. They bear flags and eagle-feather staffs during grand entry and are the subject of praiseful discourse throughout the day. As I will explore in the next chapter, honoring those who have served (and are serving) the military of a state that has pursued ethnocidal and genocidal policies is a complex affair.

Individuals are also recognized with formal positions within the powwow. For example, head dancers organize dancers and communicate directions through the emcee, who then communicates to the rest of the gathering (Gelo 1999:41). Typically experienced and even champion dancers, they do a job that requires organizational skills, leadership, and extensive knowledge of dance. From an outsider's perspective, this work seems arduous, but it is rewarded with community respect.

Powwow is also the venue to honor and confer the title of princess. Being a princess is a bit like being an arena director or head dancer. It is an honor, but it also entails obligations that are fulfilled at the powwow. Whereas head dancers and arena directors are selected based on experience, the title of princess is open to young women who apply and compete. The competition is structured much like a beauty contest, but what is sought and found beautiful has little to do with the physical qualities of the contestants (Roberts 2005:152–154). Rather, contestants strive for excellence in areas such as dance, traditional craft or subsistence skills, and public speaking (where indigenous language use is valued) (Roberts 2005:154–155). As in contest powwow dancing, competition is carefully ordered and judged, but contestants are encouraged to form friendly relations with their adversaries (Roberts 2005:155).

In execution of these competitive tasks and in carrying out obligations of the office, the princess must carry herself with utmost dignity (Roberts 2005:158–160). This emphasis on dignity finds parallel expression in dance and oratory. Traditional Shawl and Jingle Dress dances communicate female balance, control, and modesty through movement that is restrained compared with complementing male dances. Similarly, in her dignified conduct and discourse, the princess complements the often-joking tone of the emcee (Roberts 2005:160).

However, the addition of youth (or adolescent transition) to the mix distinguishes the princess from other dancers. As emergent female, the princess serves as an "icon" of what is valued in a Native woman (Roberts 2005:167). Her yearlong tour features repeated appearances and speeches at other powwows. She sacrifices opportunity for courting at powwow in favor of dignified service to the gathering and Native culture and traditions. The princess, then, enacts beauty through service to community and tradition. Such a person merits prestige and is honored in her selection and in her reception as officeholder.

Whereas honoring princesses affords a chance to recognize youthful dedication and service, powwows also honor lifelong service of community leaders as special honorees. Arena directors, head dancers, and royalty are honored *within* the powwow. Those recognized for long-term service to the community are honored *by* the powwow. The 2007 Intertribal Indian Club of Tulsa (IICOT) Powwow of Champions honored Osage assistant chief John Red Eagle. The elaborate process of honoring began with the honoree leading a dance counterclockwise through the arena (past deeds, after all, were to be recounted). The arena director accompanied the honoree and collected donations from audience members who occasionally entered the arena. Accomplishments in service to his community were recognized by a speaker selected by the honoree. As in other occasions of honoring, the

6.9. Honoring at the IICOT Powwow of Champions. The honoree is at the center of the image, back to camera, shoulders covered in a blanket, August 2007. (Photograph by author.)

person recognized does not recount his or her own deeds. Chief John Red Eagle, standing at the center, then received an honor song presented by dozens of singers, concentric circles of women with blankets or shawls over their shoulders (Figure 6.9).[4] Reiterating the theme of reciprocity, the honoree, in turn, recognized important people in his life with gifts of blankets. The cycle of exchange was extensive. Service to the community was reciprocated with honor from the community. This honor was reciprocated by the honoree with gifts to people who had supported him in his work. Overall, the ritual had a powerful effect. An individual was recognized, but in a way that emphasized what he had done for others. A notion of self that values individuals who act for the group was realized. While the esteem for the honoree was palpable, he maintained a posture and manner that stressed humility. Also, in enacting the concept of a good person, the ceremony provided a model for the good life that emphasized prestige as reward for service.

Honoring at powwow, then, is a complex process. Various types of service are recognized in formally structured ways. A common theme is of individuals who make choices to serve their communities, and that honor is the gift that extends a cycle of reciprocity between self and group. The power of positive social esteem (or prestige) to pronounce and reinforce community values is fully utilized. Material rewards for service are deemphasized in favor of social acts of recognition in exchange for service to community. The guiding force of reciprocity in honoring ritual cannot be underestimated. Honor is given in acts that are conventional to the honoree and are received and repaid in conventional ways. Moreover, honor is about the life of a contemporary person, not a romanticized past.

THE COPRESENCE OF SACRED AND SECULAR

So far I have described powwow as a festive event of honoring and reciprocity in which a particular set of representational dances and music is presented. In these elements sacred and secular dimensions are present. As Gelo (1999: 47) remarks, "sacred and secular time periods alternate during the powwow day." First I will address secular dimensions before moving to the sacred. The goal in this discussion is to emphasize how these concepts are mutually defining in their juxtaposition at powwow.

In many respects, powwow is a set of secular rituals. It deals with abstract concepts that, while not necessarily sacred, are difficult. Among these secular concepts, the nature of personhood and the multiplicity of human identity (including the challenges of pan-ethnic political identity) are the most common. Humor and competition are the two most salient secular themes at powwow.

Humor—sometimes bawdy, sometimes political, sometimes ethnic—pervades the discourse of powwow. While we must avoid assuming that all things sacred are handled with awe and reverence, humor gives the event an easy, fun feeling. Moreover, where it is expressed and where it is not help the powwow combine serious/sacred and fun/secular in a way that helps to define both.

I explore how powwow constructs identity in more detail below. Here I address one of the event's most directly secular themes: competition. Competitive dance is much like athletic competition everywhere; it works to define appropriate rules for social disagreement and conflict. Powwow, as I explored above, provides a variety of competitive dancing. Competition is resolved through careful and impartial judging. Competitors congratulate one another in the end (Axtmann 2001:13). To the general audience, the notion of fair play and good sportsmanship is enacted; individuals who come into conflict resolve their differences by strict adherence to norms and ensure that harmonious social relations prevail after conflict. Ellis (2005:9) points out that the realization of powwow competition is sometimes marked by social tension, rivalry, and social hierarchy. However, the structure of competition emphasizes fairness and friendliness, important interpersonal values in the resolution of competing visions of the future that Fowler describes (2005:68). Moreover, harmonious resolution of competition is crucial for people with limits in economic opportunity imposed from the outside.

Conceptually, we might say that cooperation is the opposite of competition. In cooperation, individuals work together toward common goals. Powwow, from its planning and organization to its music, grand entry, giveaways, and intertribal dancing, makes the most of juxtaposing competition with activities that emphasize social solidarity. Dancing particularly offers both modes; performers dance against one another (in contest dances) and with one another (in intertribal and exhibition dances). Events stressing cooperation work to undo some of the socially corrosive effects of rigorous competition. So the contest powwow, although overtly stressing competition, more subtly (but pervasively) constructs cooperation.

Where competition works to define cooperation, secular elements are juxtaposed in important ways by sacred elements. The handling of regalia in etiquette and use and the form of the dance arena suggest that powwow manifests elements beyond the five ordinary senses. Powwow dance paraphernalia is termed *regalia* specifically to set it apart from the semantic attachments to the word *costume*. Dancers do not dress up in a costume to play a character but represent themselves as living bearers of an ancestral tradition. Moreover, although I emphasize that powwow is fun, the term *costume* connotes triviality. *Regalia*, on the other hand, better carries the notion of seriousness. Additionally, knowing not to call outfits *costumes* shows a familiarity with powwow and communicates respect for tradition.

Beyond terminology, how items of powwow dance gear are handled reveals more directly sacred elements. Bustles and other components of regalia containing eagle feathers are carefully constructed and securely placed to ensure that the sacred plumage does not touch the ground. The emcee (and websites) frequently remind powwow-goers that they are not to touch regalia and that the feathers are sacred. Moreover, it is often noted that the eagle is an endangered species and that only duly enrolled members of Native nations may possess their feathers. Accordingly, the feathers carry spiritual power but also mark Native status in an unmistakable, public way.

If an eagle feather becomes dislodged and falls to the ground, a special dance and procedure are employed to recover it. When this happens, the emcee's tone shifts from light and humorous to solemn. He requests attention and silence and notes that video or audio recording of the proceedings is prohibited. My family and I observed this at an Ojibwe powwow in northern Wisconsin. The change in atmosphere was remarkable. Chatter in the audience ceased and the emcee guided the audience through the procedure. The dancer whose feather fell carried himself in a way that communicated shame and consternation that turned to relief and gratitude when the feather was recovered by a respected elder veteran. The event interrupted the jovial social atmosphere with one of solemnity.

Interestingly enough, the origin of the dance, as the emcee explained it, involved warriors who returned to enemy territory to recover a fallen comrade. They were, in turn, captured, but the enemy was so impressed with their bravery that the event precipitated friendly relations between the peoples who had been in conflict. Accordingly, intertribal cooperation, a central theme of many powwows, is given primordial origin and enacted in ritual involving powerful objects.

For peoples of the Woodland culture area, whose aboriginal kinship structures often make use of the sky and earth dichotomy, a basic categorization of the world is collapsed and reestablished in the feather-recovery ritual. Moreover, normal time and space are broken as sacred is extricated from secular. For people who must move among differing societies, clear definition and ongoing maintenance of sacred and secular categories are particularly important.

Beyond ritual treatment of regalia, the organization of powwow space and the way dancers traverse it trace onto the ground a key summarizing symbol. From the drum itself at the center, the circle and concentric circles are realized and invested with meaning. Gelo (1999:46) argues that the circular shape of Plains powwow dance is conceptualized and named as if it were a large tipi. In particular, Comanche terminology orients the entrance to the powwow arena as the eastern door, or "sunrise direction," of the tipi. From this sunrise entrance, powwow dancers generally follow a clockwise path through the arena, thus referencing the path of the sun through the sky (Gelo 1999:46). The cycle of the sun is reiterated in the cycle of life, in the accumulation of days and stages that makes up a person's life. Powwow dance, then, at one level symbolizes the path one follows in life. An abstract connection between the astrological cycle and human life and also a way of thinking about time are realized in the dance and dance arena.

Reckoning life in terms of a circle reflects a general conception of time that stresses its cyclical properties. Indeed, Axtmann argues that the powwow manifests "circular time" as well as space (2001:12). Movements executed by dancers emphasize a bodily enactment of cyclical time. Not only do they pass through the arena following a circular path, but the space immediately behind a dancer is symbolic of the past. Moreover, elements of the steps and regalia emphasize circular movement (Axtmann 2001:18). So in addition to the assertion of event-oriented time that directly challenges the autonomous clock of the settler society, powwow more subtly enacts the cyclical time. Again, effective ritual breaks with mundane (in this case lineal) time and produces in participants a sense of extraordinary time. When dancers bodily enact cyclical time in concert with one another, they can achieve "a feeling of worship," as one Grass dancer reports (Axtmann 2001:18).

Extending the circular shape of the arena, powwow sorts space into concentric circles (Gelo 1999:45). The character of the activities realized changes as we move from center to periphery. At the heart is the drum, circled first by players and singers and then by dancers. The inner rings are dominated by activities that are (at least potentially) spiritually charged. Dancers and dancers' families and friends typically occupy the first rows of seating. As we move deeper into the audience and further from the drum, spectators less socially connected to the powwow become more common. Beyond the seating typically is another concentric circle of space for the people to walk and socialize. Often vendors and community organizations set up booths on the outer boundary of this circular midway, a place for establishing new social relationships (including courting). Beyond the concession area we typically find parking and camping. The camping area, in particular, plays a role in renewing old social relations (Gelo 1999:45). Loosely speaking, sacred activities and relations of close social distance are near the center. Gelo contends that these smaller circles require "more intensive involvement in the celebration, until ultimately, through metaphoric connections suggested by the drum, contemplation is directed beyond the dance ground" (1999:47). In other words, the center of the arena is sacred space, distinct from mundane areas, evocative of a higher order. Conversely, as we move further from the drum and closer to alienated larger society beyond the grounds, activities move from relations between human and spirit to relations among human beings of community and acquaintance and to relations of politics and commerce among strangers.

Indeed, throughout powwow, sacred elements often symbolize differences between the cultures and lifeways of Native peoples and of mainstream society. This is not to say that powwow constructs Native cultures as sacred and others as profane. However, certain features of the mainstream—how it uses natural resources, its materialism, and its alienated social and economic life—seem profoundly unsacred. In working on ethnic and cultural differences, powwow also works on spiritual differences and locates close social relations immediately concentric to close spiritual relations.

Fowler (2005:68) describes powwow as "multivocal" and "condensing." That is to say, it references a variety of disparate concepts while also unifying multiple domains of experience under one conceptual framework. Drawing on terminology developed by Ortner (1973), the circle is a key symbol of powwow, exemplifying these multivalent and summarizing qualities. Among the concepts it unifies are sacred and secular, solidarity and alienation, the human life cycle and astrological cycles. As such, powwow provides content and context for construction of viable, culturally distinct identities.

In the next chapter, I further explore the multivocal and condensing nature of powwow, focusing on the nature of identity. Powwow reflects general trends in indigenous work toward self-representation. In this endeavor, powwow constructs identities that are communicated through multivocal symbols and are marked by multiplicity. It also connects individuals and communities to a larger condensed, abstract category of identity.

NOTES

1. Scholarly sources and websites emphasize healing and protection. However, some powwow enthusiasts contend that the grass is not botanical at all but symbolic of war trophies, including scalps taken from the enemy and displayed in celebration of success in battle.

2. See Axtmann (2001:18) regarding how the posture of women and men differs within similarly themed dances.

3. Not all powwows place the drum(s) in the center of the arena, although it does seem preferred. The AIC powwow in Chicago has the challenge of accommodating many dancers and many drum groups on a limited floor space. AIC places the drums on the floor immediately in front of the first row of audience seating.

4. The image of women draped with blankets and shawls is evocative of the women attending church in Highland Maya communities, where women cover their shoulders with colorful, multipurpose textiles called *perrajes*.

Seven

Powwow, Self-Representation, and Multiplicity of Identity

Warren and Jackson (2002) identify self-representation as both a goal and a strategy of indigenous movements in Latin America. The same is true in Native North America as well. In the United States, protection and enhancement of tribal sovereignty—that is, power to self-govern—are a constant theme in Native American politics and political action (Wilkins 2002). In other words, more than other issues, collective self-representation, the ability of a Native nation to speak for itself in matters of governance and to determine education policy, land-use regulation, taxation, and so forth, is identified by Native Americans as important across time and space. However, self-representation carries other meanings as well. In this media-saturated world, representing self in *image* is also a common goal across indigenous societies. It is, however, more than a superficial problem. For example, Victor Montejo identifies the destructive impact of racism on contemporary Maya and argues that combating negative stereotypes is crucial to individual and group self-image and health (2002:123–124). The connection between mental health and image is recognized in the United States as well. Moreover, Native dance is specifically identified as part of the solution. Native American leaders have promoted participation in "traditional song and dance activities as building healthy pride and self-esteem" (Thiesz 2005:88). One of the primary functions of powwow dance is the "positive embodiment of what it means 'to be Indian'" (Axtmann 2001:13).

Beyond how one is perceived by self and neighbors is how one's group is perceived by ethnic Others. For indigenous peoples who have suffered official and unofficial policies aimed at their erasure, controlling or at least influencing the construction of images of Indianness that are circulated among dominating populations is important as well. These notions of what it means to be indigenous and the nature of indigenous culture when constructed by powerful ethnic Others can become the ideological underpinning for destructive social action ranging from discrimination to ethnocide and genocide. Although states may not succeed in erasing a people physically, dominating groups tend to frame Indianness in a way that makes noble savages of indigenous people of the past and invisible living ones. As Robes Kipp (2001:32) points out, when real Native people do not conform to narrow stereotypes, their cultural distinctiveness is denied. Accordingly, for the health and survival of the group, active involvement in the construction of collective self within and Indianness without is crucial.

The most visible effort to combat stereotyped images of Indianness is the sustained and diverse campaign to retire Indian sports mascots (addressed in Part Five). Working to influence how Others represent Indianness is only part of the picture, though. Self-representation—that is, influencing the construction of images of Native culture by presenting it under Native control—is the complementing strategy. As Shay (2006:56) contends, dance is an ideal form for the expression of ethnic identity, and powwow can be understood, at least at one level, as an exercise in ethnic self-representation through dance. In other words, powwow, while having roots in ritual and dance, is also representational dance in its current manifestation. As such, I now address how powwow works to present complex and positive images of Native cultures. My discussion emphasizes the multiplicity of Native identities presented at powwow. Specifically, in three ethnographic vignettes, I explore how multilayered conceptions of Native culture and identity are constructed and presented at powwow.

To say that powwow employs self-representation to construct a positive image of Native people and culture is only a partial depiction. Part of combating stereotypes involves addressing preconceptions that seem positive on the surface but are confining in their narrowness. As such, powwow asserts not only a positive embodiment of Indianness but also a complex one. That is, it provides an avenue for expression "of a wide range of identities" (Fowler 2005:68). Moreover, dancers are afforded space and convention that allow each to construct and present "her or his own interpretation of social and spiritual power" (Axtmann 2001:19). This open conceptual space is available within and among dance categories but also in other roles attached to powwow.

The elaborate model of social structure, status, and roles enacted at powwow challenges one-dimensional conceptions of Native people and cultures, but also argues for a particular way of seeing identity in general. Human identity has a quality of multiplicity[1] that is underappreciated and masked by the dominating ideology that emphasizes singularity of identity. Powwow emphasizes the fact that we all inhabit multiple identities shaped by kin, class, region, gender, and ethnicity.

In this chapter I discuss the expression of identity at powwow in three dimensions: individual, intertribal, and national (of the nation-state). I illustrate each dimension with an ethnographic vignette, one involving a local traditional powwow, one involving a medium state/regional powwow, and one involving a multi-state regional powwow.[2] In considering the multiple levels of identity constructed at powwow, it becomes clear that participants challenge stereotypes of Native people but also the basic conception of identity commonly held in the dominating society.

MULTIPLICITY OF INDIVIDUAL IDENTITY

The Mno Keno Ma Ge Wen ("good teachings") Powwow is small compared with some that we have attended. Held on the Forest County Potawatomi reservation in northern Wisconsin, it is a traditional powwow; while there will be some prizes awarded, its main purpose is not competitive dancing. This is not to say that it is sparsely or unenthusiastically attended. Dancers and drummers crowd a tent-covered dance circle, surrounded by rows of audience. Outside the tent, across a wide, well-defined path, booths occupied by various groups and businesses define the outer limits of the event. Overall, it has the feeling of a very large family reunion, with occasional neighbors and curious outsiders dropping by.

Many of the attendees wear clothing that one way or another proclaims Native identity. Hats, t-shirts, and military fatigues adapted with Native symbols complement the most obvious form of indigenous dress: powwow regalia. Many of these folks specifically identify as Potawatomi, although a variety of other Native nations participate. The grand entry features Forest County Potawatomi veterans, Lac du Flambeau (about two hours northwest) Ojibwe veterans, and Hannaville (Michigan) Potawatomi veterans. The host drum, Smokey Town, is Menominee, whose reservation is a short trip to the south. Visiting dignitaries, who are officially introduced, include the current Oneida powwow princess (who lives about an hour south and east). Beyond the various markers of indigenous status is the occasional reference, in speech or apparel, to the Green Bay Packers professional football team.

In addition to the contingent from Michigan, we learn of folks from Birch Island, Canada, through references made by the emcee. Despite these interstate and international visitors, in many ways it is a local Wisconsin powwow. An informal survey of license plates in the parking lot reveals one from Illinois (ours), a few from Michigan, and a large majority from Wisconsin. Through this decidedly local flavor, the Mno Keno Ma Ge Wen Powwow presents a wide array of means for individuals to proclaim and to be indigenous and Potawatomi.

In this small powwow, several (most culturally, linguistically, and historically related) Native identities are presented. We hear of participation by Menominee, Oneida, Ojibwe, and Potawatomi people (the Ojibwe and Potawatomi, along with Ottawa, also holding an intermediate level of identity [Anishinaabé] between Native nation and Native American). Common to upper Midwest powwows that we have attended, cultural differences among these groups occasion the discourse. In other words, this local powwow defines the broad ethnic identity of Native American while also reinforcing specific historically and culturally connected indigenous nationalities.

How one participates in a powwow adds a further layer of complexity. In addition to various ways of dancing, one may serve the community by organizing and managing the powwow. Vendors supply tasty treats and handmade crafts and add a festive midway-like walkway to stroll. Among the various ways of participating, the emcee has the most audible presence at the powwow. He keeps the audience informed, shares jokes and experience, but also has a literal platform from which to share his views. Here he expresses his joy at seeing "all these beautiful Indian people,"[3] offers an extended and serious commentary on the necessity of honoring veterans, and at various points stresses the importance of embracing and using indigenous language. Also directly audible to the audience are the drummers and singers. Thirteen groups, including the host drum, pack the center of the tent-covered arena. They are the physical center of the space, the heart of the powwow.

There is a great deal of individual expression afforded in a dancer's choice of style and construction of regalia. At the Mno Keno Ma Ge Wen Powwow, women's shawls tend to the cloth variety and Jingle dresses are fairly well represented. Also present are a handful of Oneida Smoke dancers. Despite the small size and local feel of the powwow, its grand entry presents a wide variety of ways for individuals to realize tradition and express their Native identities. Depending on a combination of experience, talent, and choice (and, here as everywhere, these are products of one another), one can bear flags or feather staffs, be honored as a princess, coordinate dancers to activities in the arena, narrate events to the arena and audience, or dance. In the center, circled by the grand entry, more opportunities abound. Individuals can drum, sing, lead a drum group, or lead all of the drum groups. Outside the circle traced by the grand entry, sitting closest are friends and family supporting the dancers, then a wider audience, and finally

7.1. Mno Keno Ma Ge Wen (Forest County Potawatomi) Dance Space, August 2007. (Photograph by author.)

vendors and organizations. All of them, from drum core to vendors, are coordinated by the powwow's organizers.

Although considerable prize money is available at large contest powwows, at traditional powwows, small raffles and more informal giveaways predominate.[4] *Here people dance and participate in myriad ways for nonmaterial motivations: the desire of self-expression, the connection to community, and the prestige born of individual service to things larger than oneself. In the process, they reconnect to place and to friends and family who are often scattered around the Midwest and further abroad. I am reminded of Mik'maq and other Native peoples who, like the Potawatomi, practiced mobile foraging during aboriginal times. Before gaining recognition and securing tribal land in the early twentieth century, the Potawatomi survived as "strolling bands." The contemporary U.S. economy demands mobility as well, and like their ancestors, contemporary Potawatomi people draw on familial and communal ties reinforced through seasonal gatherings.*

In addition to these communal and social functions, powwow constructs a notion of personhood that emphasizes autonomy by providing individuals a wide array of ways to participate. Within the role of dancer there are many ways to be a Native dancer. However, it is not as simple as coming to a powwow and choosing a role. These ways to be Native require investment of time and effort and dedication to living tradition. To be a veteran requires military service. To dance takes skill acquired through practice and construction of regalia. While powwow does provide individuals with choice, it also recognizes individual expression in service to community. Tradition is valued but so is individual creative expression of tradition. This is not to say that powwow is always a happy accommodation of group and individual. Ellis (2005:9) points to social tensions and conflicts that play out at powwow. Moreover, Fowler (2005) emphasizes powwow as a context for people to contest and assign leadership and other social roles. Characteristic of the capacity of dance to simultaneously express continuity and change, powwow, Fowler also notes, is a place to promote and articulate visions for new directions in performance and politics.

INTERTRIBAL CULTURAL DIVERSITY AND PAN-ETHNIC POLITICAL SOLIDARITY

On the Saturday closest to Independence Day, we arrive at the Norbert Hill Center Pow-wow Grounds on the Oneida reservation in northern Wisconsin. After finding a parking spot in the shade, we grab our gear and head to the entrance booth. It is unusually hot for northern Wisconsin in early July, bright, humid, with only scant breezes. To protect ourselves from the afternoon sun, my three-year-old daughter and I have been liberally coated in sunscreen. However, I have forgotten to pack her cap and the first order of business is finding a hat to fit a toddler. As we stroll the grounds, I recognize businesses that I have seen at other powwows in Wisconsin and northern Illinois (and am reminded of the folks who travel from feria to feria in Guatemala). However, murals lining the area behind the emcee stand feature Oneida and Haudenosaunee iconography. This theme of "similar yet distinctive" will flavor the afternoon and evening.

We find a hat for Frankie, not without overcoming significant challenges. It needs to fit her, and although I wish to support indigenous business and art, I am not comfortable with clothing that overtly proclaims indigenous status. For this book, I have been researching Indian mascots and have come to be particularly sensitive to the problems of whites who, as Deloria (1998) terms it, "play Indian." A pink hat with stylized embroidered lances now on my daughter's head, we seek food and a place to sit. Fry bread and a hot dog in hand, we settle in to enjoy the dancing.

A highlight of the evening is the Smoke Dance contest. Earlier, I read about Oneida Smoke dancers who performed during halftime of a Green Bay Packers preseason football game and am interested to see a form that is generally not mentioned among powwow dances of the Woodlands and Plains. The dance and its quick tempo are said to originate in efforts to clear the longhouse of hearth smoke during gatherings (Applegate Krouse 2001:402). An introductory round of Smoke dancing features all contestants, male and female, adult and juvenile. Then the contest begins, with divisions by age and gender dancing separately. The first to dance are girls under eighteen, then boys under eighteen, then women eighteen and over, and finally men eighteen and over.

The regalia, compared with other powwow styles, is fairly unadorned. Women wear brightly colored, floral-patterned loose tunics over longer black dresses and leggings that feature piping and embroidery. Some wear simple fabric headdresses, others adorn with barrettes or ribbons, all have their hair braided. Men's outfits feature a tunic of printed material, an apron with embroidery, and leggings of solid color. A sash around the waist or over the shoulder and across the chest (or both) and a variety of jewelry round out the men's gear. A distinctive headpiece features a cap that combines both soft, flat-lying and rigid, upright feathers. The music is melodious, featuring a high-pitched drum and a single singer. Each dance starts with a slow-tempo song followed by a high-tempo piece. Dancers interpret the first song by crouching and searching like hunters or warriors. The second piece is danced with lively footwork and an upright posture. The regalia, music, and dancing are all quite enjoyable. The audience appreciates the performance, applauding it vigorously.

The emcee, who is not Oneida, describes the dance as an important and unique Iroquoian tradition. He further suggests that we attend the Grand River Powwow on the Six Nations Reserve if we would like to see more. Smoke dancing, according to Applegate Krouse (2001), is a social dance that has recently been incorporated into powwow. These varied iterations of Smoke Dance closely fit Shay's concept of parallel traditions (2006:9–14), with social and representational Smoke Dances coexisting. Moreover, anyone in the audience with a passing knowledge of Native history knows that Smoke dancing is distinctive among other dances of the upper Midwest because the Oneida were compelled to leave their homeland (now central New York state and bordering areas of Pennsylvania) in the context of that early nineteenth-century government policy charitably identified as "removal." It is not simply an expression of diversity among Native nations but also a reminder of a commonality of indigenous histories worldwide: mistreatment at the hands of states that imposed themselves on aboriginal homelands. That the dance is presented today nearly two centuries after removal speaks of survival and cultural continuity. Clearly an important tradition of the host nation, the dance was moved from the end of the program to the beginning, in front of the senior men's Traditional Dance but after a traditional music singing contest.

Ellis and Lassiter's contention (2005:ix) that powwows are not the construction of a singular "pan-Indian" culture is clearly in evidence. Smoke Dance is not about the emergence of a general Indian culture that is a bricolage of various indigenous traditions. Rather, it emphasizes Oneida cultural distinctiveness within a context of Native American political and social cooperation. Oneida remains Oneida within a general category of political pan-ethnic identity. Other Native nations and communities, by reflection, remain culturally distinctive as well. Earlier work, as Ellis and Lassiter (2005) identify, mistook the general pan-ethnic identity and its markers as the whole of various distinct groups. Moreover, such a position is based on the assumption that people live within one ethnic or cultural identity. Perhaps because globalization was not as apparent or perhaps blinded by the ideology of their own state—that identities inevitably homogenize—scholars who proposed the generalization of particular Native nations into a pan-Indian culture have misread the meaning of powwow. The emcee used the opportunity to stress that the tradition was Iroquoian (and Smoke Dance is clearly distinctive), emphasizing directly to the audience the diversity of tradition within the intertribal (imagined or political) identity of Native American. The host nation has its chance to educate me and other non-Oneida about its particular culture and tradition.

After the last of the men's contest, an intertribal dance to Smoke Dance music is opened. People from various nations and in various styles of regalia enthusiastically join, some imitating the Smoke dancers, others adapting their own steps to the music. Those who take to the arena briefly become Smoke dancers. In their bodies and faces is a sense of fun at trying something new. Overall it is an effective secular ritual, a convincing embodiment of intertribal cooperation based on mutual respect and appreciation of one another's cultures. People joined in and partook of another's culture in the context of cooperation and mutual respect. If dance is a good means to physically manifest a group's notion of how individuals are articulated to societal purposes, here individuals and their respected nations are articulated to intertribal political cooperation. Walk in another's shoes and dance her steps, political alliance through intertribal cooperation realized in dance.

MULTIPLICITY OF NATIONALITY

It is grand entry of the American Indian Center's annual powwow at the University of Illinois at Chicago. Eagle feather staffs of the American Indian Center of veterans' associations of various Native nations borne by veterans lead the procession. Following are a variety of flags representing governments and institutions. Military banners are prevalent; the standards of the branches of the armed forces and the black prisoner-of-war flag are featured. Also present are flags of the United States, Canada, and Illinois. Flags of several Native nations of the upper Midwest round out the first segment of the parade. The longest continuously presented urban powwow in the country, the AIC event takes place on or near Veterans Day. Although all powwows honor veterans, this one pays particular respect to those who serve or have served in the military.

7.2. The Distinctive Step of Oneida Smoke Dancers, July 2007. (Photograph by author.)

This multilayered presentation of symbols of loyalty, service, and governance inspires contemplation of identity. What are the messages conveyed by the wide variety of flags paraded before us? Compared with celebrations of military service in the mainstream, powwow is decidedly pluralistic. Where Memorial Day and Veterans Day are dominated by the American flag and military service is equated with patriotism and loyalty to the state, powwow honoring manifests a more complex notion of identification. The veterans who bear this array of flags are at once Americans, Native Americans, and members of particular Native nations.[5] *They served in particular units in particular branches of the armed services. Indeed, social scientists should appreciate the grand entry's take on social status and identity. Our fields have long recognized that an individual's identity is complex, contextual, and layered. At points in life, family identity is paramount; at others professional identity is central. In transnational or international settings, identification with nation-state becomes highlighted. For example, one is most acutely aware of being from the United States when one is outside of the United States (less so when socializing with kin at a family gathering).*

In addition to provoking thought on the nature of identity, the grand entry has a personally disquieting impact. In its various honoring of veterans, powwow makes me a bit embarrassed. Here I sit with my family secure that our human and civil rights will be respected. My wife and I have work that is meaningful to us and provides us a degree of economic security. However, never once have I seriously considered volunteering for military service. Yet, in our presence are Native people who, despite structures of ongoing economic, political, and cultural discrimination, have served proudly. Many Native soldiers (disproportionately) have died and many more (also disproportionately) have been wounded in military service to our country. This moment makes untenable facile notions of social justice. Honoring Native veterans goes beyond the agenda often associated with political liberals that combines economic integration with officialized multiculturalism. Reflecting an indigenous tendency to eschew right and left political categorization, honoring veterans is not conservative either. The procession of Native veterans bearing a plurality of flags counters the ideology that has dominated the mainstream and right-of-center notions of nationalism. Powwow asserts that its participants are Native and American. That is, to be an American does not require cultural conformity to the dominating society, and the military service that is honored is an undeniable claim on American identity. Who more exemplifies patriotism: a Native American who has served in the military but is also proud of his or her unique heritage, or someone who conforms to mainstream cultural norms but has not served?

I recall how my students are occasionally confounded by the high rates of Native participation in the military. It is no wonder. The cognitive models passed from their culture and taught in their formal education are often inadequate for understanding the complexities of identity. The notion that Native people participate out of false consciousness is inaccurate and rather patronizing. While economic and educational opportunities offered in exchange for military service certainly have a role, the ceremonial time and energy dedicated to and by Native veterans at powwows suggest that much more is at play. Reading Native military service as assimilation is misguided as well. From dress that combines military fatigues with Native symbols and regalia to dances that have roots in aboriginal war dances, military service is indigenized more than indigenous warriors are militarized. As such, Native veterans reflect more the notion of inclusive pluralism described by Gossen (2004) than they do the policies of cultural assimilation so often favored by the U.S. government. Moreover, indigenous veterans make the same claim of equal rights to the benefits of American citizenship that returning minority soldiers made throughout the twentieth century. Here, in this display of plurality of identity and community, they also demand inclusion on their own terms. I begin to appreciate more fully how powwow is not only about controlling perception of Native people through self-representation but also an assertion of pluralism and a notion of self that stresses multiplicity.

This secular ritual works on the difficult area of human identity. It provides what Ortner (1973) identifies as a key elaborating scenario. In the setting of powwow, multiplicity of identity is asserted and outwardly expressed. Powwow presents the ideal where the layers of identity are valued and accepted equally.[6] *It emphasizes the multiplicity of identity and deemphasizes that identity is contextual. Outside of powwow, in a society marked by social inequality and that demands much of us in our working lives, the cultural diversity is constrained. As is the case for indigenous peoples who live within states dominated by cultural Others, many present here are compelled to change levels of identity and norms of social discourse when they return to school or the workplace. These non-Native social contexts require shifts to the social discourse style of a society established by settlers.*

After the entire procession had entered the arena, the flag bearers stand at attention in formation facing the emcee stand. The emcee turns the microphone over to a priest who offers a prayer. Thanks are given for the day and the ability to come together and dance. Protection for those serving in the armed forces is requested. The prayer, however, never veers into implying divine support for political policy. The emphasis is on those serving, not the political process that put them in harm's way. It leaves plenty of space for both those who back war and those who do not. Indeed, at powwow, one can and is expected to support and honor the troops. However, powwow speakers avoid the facile equivalence, common in mainstream political discourse, made between supporting state policy and supporting those who serve.

While listening, I recall another prayer that opened the American Indian Center powwow during an earlier phase of the Iraq War. It asked for protection and blessing of civilian populations affected by war as well as for the troops. The officiant reminded the audience of a long history of wartime suffering by indigenous women and children. At a moment when the "collateral" death and dismemberment of Iraqi civilians

7.3. Multiple Markers of Service and Loyalty. Next to the emcee table and in the center of the image are four eagle feather staffs. At right is an array of flags representing the United States, Native nations, and Native and non-Native veterans' groups. American Indian Center Powwow, November 2006. (Photograph by author.)

were making the news, the humble prayer contained a powerful call to consider more thoughtfully the realities of war. In addition to the multiple layers of identity represented by the flags of nations, states, and institutions, the prayer asked us to consider the loyalty we owe to humanity.

The preceding three vignettes and Part Three in general demonstrate multiplicity of identity as a pervasive theme, we might say a key, concept and key scenario elaborated in powwow. The obvious question then is, why so much emphasis on multiplicity of identity? The answer involves factors particular to Native North America and common to indigenous political and identity struggles. Although varied from group to group, Native North American concepts of personhood generally place a strong emphasis on individual autonomy within tightly knit kin, social, and communal groups. Powwow as an event and powwow dances engender a wide variety of expressive possibilities, giving the individual many paths to discover and follow. Moreover, indigenous people are often compelled to adapt to a variety of social settings, some constructed according to the norms of cultural Others. Powwow works on this problem and suggests ways to minimize its dislocating consequences. In converting square spaces to circles, and in constructing a notion of time that is both event- and clock-oriented, the powwow carves out a Native social setting that may be shared by non-Native audience members. Honoring Native veterans contests the ideology of the "real American" and asserts a notion of patriotism that embraces cultural pluralism. The construction of multiplicity of identity at powwow works also on the challenge of pan-ethnic cooperation. In addition to being a member of a particular Native nation and of the imagined political community of the larger society, indigenous powwow participants belong to the pan-ethnic category of Native American. Many powwows deliberately bring together people of varied Native nations and construct a space where local identity is affirmed and intertribal cooperation is built. In the simultaneous construction of diversity and commonality, the powwow further contests notions that to be an American in a general sense requires the adoption of the culture of the white mainstream. It creates a model of cultural pluralism that is inclusive. In short, as often in the case of ritual, the multiplicity in powwow reflects the experiences and aspirations of its participants. Indigenous people often must draw heavily on the human capacity to create complex, multilayered identities. Powwow participants work to control and make more meaningful and satisfying this process of multiplicity.

Beyond multiplicity of identity, powwow is multiple in function. First, powwow is fundamentally an event of cultural and political self-representation. Individual dancers represent themselves, and the powwow represents particular Native communities and nations as well as Native Americans in general. In the process of self-representation, reciprocity of material and social esteem builds mutual aid and support and powwow takes on economic functions well suited to people who face material poverty at higher rates than other U.S. groups. Powwow is also about connecting the past, present, and future and constructing and contesting the direction of particular communities and Native America in general. Dancers express both tradition and change, a particularly challenging endeavor given the ill-defined and unequal expectations of authenticity often placed on indigenous people. The mainstream folk theory imagines Indians as one-dimensional Plains Indians. Powwow counters with Native nation–specific culture. Rather than the Indian of the white imagination, powwow articulates intertribal cooperation among complex and varied Native nations and individuals.

So far in this book, I have considered genres in which indigenous dancers represent indigenous culture and community. Through the next two forms of dance we enter arenas where representations of indigenous culture are enacted by dancers who are not indigenous. The act of dancing moves from self-representation to Other-representation. In my treatment of this contested social space, I consider not only Other-representation but also indigenous responses to the appropriation of images of culture in dance. I endeavor to give greater context to powwow and K'iche' Maya traditional dance, but also to understand why the nonindigenous feel compelled to dance Indian.

NOTES

1. See Montejo (2002) regarding multiplicity of Maya identity and culture.

2. This division reflects Albers and Medicine (2005:26–30).

3. Gelo (1999:49) reports that discourse stressing the beauty of Native music and people is common among powwow emcees on the Plains as well.

4. See DesJarlait (1997) for more detail regarding the distinction between traditional and contest Woodland powwows.

5. Early to mid-century Ho-Chunk performances of the Stand Rock ceremonial for tourists at Wisconsin Dells featured dramatic, overt expressions of state patriotism (Arndt 2005:56). Fowler (2005:74) notes the deliberate exclusion of symbols of the American state from Gros Ventre and Assiniboine powwows during the Indian pride movement of the 1960s. Both exhibited less of the subtlety of identity than contemporary powwow's take on nationalism.

6. Kracht (1994) and Ellis (2005:9–10) disagree on whether powwow is well understood in terms of Victor Turner's concept of *communitas*. As seems characteristic of all human ritual, certain ideals are constructed in ritual that are less evident in the social reality referenced. Here, inclusive pluralism and multiplicity of identity are idealized.

Part Four

Folkloric Dance

Eight

Folkloric Dance, Modernity, and Appropriation

It is a bright, pleasant Sunday morning in Melrose Park, Illinois. The September sky is a clear and deep blue, the fall air dry and slightly breezy. Nineteenth Avenue, the main commercial street of this near-west suburb of Chicago, is closed for Hispanofest. Normally dominated by automobile traffic, la decinueve, *as local residents are apt to call it, now features families, couples, and groups of friends out for a leisurely stroll. They amble past booths rented by local businesses, community organizations, and national and multinational corporations. At the Lake Street intersection of 19th Avenue, a large stage with sophisticated sound and lighting systems marks the north end of festivities. A long block to the south, Main Street crosses 19th Avenue. To the east on Main we encounter carnival rides and two additional, smaller stages. The grade-level intersection of Broadway by the Union Pacific railroad, its crossing gates lowered, marks the south end of the fair. The atmosphere is altogether agreeable—festive yet relaxed. Later in the day, after families have returned from church and had lunch, the festival will pick up intensity and the crowd will grow large.*

My wife, Christa, and our two children are along with me today. After a three-year stint as director of a large adult-education ESL (English as a Second Language) program serving Melrose Park and other western suburbs of Chicago, I now return my attention to ethnography. We are at Hispanofest so I can more directly investigate immigrant communities in the Chicago suburbs. As we stroll about the festival, I am reminded of my fieldwork experiences at ferias *in highland Guatemala. While the two events are distinct, they have some commonality, and their differences often seem inversions of one another. Uniform, mass-produced collapsible booths in neat rows line the streets of Melrose Park during Hispanofest. Ramshackle, individually improvised booths of laminated metal roofing panels, rope, and lumber dominate Guatemalan* feria. *In the highlands, mini cinema booths show excerpts of action films, but here in the suburbs, a semi-tractor trailer converts itself into a movie palace, marquee and all, where audiences learn about the wonders of the Internet. Both Hispanofest and* feria *communicate a strong sense of social connectedness, although the spatial dimension of connection varies. My temporary inclusion in this glocal*[1] *community comes in the form of short conversations with former ESL students. I am pleased to hear of progress toward both language proficiency and fulfillment of life goals. In these chance meetings, Hispanofest provides (much as fieldwork in highland Guatemala does) a welcome departure from the often stark anonymity of public space in mainstream U.S. society.*

After a lunch of festive foods, we move to the stage and carnival ride area of Hispanofest. While my wife and soon to be three-year-old son enjoy a carnival ride, I push our five-month-old daughter in her stroller to a good vantage point to watch and photograph folkloric dance presentations. My daughter, tucked under a soft blanket, enjoys a late morning nap as I observe two dances. In one, male and female dancers, in costumes that seem inspired by both contact-era codices and images from contemporary marketing, depict a ritual of Native Mesoamerican cosmology (Figure 8.1). Employing shell-rattles on legs and arms, the dancers repeatedly face and address the four cardinal directions in succession. At each point, one of the dancers blows a loud note through a conch. In another performance, couples dance in courtship, their costumes reminiscent of colonial-era Mesoamerican Natives (and vaguely of contemporary Highland Maya). The men wear wide-brimmed straw hats, white shirts, and white pants. The women have their hair up, elegantly wrapped in brightly colored bands. Frilled white blouses nicely match flowing and colorful skirts.

I have seen similar performances many times here in the United States and in Guatemala. However, now I begin to directly and consciously consider identity and indigenism. In the Native Americans course I am teaching, we are having an ongoing discussion of racial and ethnic classifications. Questions similar to the ones we have been struggling with come to mind. Should Mexican Americans who explicitly embrace Aztec, Mexica, or other indigenous heritages be counted as Native Americans, indigenous, Latino, or some combination of terms?

In Parts One and Two, I considered forms of representational dance in which indigenous peoples dance, manifesting and controlling their own culture. Here, I begin to address forms in which indigenous people, life, and culture

8.1. Folkloric Dancers Portray Pre-Columbian Ritual. Hispanofest 2005. (Photograph by author.)

are referenced in dance that is performed by people who are not necessarily indigenous. Folkloric dance, the form I address presently, is performed by people whose ethnic status ranges from clearly nonindigenous, to people who feature themselves as descendants of indigenous people, to those who are indigenous by their own reckoning and by that of their neighbors. What most certainly began as sometimes fanciful and often unrestrained elite appropriation of indigenous forms has, over time, been counter-appropriated by non-elite immigrants and even indigenous dancers. Presently, I address these multiple manifestations of folkloric dance, considering state-sponsored groups, immigrant groups, and indigenous groups. I examine these as parallel forms, coexisting and co-influencing, but rarely on equal footing and often with divergent purposes.

In the spirit of the comparative approach that guides this work, I begin with brief reflection on the differences and similarities between folkloric dance and traditional dance. For purposes of clarity, I rely on a distinction that Guatemalans make between *baile folklórico* (folkloric dance) and *baile tradicional* (traditional dance). Typically short dances with a theme—washing clothes, courting, marriage, and other idealized aspects of indigenous life—and frequently presented with recorded music, Guatemalan folkloric dances often require costumes. *Bailes folklóricos* differ from traditional dance in several important ways. Perhaps most crucially, they are much shorter (lasting four to ten minutes as opposed to six to eight hours) and directly theatrical. Moreover, they are not as narrative and they are not ritual in the way that traditional dances are. Most of the time, masks are not employed. Perhaps most importantly, folkloric dances feature both indigenous and nonindigenous performers. In fact, folkloric dances are often performed by nonindigenous people who take on costumes and perform Indianness. As the costuming content and identity of the performers vary, so does the context of performance. During my visits to Guatemala I have seen folkloric dance performed for tourists and at culture festivals, *clausura* parties,[2] school assemblies, celebrations of national holidays, and other similar public functions.

While the distinction between folkloric and traditional dance is not as clearly marked outside of Guatemala, the folkloric-traditional classification system serves well. Folkloric dances are performed both in their countries of origin and internationally. They typically draw on and present images of indigenous culture and elements of what Guatemalans would identify as traditional dance. However, the relationship between the forms is complex and global and requires some sorting.

First we should briefly explore the term "folklore" in relation to the term "tradition." These terms, as I argued concerning so-called authenticity, must be understood as products of colonial expansion and imperialism (Graham 2002:188). With the spread of colonialism across the globe, Europeans encountered peoples and lifeways quite distinct from their own. The cultural diversity encountered by the colonizer needed explanation (and colonial presence required justification). Why were the colonized so different from their colonizers? A good deal of the attempts to understand these widely varied ways of life were (and continue to be) loaded with racism and ethnocentrism. Rarely were these differences considered as equally appropriate expressions of being human. This is not to say that all explanations and descriptions of human diversity are loaded with negative stereotypes. A degree of ambivalence has marked elite estimations of those whom they dominate. The colonized other has been considered savage and primitive, but also noble, exotic, and interesting.

From the perspective of the colonized, the questions presented by European expansion were more immediate. Societies of relative stability experienced the instability caused by loss of life to war or disease, destruction of economic bases, and great restrictions on political autonomy. Colonization fundamentally disrupts the cognitive and social structures necessary for human well-being. While the colonized certainly commented on the odd ways of their colonizers, how Europeans became Europeans was less important than how varied, distinct peoples became Indians. Who will we become and who were we are questions that continue to mark the identity of those who have been dominated by others.

Some in European and subsequent settler societies recognized (some even with great consternation) the pervasive impact of their colonial presence. It is in this colonial context that the concept of "tradition," as it is popularly applied to non-Western groups, was fundamentally shaped. To Europeans, tradition became those aspects of their colonized subjects that were not European. Said elements were assumed to have been stable, essentially unchanged from a deep imagined past before European presence. However, given the oppressive reality of colonialism (or because of "progress"), tradition was also assumed to be disappearing as the Other would become inevitably Western. When such things do not disappear quickly enough, the colonizer works to hasten their disappearance. When they disappear too quickly, we lament their loss, blame ourselves, work at preservation, or even admonish the tribe for not being tribal enough. Conservation, maintenance, or revitalization of culture and society by the colonized Other elicits responses ranging from disdain and religious intolerance to admiration and hopeful romanticism. Rarely is it viewed as pragmatic or realistic. As such, traditional cannot be divorced from colonial. On the other hand, to the colonized, tradition means something else. It answers the question, who were we? For some, traditions or at least elements of the traditional remain crucial to who we will become. As I explored earlier, this is precisely what the Highland Maya do with traditional dance, enacting, in the present, forms that have both deep roots and obvious signs of change over time. Any practice, even one that dwells on tradition, is alive and well when it helps people understand the present.

However, by the nineteenth century, Europeans societies were experiencing profound changes of their own making (or at least that of powerful elites and global transformations). Industrialization, urbanization, and modernization fundamentally changed Europe as well as the settler societies it founded through colonization. While not as threatening and debilitating as the loss of political autonomy, destruction of economic base, and outright extermination faced by colonized peoples, those in the industrializing world faced (and continue to face even after industrialization) some profound challenges to meaning and identity. Those in the wealthy core states must frequently reconsider themselves and their place in the world. Depersonalized modern society—filled with strangers, objects without unique histories, and places of impermanence—triggers in many a longing for things traditional and a meaningful, local sense of place in the world. Those whose basic needs are adequately met find time to contemplate the alienated urban societies they inhabit. In early industrialization, a more satisfying existence could be built from an imagined rural past. It is in this context of increasingly alienated society that folklore became a field of elite urban interest.

Earlier, I defined authenticity as a folk theory about the folk. The related concepts of tradition and folklore evince a similar pattern in popular deployment. They are concepts that help social actors understand change that takes on political dimensions when they are applied to a folk Other. Who exactly the folk are, of course, varies. However, constant in construction of folk is their status as Other and of perceived and real economic and social differences. Otherness of the folk has come from distances of time, space, and class. Folk can be rural Others to an urban elite, Indian ancestors to settler societies, and old-country villagers to immigrants. In all of these cases the folk have become the source of authentic tradition to be romanticized, admired, and appropriated. Much as in the process of colonization, the inherent inequalities (and occasional violence) suffered by the people who are the source of notions of folk are obscured, bemoaned, or romanticized to secure and enhance the authenticity of what is appropriated. As such, consumption of folklore involves recovering the past, idealizing the peasant or Indian, and romanticizing and repackaging it all. The process makes the arbiters of authenticity urban elites rather than the people who live the culture that is identified as authentic (or once authentic).

If traditional is a category designed to help us understand change, the study of folklore is a means to understand those objects, beliefs, and practices that make up the traditional. Indeed, folklore has placed into the same rubric the practices and beliefs of the exotic other of distant shores and the illiterate other closer (but socially distant) rural hinterlands. Think of Liszt and his Hungarian dances. The context of this consideration of the folk and their culture is one marked not only by inequality but also by notions of progress and social evolution that make natural social inequality and inevitable cultural homogenization. Within the concept lurk preconceptions of the Other as noble savage, brute, or simpleton. So, just as traditional dance is a product of colonialism, folkloric dance is a product of the struggle for meaning among the modernized and modernizing. The forms are not as independent, however, as they seem.

In *Choreographed Politics* (2002) and *Choreographing Identities* (2006), Anthony Shay develops the concept of "parallel traditions" to deal with the subjective loading and other shortcomings of the concept of authenticity that I explored in Chapter 2. Shay argues that we should not privilege one form of dance over another (2006:9). Rather, "theatricalized dance" and "dance in the field" should be understood as forms that (at least starting with industrialization) develop concurrently. Dance in the field, what I identify as "traditional dance," is the source for the creation of "theatricalized dance," what I term "folkloric dance." However, folkloric forms eventually acquire a life of their own and even occasionally influence the execution of traditional forms (Shay 2006:44). Presently, in Part Four, I argue that parallel forms representing indigenous Mesoamerican cultures vary in ways that reflect the context of their production and the needs of the dancers and their audiences.

Shay also identifies distinct phases of development in theatricalized dance. *Choreographed Politics* (2002) deals primarily with dances developed by state-sponsored companies that modified the dances of the field into performances meant to instruct national identity and nationalism. In *Choreographing Identities* (2006), Shay deals with transnationalist parallel traditions and folkloric dances performed by immigrants in U.S. society. In early twentieth-century immigrant communities, dances were created to represent ethnic identity from whatever resources in knowledge and material were available, often with little reference to actual "dances in the field" (2006:36–37). From the mid-twentieth century on (1950–1990), folkloric dances were created and performed by state-sponsored dance companies. In turn, the dances created by state-sponsored companies were adopted and adapted by immigrant dance groups in the United States. This phase, which dedicated attention to accurate mimesis (Shay 2006:39), involved both official state presentation of *national* culture and immigrant community representations of *ethnic* culture.[3] In these initial phases, educated elites enjoyed the authority to construct the dances that would represent their respective cultures (Shay 2006:36–42).

Appropriations of folklife to construct satisfying national and ethnic identities were done with a degree of disdain for the primitive rural Other (Shay 2006:36–42). In other words, from its inception, folkloric dance has had a conflicted relationship with its source cultures and peoples. Rural peasants are authentic, but they are also backward. If the folk Other and folkloric consumer inhabit the same society, then appropriation takes a while, distancing itself from its source.[4] This ambivalence stems from idealized notions and images of the folk. The actual people who are the source of such appropriations are never as simple and romantic as they are imagined.

The mid-century U.S. culture and economy embraced uniformity and technification, creating for immigrants a rather conflicted climate. One should be modern, look forward, and abandon the past. However, the present (to say nothing of the future) seemed void of authenticity. Referencing the rural peasant by European immigrants and indigenous people by Latin American immigrants under such conditions is satisfying but dangerous. Consequently, immigrant folkloric dancers created authentic performances that involved the risk of making their performers appear as backward or, worse, as unassimilated greenhorns.

In this book, I address a third parallel folkloric form in addition to the two identified by Shay (2002, 2006). In loose chronological order, folkloric dance began with state companies that performed official versions of national identities. Second, immigrant dancers deployed folkloric-like dances to educate and influence the images of their culture and identity circulated in the receiving country and across national borders. Third, and similar to the way powwow dancers have adapted elements of rodeo and the Wild West show, indigenous dancers now number among the genre's performers.

I explore this third parallel tradition through K'iche' Maya use of various theatricalized short dance forms. In Guatemala, both indigenous and nonindigenous people present folkloric dances, though at least to the present moment, it is a predominantly nonindigenous form. As I discuss below, folkloric dance has important roots among the elite of 1950s Mexico City and later among the elites of 1960s Guatemala City. While traditional dance has indigenous ancestry, folkloric dance does not directly. Therefore, K'iche' Maya participation in folkloric dance is a venture into the nonindigenous realm of performance. Some indigenous folkloric dancing is a counter-appropriation of widely circulated and highly salient dance created by professional touring companies. Some are adaptations of contemporary traditional dance into the structure of folkloric dances, fitting a smaller number of masked dancers into a shorter time frame.

Folkloric dance, once firmly in the hands of the elite, has been wrested from its originators and counter-appropriated by dancers and groups who differ in both class and culture. Accordingly, in this chapter, I consider the roots of folkloric dance in mid-twentieth-century Mexico City. In the following chapter, I explore immigrant folkloric dancing in the United States. In the third chapter of Part Four, I discuss folkloric dance as counter-appropriated by K'iche' Maya dancers in Guatemala.

At the recommendation of Elsa Figueroa, director of Nuevos Horizontes (the Melrose Park community education center), we have acquired tickets to see the Ballet Folklórico de la Universidad Veracruzana. We have also arranged a babysitter (Grandma), driven to downtown Chicago, and parked in the spacious garage attached to the Music and Dance Theater of Chicago. It is our first night out without the kids in some time. I will not be able to take notes or photographs as I did in highland Guatemala or suburban Chicago, but I am hoping to combine ethnography with an enjoyable "date" with my wife. We are not disappointed. The dances are crisp and energetic, the music moving and excellently performed. A good time is had by all.

One of the dances features a military theme. Although it is difficult to determine the ethnicity or religion of the characters—the costumes seem to vary only by color with identical form, adornment, and iconography—the dancers of the two sides engage each other in combat. They form two circles that turn in opposite directions, and the dancers exchange blows, their formations articulating like interlocking gears. I glance over at my wife. Having proofread my dissertation several times, she also sees the connection to the way the K'iche' Maya dancers of San Cristóbal Totonicapán represent combat between Spaniards and Mayas in the Dance of the Conquest. I am struck and realize that a traditional dance is being presented within a folkloric dance, and contemplate the possibility that the K'iche' dancers of San Cristóbal have incorporated an element of folkloric dance into their realization of the Dance of the Conquest.

The precise origins of folkloric dance are not easily defined or determined. Indeed, dances representing the lives and cultures of Natives of the Americas began soon after the extension of Spanish political control. Baumann (1995:240) describes a sixteenth-century performance, certainly under elite control and possibly enacted by Spaniards: "In October 1571, during the visit of the Duke of Alcalá and his wife in Alcalá de los Gazules, a night masquerade on the main square evoked the conquest of Mexico with over 200 men costumed as Indians. An embassy sent to Montezuma by Cortés preceded a great battle which included artillery fire and ended in the capture of the Aztec emperor." Representation of indigenous culture in dance under elite control appears again in the following century in neighboring Guatemala. Montoya summarizes a 1680 description by Domingo Juarros of a dance performance in honor of the dedication of the Catedral de Guatemala:

> *[D]onde ya encontramos una mezcla de personajes y danzas indígenas y españoles . . . Hacemos notar que niños y niñas de la primera nobleza de Guatemala, aprendieron danzas, imitaron vestuario y representaron personajes indígenas, lo que indica una fusión en las manifestaciones de teatro y danza de ambas culturas.*

> [W]here we already find a mix of indigenous and Spanish characters and dances . . . We note that children of *the first nobility of Guatemala* learned dances and imitated dress and presented indigenous characters, which indicates a fusion in the manifestation of theater and dance of both cultures. (1970:35, emphasis in original)

Indigenous and nonindigenous alike have been dancing to represent Mesoamerican indigenous culture in various ways since the Spanish invasion. The events above are best classified as rituals of the state (or empire). They enact official history and ideology in a context that marks or recognizes elite authority and state accomplishments. They, like the folkloric dancing explored presently, are also secular rituals, focused on identity, social order, and the justification of its hierarchy. However, *baile* or *ballet folklórico* of the present combines these pervasive representations of Indianness in dance with theatrical venues and professionalized dancing of later origin. What I examine in the following paragraphs is the standardization and proliferation of *ballet folklórico* as an internationally salient genre of dance.

By the mid-twentieth century, Indianness would come to be a predominant theme in theatricalized representational dance forms created in Mexico. Among the most influential presenters of folkloric dance is the El Ballet Folklórico de México, founded by Amalia Hernández (Nájera-Ramírez 1989:21). According to Julio Solorzano-Foppa of El Ballet Folklórico de México, "The concept of Ballet Folklórico was developed by Amalia [Hernández] herself . . . Before her, those two words were never together" (Burke 2001). Whether the combination was unique at the time is not entirely knowable. However, Hernández seems to have been one of the first to combine elements of indigenous life and dance with modern dance form, choreography, costuming, and venue (Anderson 2000). Perhaps as important, she was the first to have such dancing embraced by mass-media audiences.

A formally trained dancer, Hernández founded El Ballet Folklórico de México in 1952 (Anderson 2000). By the mid-1950s, the group was making regular appearances on Mexican television, presenting some sixty-seven programs to enthusiastic audiences (Nájera-Ramírez 1989:21). The group was sponsored by Mexico's Department of Tourism and was "made the official cultural representative of the Mexican government" (Nájera-Ramírez 1989:21). Before the end of the 1950s, the company was traveling outside of Mexico to perform in the United States, and in 1961 it was "an official representative of the Mexican government at Paris's Festival of the Nations" (Ballet Folklórico de México 2005a).

Beyond presenting folkloric dance, El Ballet Folklórico de México trains performers. According to its website, "From the beginning of the 1960s, Amalia

Hernández conceived of the idea of creating a School of the Ballet Folklórico, to promote and strengthen its artistic expression, as well as to prepare dancers who would be capable of responding to the company's needs" (Ballet Folklórico de México 2005c). By the end of the 1960s the Ballet Folklórico had its own school building and in 1973 it added an annex. To date, the school has trained more than 25,000 performers (Ballet Folklórico de México 2005b). The impact of Amalia Hernández and the school she founded on folkloric dancing cannot be underestimated. Through mass media, international touring, and training thousands of performers, the school and its founder are a central part of contemporary Mexican folkloric dancing (Nájera-Ramírez 1989:21).

While *ballet* or *baile folklórico* may have been initiated by Amalia Hernández, it would take on defining characteristics from other sources. Hernández formed her company in the early 1950s, and by the next decade, Florencio Yescas became an important collaborator (Shay 2006:82). A Conchero dancer[5] from Mexico City, Yescas moved to the United States in the early 1960s. He is credited with initiating an Azteca dance movement that made reference to an imagined pre-Columbian past free of Spanish influence (Shay 2006:84). Where Hernández focused primarily on the indigenous folk of the present and colonial past, Yescas was concerned with the aboriginal Aztec imperial past. The Gran Tenochtitlan suite, an homage to the pre-Columbian Aztec, became an integral part of Ballet Folklórico's program and was born of cooperation between Yescas and Hernández (Shay 2006:82). Thus, Mexican-influenced folkloric dancing would reference indigenous culture from a range of pasts. It would influence immigrant dancing in the United States, but in its incorporation of pre-Columbian culture, it also drew from immigrant dancing.

The success of Ballet Folklórico de México no doubt influenced the formation of other Latin American national dance companies. Ballet Moderno y Folklórico de Guatemala was formed in 1964 by the state education ministry. Much as its Mexican counterpart, the Guatemalan company enacts Indianness through theatricalized vignettes performed by professional dancers. Description of a 2008 performance at the Million Dollar Theater in Los Angeles titled "Guatemala: Colorful and Friendly" emphasizes "ancient native cultures" and specifies performances that portray "Mayan ritual dance practiced 1,000 years before the birth of Christ" (Schieber 2008). Ballet Moderno y Folklórico de Guatemala's mixture of genres (modern and folkloric) nicely captures the central tension of Guatemalan nationalist ideology. As ethnic categories, modern-Ladino and folkloric-Indígena frame social hierarchy as a reflection of such progress. The issue contested by Guatemalans is whether this combination of modern and folkloric is one of assimilation of indigenous cultures to a homogeneous national culture or of pluralism that accommodates robust diversity.[6]

Not surprisingly, non-Mexican Latino dancers offer varied accounts of the origin of folkloric dance, depending on the histories of their home countries. For example, a folkloric dancer from Bolivia understands the rise of folkloric dancing in her Andean homeland as a reflection of a period in which the strict alignment of caste (indigenous, mestizo, white) and class (poor, middle-class, elite) began to break down. Under this theory, dances of the field performed in Aymara communities became folkloric dances presented by people from all strata of society as part of an organic social transformation.

A similar process likely took place in Totonicapán. La Vanguardia Indígena Totonicapense was formed in 1950, contemporary with the formation of El Ballet Folklórico de México and several years before Guatemala's state dance company was formed in 1964. Documents concerning the founding of the group held by its current president, Alfonso Sastre,[7] speak of preservation of culture and tradition through dance in theatrical settings. It is clear that community leaders, both indigenous and nonindigenous (certainly with occasionally divergent motivations), were concerned about changes occurring in Totonicapán at mid-century. The process that would make (and continues to shape) Totonicapán into a center of production for local, national, and international markets was well under way. The Vanguardia Indígena, in certain respects, was formed to accommodate this process of change by guarding and enacting tradition. The notion that indigenous culture was sure to disappear if action was not taken shaped the founding of the Vanguardia. It continues to inform the discourse of many Totonicapenses. However, in true parallel fashion, short (five- to ten-minute) theatricalized folkloric performances and long (six- to eight-hour) semi-ritualized traditional dances are a part of the social and cultural life of Totonicapán and its surrounding hamlets more than sixty years after the foundation of the Vanguardia Indígena.

My purpose here is not to provide a definitive history of folkloric dance but to consider the context in which the genre expanded and became part of national and international consciousnesses. The political and cultural currents of the 1930s and 1940s certainly encouraged forms like folkloric dancing. In particular, Mexican indigenist policy emphasized assimilation of indigenous groups while appropriating selected elements of their cultures in a new, unified national identity. Additionally, many of the elements of globalization and modernity are a part of the process. The occupational specialization that professional dancing and formal dance training entail is another hallmark of complex modern society, and the postwar represents for Mexico a period of change and industrialization. Ballet Folklórico de México, with the resources that come with state sponsorship, reached a wide audience through mass media and a system of accelerating international travel, both features commonly attributed to globalization. By promoting an official version of

Table 8.1. Comparison of K'iche' traditional dance and Latino folkloric dance

		Traditional Dance	*Folkloric Dance*
Performers and Performance	Ethnicity	Indigenous	Indigenous and Nonindigenous
	Training	• Embedded in kinship • Nonprofessional	• Formal classes • Professional training • Professional and nonprofessional performers
	Context of Performance	• Fairs in honor of the patron saint of particular concrete communities • Traditional dance festivals • Almost always outdoors	• In United States and in home countries • Ethnic festivals for transnational communities • School events as part of cultural and multicultural education • Formal dance and music venues
	Length of Performance	Four hours to several days	Ten to twenty minutes, presented one after the other
Paraphernalia in Performance	Masks	Central element of paraphernalia	Masks typically absent
	Regalia	• Abstract • Symbolically loaded • Some individual expression	• Realistic • Pleasing to the eye, not as symbolically loaded • Little individual expression
Meanings in Performance	Ritual?	• Often ritual as well as drama • Ritual treatment of masks and costumes • Ritual avoidances observed before performance • Spirits of important figures present during performance	• May portray ritual, but is not ritual itself • Sacred elements absent or not apparent
	Pre-Columbian References	Encoded in costumes, character names, and covert themes	Explicitly presented
	Religion	Outwardly Christian with indigenous religious belief and practice coded or hidden from outsiders	Beliefs and practices are presented as images of indigenous life and culture
Challenges		Colonialism	Modernity and ethnic discrimination
Responses		• Typically through strong communities • More recently through pan-Maya cooperation • Pan-Mayanism not much expressed in dance yet	• Unique national and regional identities expressed • Dances performed in context of cultural diversity within social and political unity

nationalism that incorporated images of indigenous culture, state companies addressed some of the cognitive and emotional challenges of modernity, making the construction of official identity compelling to a wide variety of audiences. Performances continue to evoke national pride, but also a sense of deep-rooted tradition as antidote to rapid change.

Also by the early 1960s, the issues of identity and economy that transcend state borders so prevalent today were taking root. The "Mexican miracle" of postwar economic development resulted in a greatly expanded economy, increased participation in wage labor, and other markers of modernity. It also fostered dependence on foreign investment and engendered growing social and wealth inequality. The foundations for the North American Free Trade Agreement and intensified flows of Mexican workers to the United States were well in place. With these came intensified challenges of identity. Images of Indians, as Deloria (1998) notes, are deployed during periods in which received notions about identity are challenged by shifting social and economic realities.

At present, folkloric dance continues to construct national identity and negotiates modernity and transnationalism. Accordingly, I now address contemporary iterations of *ballet folklórico* that have roots in state-sponsored companies. I draw on dance programs and performances of three government-supported professional touring dance companies based in Mexico. The first program I employ is from a 2002 performance of El Ballet Folklórico de México in Berkeley, California. I also draw on the program and performance of a 2006 appearance of the same company at the Auditorium Theater in Chicago that I attended. The second written text I consult is from a repertoire of the Ballet Folkórico de la Universidad Veracruzuana. This troupe also tours extensively in the United States, and I attended a performance at the Chicago Music and Dance Theater in 2004. Additionally, I attended a performance of the municipal folkloric company of Guadalajara at an interethnic community festival in Melrose Park (programs were not available). Using these sources, I first consider a general theme that unites folkloric presentations. Second, I examine how a specific aspect of this general theme is expressed in folkloric dances.

The first impression that *bailes folklóricos* often make is of an era past, a bucolic simpler time. The costumes reflect rural pastimes and rural sensibilities. The programs of the Ballet Folklórico de México make repeated references to "village fiestas" and rural settings. The Universidad Veracruzana repertoire listing describes rural *pueblos* and *ferias* and *costumbres ancestrales* (ancestral customs, rites). Interwoven into these descriptions of a rural premodern past are direct and indirect references to indigenous people and peoples. Although some dances do not include representations of the first peoples of the Americas, allusions to indigenous life and culture are rarely absent. Ballet Folklórico de México's programs refer to "indigenous culture" and Indians. They also specifically mention several indigenous groups, including the Yaqui, Mixtec, and Zapotec. The repertoire of Universidad Veracruzana includes dances with titles such as Boda indígena, or Indigenous Wedding. It mentions particular indigenous groups as well, including Nahuatl and *los huastecos*, who are identified as *hermanos étnicos de los mayas* (ethnic brothers of the Maya).

Presentation of images of indigenous life and culture are not limited to the recent past. Folkloric dance frequently attempts to reconstruct the pre-Columbian era. Ballet Folklórico de México describes the "ancient" roots of many of its dances. The program for the 2006 performance in Chicago proclaims that some of the dances "encompass pre-Hispanic rituals." Los Matachines, for example, "dates from pre-Hispanic times and reflects the custom of dancing with one's gods." According to Ballet Folklórico de la Universidad Veracruzana, the dance known as the Huahuas or Guaguas is *indudablemente una danza prehispánica a los cuatro puntos cardinales* (undoubtedly a pre-Hispanic dance of the four cardinal points). Performances of the Guadalajara company featured a representation of a pre-Columbian rite.

These references to indigenous life also include indigenous dancing. Both companies present versions of contemporary traditional dance, including the Dance of the Moors and the Christians (Moros y Españoles). The text of the Veracruz company also explicitly references contemporary flying pole dances (*[e]sta danza perteneció al complejo de el Volador*). It also claims origins for Danza de los Matachines in the Dance of the Conquest.

So what are we to make of all these references to indigenous culture? In *The Predicament of Culture*, James Clifford argues that modernity brings with it a sense of lost authenticity (1988:4). Large-scale, complex modern (and post-modern) industrial (and post-industrial) societies do foster experiences that are cognitively dislocating. We often encounter more unknown faces than known ones; moving about outside of the home or workplace can be a profoundly impersonal and anonymous experience. We have momentary interactions with people we may never see again. The hyper-specialization of our economy makes even the people we know sometimes unknowable. We are befuddled, asking what was it, again, that he does? Many of the objects that we encounter are mass-produced, identical to thousands if not millions of others. The spaces we pass through and inhabit can and do change frequently, a seemingly permanent building reduced to an empty lot in the space of a week, a farm converted into a subdivision in mere months. What were landmarks of navigation and memory disappear before our very eyes.

Depersonalized experiences like these evoke a strong sense of disconnection from people, places, and objects. Human beings are, however, creatures that need meaning and often prefer to get and express meaning in local, personalized connections. In other words, life in large-scale, complex, and anonymous societies compels many to seek experiences that feel "authentic." Clifford (1988:4–14) also argues that the moderns often seek, locate, and find authenticity and purity in non-modern, exotic Others, the indigenous. Clifford's insight goes a long way toward explaining why folkloric dances are so loaded with images of indigenous peoples and cultures. As I remarked earlier, the florescence of folkloric dance corresponded with a period of great urbanization and industrialization, key components of modernization. It is no accident that a daughter of elite society in a great industrial and urban center founded Ballet Folklórico de México.

Just as K'iche' Maya traditional dance and Native American powwow dance have important origins in the colonial period, folkloric dance has roots in globalization and modernization. The colonial period saw a conversion of aboriginal dances into traditional dances. Globalization and modernity saw the creation of folkloric dance. While I continue to identify traditional and folkloric dance as parallel traditions, both do deal with and react to prominent forces distinct to their respective eras of initial creation. Moreover, the continued practice of both reflects the realities faced by their dancers. Transnationalism made the formation of companies in the United States inevitable.

In the next chapter I consider enactment of folkloric dance by immigrants (and their children) in the United States. Whereas state-sponsored companies respond to modernity and emergent and shifting senses of nation-state identity, immigrant dancing concerns transnationalism and its challenges.

NOTES

1. The community manifests the transnational flows of people and culture characteristic of globalization. However, it is neither a replication of a Mexican town nor like the white and African American suburbs that make up other parts of the inner ring of suburban Chicago. Influenced by globalization but also local, Melrose Park is best termed *glocal*.

2. A party to mark the end of a course, a conference, or other event or series of events that has brought a group of people together with a common purpose.

3. As I explored in Part One, these ethnic and national references evidence a similar kind of identity based on shared culture and history. National ethnic identity of the nation-state differs from ethnic identity of the ethnic group within the state in degree of abstractness (remoteness from actual concrete community or group) and in attachment to power of the state.

4. See Rostas (2009:202) regarding "Mexica" folk dancers from Mexico City, who have limited awareness of or concern about indigenous suffering under the exercise of Mexican state policies.

5. "Conchero" references the conch-bodied guitars used in a popular genre with indigenous roots danced by Mexicans of various backgrounds (Rostas 2009).

6. Reflecting differences of scale in their patron states, Ballet Moderno y Folklórico de Guatemala does not enjoy the same degree of support as the Ballet Folklórico de México. It tours internationally only rarely, and as a result, finding programs and performances is a greater challenge. My description of the Guatemalan state company relies on notes published by Centro de Reportes Informativos sobre Guatemala (CERIGUA), a nongovernmental press agency dedicated to more accurate and complex news reporting on Guatemala (www.cerigua.org). I also rely on video recordings of the troupe's performances posted on YouTube and other Web-based sources of video.

7. Alfonso Sastre is a pseudonym.

Nine

Appropriation, Round 2: Immigrant Folkloric Dance

Triton Community College features a large, high-ceilinged, adaptable open space that is flanked by the student service center and the bookstore. During the day it serves as a cafeteria. On this evening, teachers and students of the English as a Second Language program have gathered for a night of international culture. Fliers were distributed to the classes and posted around campus. Tables have been rearranged to accommodate displays of art and samplings of food. Against the solid west wall of the space a set of risers forms a stage. The district encompasses large Eastern European and Latino immigrant populations and the evening reflects the demographics of the surrounding communities. Polish and Mexican folk culture is presented as art, food, and dance. I take some pictures and talk with some former colleagues. The event, as teachers report to me, occurs largely because of student impetus; teachers assist in the organization, but it is students that really make the evening happen. It is a most public and direct expression of the kind of cultural exchange that pervades the transnational ESL classroom. Students learn about the English and culture of the United States. Their teachers and classmates learn about peoples and places from all over the world. Here, the whole campus is encouraged to join the exchange.

After a suitable period of mingling and visiting, the dances begin. I am struck once again by how often dances are employed to represent ethnic identity. As Shay points out (2006:158), immigrants and those who assist their adaptation to U.S. society have long used dance to reaffirm their cultural identity to themselves and their children and to express it to others. In addition to adapting an event of the immigrant settlement house era to the community college, the event is a small-scale iteration of the large folk festivals held in St. Paul and Los Angeles and through the Smithsonian (Shay 2006:155–220). At the Triton culture night and at large festivals, food, art, and dance are the three means of defining, expressing, and experiencing cultural diversity.

According to dancer David Rojas, there are more than 2,000 folkloric dance groups in the Los Angeles area alone (Preston 1997). Hispanofest,[1] which regularly features a variety of dance groups, taps an extensive community of folkloric dancing in the Chicago area. Indeed, in and around Chicago, professional and amateur groups perform at weddings, graduations, and even at the mega-festival Taste of Chicago. An informal survey of folkloric dance websites reveals groups and performances in other expected places. The Anita N. Martinez Ballet Folklórico is based in Dallas, Texas. The Aztlán Dance Troupe makes its home in San Jose, California.

Immigrant folkloric dancing also appears in unexpected places. The December 20, 1999, issue of the *Honolulu Star Bulletin* includes a brief story describing a "Hispanic Christmas" celebration in which a dance "native" to Veracruz was presented (Honolulu Star Bulletin 1999). The Quad Cities area of eastern Iowa and western Illinois is home to Quad-Cities Ballet Folklórico. An organization that strives to teach the children of immigrants about their Mexican heritage, Quad-Cities Ballet Folkórico was formed over twenty years ago (Speer 2004; Willard 2004). Students at New Jersey's Ivy League university perform in the Ballet-Folklórico de Princeton. Indeed, educational settings seem to be quite common to folkloric dancing. In addition to the heritage education goals of the Quad Cities group and the elite higher education context of the Princeton group, high school and community college folkloric dance clubs can be found on the Internet.

Folkloric dances are presented in and out of doors in a variety of settings. Venues include churches, grade and high school auditoriums, stages at Latino ethnic festivals, and university and community theaters. Facilities range from modest and simple stages to highly elaborate, acoustically designed multimillion-dollar venues such as the Music and Dance Theater of Chicago. Suffice it to say that there is an abundance of folkloric dancing in the United States presented in a wide variety of communities and settings.

In the previous chapter, I argued that we must take into account forces of globalization and modernization to fully understand the florescence of folkloric dancing starting in the mid-twentieth century. Here, after brief review of

9.1. Transnational Folkloric. A member of the municipal folkloric company of Guadalajara performs at Taste of Melrose Park, September 2006. Melrose Park is a majority Spanish-speaking community in suburban Chicago served by the community college described above. Note the symbols of the peasant farmer: machete, headscarf, and sash belt. (Photograph by author.)

some of the common themes in immigrant folkloric dance, I consider transnationalism, the formation of pan-ethnic identity, and marginalization and discrimination as significant forces that inform and motivate folkloric dancing in the United States. I finish the chapter with consideration of the controversy surrounding the representation of indigenous culture in dance.

IMMIGRANT FOLKLORIC DANCE: THEMES AND SYMBOLS OF IDENTITY

As most performances by immigrants are organized through semi-formalized groups without government sponsorship, I rely on interviews with two folkloric dancers who perform in two different semi-professional dance groups based in the Chicago area and a variety of performances that I have attended in and around Chicago. These include several performances at Hispanofest (2004, 2005, 2007, 2010), dances at a culture night at a suburban community college (described earlier), a presentation by the Mexican Dance Ensemble of Chicago at the Taste of Chicago (2006), and a joint performance of the Mexican Folkloric Dance Company of Chicago and Sones de México Ensemble of Chicago (providing live Grammy-nominated music) in February 2008.

Despite a diversity of location and organization, there is considerable thematic overlap between state-sponsored companies and immigrant dance groups (the former tending to present in one program what the latter specialize in by group). The context and the purpose of presentation differ significantly between state-sponsored companies and immigrant groups. Again, references to indigenous culture, the colonial and the pre-Columbian, are rarely absent. Indeed, the Bolivian dancer I interviewed acknowledges that all of the folkloric dances of her home country have origins in indigenous life and indigenous dance performance. Many of the dances that I observed at Hispanofest and two performed at the Taste of Chicago depicted indigenous courtship and marriage. Also at Hispanofest, as I described above (and certainly inspired by the tradition begun by Yescas), an Aztec ritual concerning the four cardinal directions was depicted. Another group that presented at the 2004 Hispanofest identifies itself as Ballet Folklórico de Tenochtitlán, referencing the pre-Columbian Aztec capital. Another group at the 2005 Hispanofest featured a performance representing pre-Columbian religious ritual. The performance of the Mexican Folkloric Dance Company of Chicago began with a representation of an Aztec ritual dance. Beyond Mexican American groups, my Bolivian dance consultant describes a dance called Los Incas, which depicts the pre-Hispanic Andean past.

While expanding modernity well explains the rise of folkloric dancing in 1950s Latin America, it only partially explains the popularity of folk dancing abroad. Granted, life in the United States presents as great a challenge to authenticity as any other place. It is bewildering to the native-born, who increasingly manifest signs of profound social and cultural confusion. (Yearning and demands for a "return to traditional values" are only a symptom of the problem.) However, for the newcomer, such difficulties of meaning and place are more profound. Maria Rodriguez describes how folkloric dances "have great currency among Mexicans living outside of their country who are asking themselves, 'Who am I? What am I doing here?' " (Preston 1997: E2). To the difficulty of finding meaningful identity posed by modernity is added the challenges of the cultural, social, and physical dislocations that are a part of being an immigrant. Transnationalism, with places and identities that are both here and there, further fosters the potential for dislocation and meaninglessness.

After finishing my dissertation fieldwork and moving to Chicago, I began work in adult education ESL. The notion that the teacher learns at least as much as the students is particularly true in ESL classes. Part of what I gained was an appreciation of the popularity of folkloric dancing in immigrant communities in the United States. I have come to understand folkloric dancing as one of many ways that Latino immigrants deal with the challenges of life in the United States. As such, it should come as no surprise that folkloric dance is often presented at community festivals.

The nationalist identities promoted by state-sponsored folkloric companies, when presented in the United States, become subethnic categories. In the process, what was meant to instill a sense of unity in the sending country becomes a source of ethnic diversity in the receiving country. Folkloric dances performed by immigrants promote unique, specific identity within broad, imagined political identity. Where Mexicans predominate in the Latino population, as is the case in Chicago, folkloric dances of other Central and South American countries provide a means to assert a version of Latino that is not Mexican. Although being Latino provides some political power by virtue of the alliance of people of varied backgrounds, it is not as local and satisfying as being from a particular place with its own unique history and culture. Moreover, the process of identification is more than simply being different from whites or African Americans or Asians. Rather, how one identifies oneself in the sending country must seem upside-down from how one is identified in the receiving country. In the home country, state, department, or *pueblo*, identity starts locally and builds outward. For example, my indigenous consultants in Guatemala are Totonicapenses (for their home community), then K'iche', then Maya, then Guatemalan, and, finally and most remotely, Latino. In the United States, the ordering of layers of identity is inverted. To white mainstream society, the same person is Latino, Hispanic, or Latin American first and primarily. Moreover, the other, more local layers of identity—the ones that tend to be more satisfying—are often unseen, ignored, or misunderstood. In the States, people from Central America are labeled "Mexican"; Mexicans are labeled "South American"; Brazilians, "Spanish"; Dominicans, "Black"; and so forth. For children and grandchildren of immigrants, Latino becomes a more natural category of identity, as they have as much or more experience being Latino within the United States as being from a particular community in a specific Latin American country. It becomes a lived category as they circulate with other Latinos and absorb and adapt to the mainstream propensity to paint ethnicity with broad strokes. For their parents and grandparents, however, references in folkloric dance to indigenous peoples and cultures from particular regions of particular countries work on the cognitive problems of the abstract and general category of Latino.

I return to Hispanofest to illustrate the point. Although the great majority of the Latino residents of Melrose Park are Mexican, Hispanofest works to promote an inclusive sense of Latino. The ideals of the festival are communicated well in a painting prominently featured at Nuevos Horizontes, a community education center based in Melrose Park. Titled *Hispanofest*, the piece portrays the Gran Desfile, a parade that initiates the fair. Individuals carrying the flags of various nations of the Americas, from Argentina to the United States, lead the procession. It nicely conveys the notion of unity through diversity and the process by which those who live in Melrose Park construct new layers of self and political identity. In general, parades are similar to dance, with the individual body conforming to group activity. This great parade enacts the addition of pan-ethnicity to other layers of cultural, regional, national, and linguistic identification.

The styles of music presented at Hispanofest reflect an interesting negotiation of local (la Melrose)[2] and Latino. While the bands provide a variety of styles—*banda, norteño, cumbia, salsa, merengue, bachata, mariachi*, and so forth—many of the groups are from Durango, Mexico, or play *duranguense* music, a form evocative of Durango but created in Chicago. Such a lineup of bands embraces diversity within the broad, abstract category of Latino. It also reflects, however, a local community that has strong connections to Durango through the regular flows of people, meaningful objects, and meaningful activities.

Moreover, Hispanofest has hosted folkloric groups that present the traditions of Bolivia, Puerto Rico, and various parts of Mexico. As the Gran Desfile and the musical variety concern identity and transnationalism, so do folkloric dances. They all are about placing some of the local from "there" in the local "here." Doing so stresses diversity within the broad, pan-ethnic identity of Latino, working on the paradox of a singular category that is full of variety.

As an avid performer of Bolivian dance puts it, Latino means *una raza unida de muchas ramas* (a united people[3] of many branches).

However, to be Latino may also mean enacting an appropriate specific identity. Upon asking an amateur Mexican dancer to describe how he came to *baile folklórico*, he replied that, like most in his estimation, he started dancing after moving to the United States. His participation in the genre has included dancing in different groups, one of which was Bolivian. He describes the experience as follows:

> *[E]n ese grupo aprendi muchisimo de esa cultura tan diferente a la mia y con ellos estuve bailando unos 4 años. Una anecdota que puedo contar haserca del balet Boliviano es que participe 3 años concecutivos en los desfiles de independencia de los USA (4 de Julio) y al yo estar en representando este pais me hacia sentir muy bien, pero en estos mismo desfiles habia un ballet folklórico Mexicano participando y cuando yo los veia pasar habia algo en mi interior que me hacia sentir mal. Pues yo estaba representando una cultura que no era mia, era solo una mascara, ahora que me pongo a pensar lo que en ese momento sentia, pienso que es por que indirectamente yo deseaba estar ahi en ese desfile representando mi propia cultura.* (personal communciation, March 2005)

In the passage, the dancer relates how he learned a great deal about a Bolivian culture that is quite different from his own Mexican culture. He describes how marching in a Fourth of July parade gave him mixed feelings. He felt quite good about this participation; however, upon seeing a Mexican folkloric group in the same parade, he felt bad. He concludes that he had been representing a culture that was not his. He decided to leave the group and currently participates in Mexican *ballet folklórico*.

The ability of folkloric dances, through their frequent reference to indigenous peoples, to express specific national identities is occasionally extended to specific regional identities. Although it should not have surprised me, I was struck by how much *regional* pride was expressed at a performance of the Ballet Folklórico de la Universidad Veracruzana. Before the performance we learned that among the dignitaries present was a government official of the state of Veracruz. Furthermore, as the program was introduced, references to Veracruz were met with enthusiastic whoops and applause from an audience of immigrants and descendants of immigrants. During the performance it was clear that the indigenous people of and near Veracruz were predominant, with multiple references to the native culture of the Huasteca region.

We return again to Clifford's observation that modernity lacks authenticity and that denizens of modern complex societies seek and find authenticity in indigenous culture. The challenge of authentic identity here lies with the abstract nature of a pan-ethnic category that results from globalized flows of people of varied backgrounds to the United States. Such imagined political identities provide little of the unique local material from which human beings create satisfying identity. Thus, immigrant folkloric dances express cultural distinctiveness by emphasizing diversity of national cultures. To make these national cultures authentic and unique, folkloric dances frequently reference the indigenous people of the respective nation-state or even a region within a nation-state.

FOLKLORIC DANCE, PAN-ETHNICITY, AND SOCIAL INEQUALITY

So far, I have stressed a certain cognitive challenge presented in attaching to multiple layers of ethnic identification. I noted that Latino is a broad abstract pan-ethnic category. That is to say, one must be from or trace ancestry to a particular Latin American country (or countries) to be considered Latino. There is no concrete place or community, no Latinolandia or Ciudad Latino outside of the United States. The obvious question then is, why do people of varied class, culture, language, and historical backgrounds, encompassed in dozens of states and many more regions, embrace a common category of ethnic identification? No doubt Latino as a category is somewhat imposed by a dominant society with a tendency to form a broad, if clumsy, classification of social reality. More of the answer lies, however, in the political potential that resides in pan-ethnicity. Political cooperation is facilitated by shared identity. Moreover, working together to combat stereotypes and discrimination includes improving the images and ideas associated with the broad pan-ethnic identity and its constituent identities. In the following paragraphs I will explore how immigrant folkloric dance, by referencing an imagined noble indigenous past, works to counter negative stereotypes in the present. As such, folkloric dance also responds to discrimination and marginalization in addition to modernity and transnationalism.

Shay (2006:79–90) describes the intersection of the promotion of Mexican national culture through Ballet Folklórico de México with rising Chicano political activism beyond the home countries and well in advance of the immigration of the 1990s that shaped the current Latino populations and politics. The 1962 performance of Ballet Folkórico de México at the Hollywood Bowl "strongly resonated in the Mexican American community and directly helped launch the Chicano movement" (Shay 2006:81). The establishment of folkloric groups at all levels of the public education, one of the demands of late 1960s Chicano student strikes, was largely achieved. By 1970, hundreds of groups had been founded in the U.S. Southwest. Eventually (and probably inevitably) touring company dancing and immigrant group dancing would diverge as Mexican immigrant and ethnic communities expanded and generated their own institutions and culture. As I noted earlier, immigrants have introduced to the folkloric repertoire dances that specifically reference the pre-Columbian era. Deployment of symbols from time immemorial responds to challenges of identity but also to more concrete issues of politics and economy faced by immigrants.

These political and economic issues have roots in immigration policy that formally or informally loosens control of the inflows of workers when labor demands are high. A general cycle that mirrors the economy emerges; weak borders during economic expansion are alternated with increased border control and anti-immigrant sentiments during economic stagnation. The latest cycle fundamentally informs the context of contemporary folkloric dancing in the United States. The economic boom of the 1990s generated demand for labor that attracted immigration flows from around the globe. However, even as economic expansion came to depend on inflows of low-wage workers, the public and government policy expressed ambivalence toward jobholders from Latin America. Mass marketing began and continues to revel in "Latino" as a style and audience. Conversely, California's 1994 Proposition 187 and congressional passage of the Illegal Immigration Reform and Immigrant Responsibility Act (IIRIRA) in 1996 signaled an attitude hostile to both documented and undocumented immigrants. Although only the latter became law, both sought to restrict access by undocumented immigrants to public benefits, and IIRIRA significantly curtailed access to federal programs for documented immigrants. Nevertheless, through the 1990s, the economy created jobs and immigrants arrived to fill them.

During the George W. Bush administration, the U.S. economy frequently failed to generate a sufficient volume of new jobs for all of the workers entering the workforce. As a result, jobs became scarce and the unofficial policy of lax immigration enforcement of the economic expansion of the 1990s came under scrutiny. Efforts by the Bush administration to legalize present undocumented immigrants and assert more control over future flows (i.e., guest-worker programs and the like) were met by strong popular opposition from within the Republican Party's own base of support. Fueled by ardent and continual anti-immigrant rhetoric of mainstream media personalities such as Lou Dobbs and by outright hate speech broadcast through less official AM radio programs, failures of policy and of government became a problem of Others who are "illegal." In turn, pan-ethnic immigrant institutions organized marches and did other less visible work to promote reformation of immigration policy in a way that recognizes social reality and complies with human rights standards.

Not surprisingly, as anti-immigrant bigotry continues, so do references to the pre-Columbian past in the art and discourse of Latinos. In fact, so salient is this connection of present to past for Mexican Americans that it has been identified by a specific term. Aztlán refers to the northern fringe of Mesoamerica that during the pre-Columbian period was inhabited by nomadic foragers known to the southern urbanized societies as rather wild. According to the Aztec origin story (and supported by linguistic connections), the original Mexica came to the Valley of Mexico from Aztlán. The group that would come to politically dominate much of northern Mesoamerica in the period immediately before the Spanish invasion likely has roots in what archaeologists identify as the Greater Southwest. This place of origin may be in what is now popularly identified as the American Southwest.

The deployment of the Aztlán complex through a variety of forms reflects an ongoing effort to counter persistent negative depictions of Mexico, Mexicans, and Mexican Americans. Moreover, assimilation, the alternative to maintaining a distinctive identity based on connection to the sending country, has its own problems. Assimilation to the mainstream for many groups has delivered only part of its promise. Even after meeting the challenge to learn and adapt to mainstream cultural norms, outsiders to the mainstream, whether African American, Native American, or Latino, find continued discrimination on the inside. An obvious response to such experiences is to assert a more positive version of ethnic identity and to take pride in cultural and social distinctiveness. In the present case, rather than accept a kind of semi-acceptance as an assimilated Mexican, embracing and representing pride in being distinctly Mexican American offer more.

Additionally, the Aztlán complex directly challenges the ideology of the "real American" and the notion that the changing ethnic composition of U.S. society is something new. By deploying images of pre-Columbian origin, dancers stake a claim to legitimate presence on the continent. Aztlán predates not only Anglo settlement of the U.S. Southwest but also Spanish colonialism. Mexican dancers who reference Aztecs reference a story that places the aboriginal roots of Mexican identity within the borders of the United States. Such performance constructs a past that asserts a time-immemorial Mexica and Mexican presence in a place where shifting government policy and popular opinion strive to exclude actual Mexicans. Folkloric dance then provides a means to construct and present positive specific ethnic identities and contest negative stereotypes. It has at its disposal varied indigenous, aboriginal, and pre-Columbian peoples to reference, claiming identities that are local, historically deep, and authentic.

Beyond specific national identities, the category Latino presents political and perceptual challenges from within and without. A Bolivian folkloric dancer argues that dance presents both the national cultural patrimony of her home country and Latino identity. She stresses the inability of outsiders to understand the great diversity within the category Latino as the root of her motivation. She dances to help whites better understand Latinos as much as to help Latinos better understand one another. As such, Latino folkloric dancing involves at least three distinct audiences. First, and most likely communicative of multiple layers of meaning, are audience members who share national or regional origin with the dancers. Second, and more apt to read dance as an expression of the paradox of pan-ethnic identity, are other Latinos. Third, and ideally disabusing themselves of stereotypical notions of Latino, are non-Latino Others. Uniting these varied audiences is the process through which the meaning of Latino is negotiated, created, contested, and shared. Representational dance, through its combination of body conformity, symbolically loaded dress, and evocative music, is an ideal form for the communication of multilayered messages to a diverse audience. It is employed to convey complex messages across social, cultural, and linguistic boundaries.

Also a common trend of globalization is anxiety among the privileged, as they must compete more rigorously for jobs and resources within global and glocal workforces. The process is one in which boundaries, political and cognitive, seem to shift and disintegrate. Not only are jobs "outsourced" to workers abroad, but economic anxiety is coupled with identity anxiety. An imagined America, one that is white and culturally homogeneous, seems imperiled by flows of people and custom. Accordingly, I briefly address a common criticism of cultural diversity, as folkloric dancing is a salient outward expression of such diversity. It is ill-informed to describe cultural enactment of local and pan-ethnic Latino identities as some kind of tribalism resistant to appropriate modernization or assimilation. First, there is nothing natural or inevitable about cultural homogenization. Globalization has not, as some in the core countries have predicted (and perhaps wished), created a uniform worldwide culture. Indeed, more often than not, cross-cultural interactions so characteristic of globalized networks of travel and communication have provided opportunities for more specific understanding of self through reflection in Other. That is to say, encountering Others often helps us more consciously define ourselves, and this process seems unlikely to generate cultural uniformity.

Second, pan-ethnic identification, whether under the term "Latino" or "indigenous," is a response to political needs derived of social inequality that itself is the barrier to political and societal (not necessarily cultural) unity. It is persistent discrimination and marginalization that motivate such political alliance. It is not diverse cultural identification but negative valuation, stereotypes, and misunderstanding of cultural diversity that drive marginalization and the strategies to counter it. Perhaps in a society free of such forces, immigrants would not feel compelled to self-represent collectively and form political alliances. However, suggesting that such responses prevent the realization of an equal and integrated society confuses cause and effect.

PROBLEMS AND CONTROVERSIES OF REPRESENTATION

Perhaps appropriately, a response to social inequality raises concerns about other inequalities. Deploying images of indigenous peoples and their cultures in dance generates difficulties for other Others. Representation of culture and identity in the global era is a complicated affair. People already equipped with multiple status and roles act in a widening array of social settings, some real, some virtual. The paradox of constructing an image of self that is derived from the culture of an Other complicates things further. Representing indigenous culture in folkloric dance enters the complex arenas of nation-state ethnicity, of social inequality, and of ill-defined authenticity.

First, state companies and the immigrant groups they inspired emphasize nationalism and mask regional class and ethnic diversity within Latin American countries. Southern Mexico and Guatemala feature populations that are diverse with a large indigenous presence. In such contexts, national identity is contested. States and elites have tended to emphasize a nationalism that stresses cultural homogenization (to their particular worldview and social patterns), while indigenous populations, either through conscious political movements or through more diffuse struggles to live life in ways that are meaningful, have tended to reject the ideology that assumes cultural homogeneity is necessary for national unity.

This difficulty is particularly illustrated in some venues. Shay (2006:166–220) explores the construction of ethnicity at folk dance festivals in Los Angeles, St. Paul, and San Francisco and at the Smithsonian. A recurrent theme in his discussion is social inequality. Festival organizers (or groups of experts that they sanction) enjoy the privileged position of selecting dance groups to represent various countries in dance. These festivals express rather unexamined notions that nation-state is the primary level of cultural or ethnic identification and that something as broad and diverse as "national culture" can be determined, distilled, and presented in short dance programs, distinctive forms of dress, and particular cuisines. The contested nature of national identity goes largely without comment, as does the reality that those able to mount a professional-quality presentation are likely themselves elites. What gets presented as popular culture may indeed be a construction by the socially privileged of "their folk" (with all of the baggage that accompanies such labeling). Not only are the nation and state of the sending countries conflated, but a model of cultural diversity within the receiving country is asserted. As such, the folk or ethnic festival to the mainstream white viewer confirms the possibility of culturally unified nation-states against the real backdrop of persistent cultural and social diversity within states. In a sense, this is wishful thinking that constructs a place where it is comfortable to be privileged. Indeed, Shay (2006:166–220) argues that liberal consumers of folk festival performance confirm their tolerance while defining what is to be tolerated. What are to insiders markers of an abstract level of identification are framed by mainstream consumers as the essential elements of authentic culture. In other words, signs and symbols certain groups have invented and adapted to signal their ethnic identity become the culture of Other to festival organizers and audiences.

Moreover, the festival gives the ability to define the bounds of appropriate expression of ethnicity and cultural diversity to mainstream cultural insiders. These boundaries reflect larger notions of what makes cultures diverse (food, dress, and music and dancing) and also controls their expression. In short, the folk festival is the reification of what we might call "weekend diversity." In certain contexts, folksy and artistic expressions are tolerated if not always embraced. However, the folk festival, by setting such expressions apart from everyday life, communicates the idea that quaint costumes and overt public expressions of identity are to be stowed while participating in the larger society. White ethnic identity becomes the norm, a kind of *cultura franca,* and is equated with democratic universals. In the end these expressions of multiculturalism also mark and foster assimilation. As I explored earlier, such limited expression of culture falls short of what indigenous movements typically envision.

Second, there are inherent problems in the representation of oppressed peoples by their dominating societies. In settler and postcolonial societies, the middle-class mainstream and ethnically privileged have much invested in imaginary Indians. The portrayals of Native people that develop in such contexts are bound to be inaccurate and sometimes construct intentional or unintentional stereotypes of indigenous societies. In the worst cases, what may seem like harmless fun can become deeply offensive to indigenous people, reinforcing stereotypes that have justified oppression and neglect. If getting the basics of culture and history right is rare, much less common are portrayals of indigenous people as living, culturally distinctive, complex human beings. For example, as I will explore later, the University of Illinois "mascot" Chief Illiniwek is at the center of an ongoing and often bitter debate. This portrayal of Indianness by white college students has drawn the ire of many Native Americans and non–Native Americans not only because the portrayal is inaccurate, but also because it is one-dimensional. Native people struggle to overcome this narrow framing through self-representation in dance, and presenting self must compete with presentation of self by powerful Others. Popular conceptions of Native people and their attached mythologies serve nationalism and generate positive self-identity for large portions of the mainstream population. Consequently, they are entrenched and carefully guarded.

Third, and related to the second problem, is the notion of authenticity in general and of particularly materialistic concepts of authenticity. As I explored earlier, folk theory of authenticity (typically expressed in dance programs) rests on a static, essentialist model of culture. Through such a lens, actual lived indigenous culture (and any human culture, for that matter) can be judged as inauthentic as it reflects adaptation over time. However, the focus of folkloric dance, not surprisingly, is on the past. Moreover, it is subject to assuming that accurate imitation (in step and cultural artifacts) generates something that is objectively authentic. Accuracy no doubt is important, but it is not enough. In fact, hyper-attention to accuracy of object and act (mimesis) implies that a theatricalized representation is more authentic than the parallel tradition it claims to represent. Charting, formal training, rehearsal, and other methods of theatrical performance, not surprisingly, produce forms that are stable over time. Video and audio recordings (widely available and frequently circulated on YouTube) foster both replication and stability. Folkloric dancing, as such, runs the risk of become self-perpetuating "authentic fake," painstakingly replicated yet divorced from communal context and social relations of life lived in social reality and that pervade indigenous dances of the field.

Folkloric dances reference indigenous culture because its performers and audience, craving authentic experience in rather alienated modern life, believe they will find something real in Native life. These hopes and expectations impose costs. Ronald Niezen (2003) and Laura Graham (2002) both note that these expectations of authenticity place special burdens on indigenous leaders. In discussions with the powerful ethnic Others, the indigenous must engage in a "hybrid discourse," one that is intelligible to the outsider but also meets the outsider's preconceptions of authenticity (Gow and Rappaport 2002). The problems extend beyond the leaders of indigenous groups into their communities. Being an environmental steward, or maintaining a rich ritual calendar, or complying with any number of other ideals of indigenousness can be quite difficult in communities that suffer under grinding material poverty and the attached persistent social and public health problems. By seeking authenticity in indigenous Others, we ask people who face real economic and political discrimination to do our cognitive and affective work. Should not we, who enjoy the benefits of globalization modernity, find our own way to deal with its difficulties?

The issues of representation and authenticity do not go without comment among audiences, critics, and dancers. Julia Preston (1997) of the *New York Times* describes an ongoing controversy of authenticity among folkloric dancers that Olga Nájera-Ramírez documents in the late 1980s and locates in the manner in which indigenous practices are incorporated into folkloric performances (1989:22). Not surprisingly, Amalia Hernández has been at the center of the discussion, and until her death in 2000, she was often a target of criticism. David Rojas, an avid dancer, relates how the Ballet Folklórico's adaptation of the Yaqui Deer Dance is offensive to the indigenous dancer who initially shared the tradition with Hernández (Preston 1997). The inspiration for other interpretations of traditional dance into folkloric dance includes some rather creative ethnohistory (Nájera-Ramírez 1989:22). Interviewed by Preston (1997), Hernández describes how her method of concentration uncovered the name of a Maya deity: "One of their gods was named Onichac. The god Onichac is not in any book that I have found. But I am sure I heard the name Onichac. Where did it come from? From my concentration." She also asserts that she had no way to learn about ancient Maya dance other than concentrating on pre-Columbian monumental art (Preston 1997). Such statements make anthropologists—especially ethnographers of the contemporary Maya—cringe. For living Mayas, it is much worse. Her discourse becomes another example of their continued misrepresentation, stereotyping, and invisibility by and to powerful outsiders. Why not ask a Maya dancer about Maya dance? On the other hand, Hernández, in the *New York Times* interview and in quotes appearing on the company's Web page, does not claim accuracy or that her pieces are the same as their in-the-field inspirations.

Nonetheless, Rojas declares "nil" the authenticity of Hernández's interpretations (Preston 1997). Here, we again return to the highly subjective nature of authenticity, an emotional response to an experience rather than anything quantifiable or unbound to a particular context. The problem is that all societies and their cultures change, sometimes rapidly, sometimes slowly. As such, what is now traditional was, at some point, innovation. Moreover, the notion of an unchanging, timeless society is an illusion, perhaps imagined to have in the world something permanent, a place to escape rapidly changing and anonymous modernity. In the end, to compare and judge the authenticity of the parallel traditions creates more problems than it solves. It is, in effect, an intellectual dead end. If authenticity is as much an illusion as I suggest, it is impossible to judge other than in terms of the response of those who feel they have experienced it. It is clear, however, that indigenous dancers recognize the power of folkloric dance (and dance in general) as a medium of representation and misrepresentation. In the following chapter, I consider indigenous involvement in folkloric dance and how it manifests this struggle over representation.

NOTES

1. Described in the vignette that opens Part Four, Hispanofest is held each September in Melrose Park, one of three suburbs of Chicago that feature a majority Spanish-speaking population. Local business owners and government officials organize the fair. Major sponsors include local Latino media outlets and multinational

corporations such as Pepsi. Minor sponsors include Latino-owned local businesses. Hispanofest Inc. "promotes the advancement to the Hispanic community through educational and leadership development" (http://hispanofest.org). The festival itself celebrates local community, presents Latino identity, and deals with issues of transnationalism.

2. La Melrose refers to Melrose Park, as it is occasionally identified by its Spanish-speaking denizens. An alveolar flap is added to the *r* and the voicing eliminated from the word-final consonant.

3. I deliberately choose "people" instead of "race" because in English "race" is loaded with inappropriate folk biology. *Raza*, however, is more social and cultural (and, from the social scientist's perspective, more accurate).

Ten

Back to the Field: Indigenous Folkloric Dance

How I came to appreciate and better understand the role of baile folklórico in Totonicapán is an example of the way that my consultants helped me see what is important. I was never directly told that I ought to expand my focus or pay attention to this or that or to ask different and better questions. This would have impinged on my autonomy in a way (as I would come to recognize) that does not square with K'iche' notions of personhood or norms of social interaction.

Members of Totonicapán's Vanguardia Indígena occasionally invited me to attend their performances during fieldwork in 1994 and 1995. Through la Vanguardia, K'iche' Maya indígenas *represented Maya indigenous life by performing folkloric dances. Rather than concede the domain of folkloric dance to the nonindigenous, la Vanguardia began to control and share images of Highland Maya life and culture on their own K'iche' terms. Employing equipment from the regalia shop where I was an apprentice, la Vanguardia's repertoire included portrayals of central traditional dances. Their performance was infused with ethnic and community pride. Without directly saying that my field research needed adjustment, dancers of la Vanguardia helped me recognize that I must more directly consider indigenous participation in folkloric dance.*

10.1. Deer Dancers of the Vanguardia Indígena. Employing the regalia of a "field" dance in a theatrical venue, K'iche' Maya Totonicapenses perform in Puerto Barrios, September 1995. (Photograph by author.)

As folkloric dances occasionally return to "the field," so do I. The particular spaces examined here are in Guatemala, some in the community of my initial fieldwork, some beyond Totonicapán to other spaces, often profoundly interethnic. K'iche'-Maya Totonicapenses dance selected aspects of their culture for audiences of their indigenous neighbors and for ethnic Others far and near. During fieldwork, my first encounters with folkloric forms were at events, often celebrating local social organizations. For example, a course in basic English ended with a *clausura* party, students and teacher sharing food and drink and enjoying folk dance performances. However, the form was also taken out of the community and put to a wider variety of purposes. In addition to the trip to Puerto Barrios, during my initial fieldwork I traveled to see Totonicapense dancers represent K'iche' culture in three predominantly nonindigenous spaces, including the capital. More recently, reflecting related changes in Guatemala's political system and increasingly globalized tourism, I have observed several performances offered to international tourists visiting Totonicapán from the Netherlands, Belgium, and the United States. In the following sections, I examine this counter-appropriation as an effort to construct Mayaness on both sides of parallel traditions. Not surprisingly, these acts of self-representation in dance respond and reflect changes in macro-social forces.

In essence, folkloric dance done by K'iche'-Maya Totonicapenses has three distinct purposes: teaching and reinforcing local culture to its own community, presenting a positive image of K'iche' culture to tourists and other visitors, and influencing the construction of Mayaness in arenas where nonindigenous dancers regularly present appropriated Maya forms. All of these reflect goals of a people who experience economic and social currents that resonate well beyond the local community. Broadly, K'iche' dancers employ folkloric forms to deal with related challenges of modernity and globalization and of the ongoing legacy of colonialism. Moreover, K'iche' folkloric dance is consistent with broader economic, political, and cultural efforts by other indigenous peoples.

SELF-REPRESENTATION TO LOCAL COMMUNITY

Sometimes I joke with my students about James Clifford's contention that modernity lacks authenticity. To all of us feeling overwhelmed with tasks, study, and work, what really is lacking is time. For those who live under the autonomous clock (certainly part and parcel of modernity), life can be an unsettled series of tasks and obligations for which there is insufficient (and wholly commodified) time. In "developing" countries, as the global market more profoundly penetrates local lives, it brings wage-based tasks and demand for bureaucratized knowledge that comes from formal education. As a result, time becomes commodified, scarce, and less under the control of individuals and kin groups.

Miguel, a K'iche' Maya *morero* (regalia shop manager), emphasizes the advantage of time in what he identifies as *estampas folklóricas* (folkloric stomps). As we share a meal in a Totonicapán restaurant that accepts credit cards, features Pepsi products, and shares its building with an Internet café, Miguel relates his involvement in folkoric dances. It began not long after he and I and two other young K'iche' Totonicapenses began our apprenticeships to the *morería*. Miguel went on to become the *morero*. In this position, he noted that among the most frequent visitors to the shop were local schoolchildren who needed outfits but also wanted to learn more about traditional dances and the community's culture in general.

From the beginning of his discourse about dances, Miguel emphasizes the short format of these *estampas folklóricas*. They are of great utility to present the ideas manifested in much longer traditional dances, but in a few minutes rather than six to eight hours. In particular, he finds value in working with schoolchildren. Whether they stop by the *morería* to ask him a few questions about dance, rent an outfit, work with him in a formal group, or view a dance presentation he has organized for the classroom, helping young people gain a greater appreciation for their culture through dance is foremost among Miguel's purposes.

Miguel is not alone among his local community or among indigenous activists globally. This use of the formalized settings and methods of modern education to pass important cultural knowledge is a common indigenous strategy. For the great majority of human existence, language, music, healing, and art have been passed generation to generation informally and fully embedded in kinship. As the demands of the modern global economy and assimilationist government policies particularize kinship structures, threatened knowledge is passed and learned through family. The replacement is formal education that has tended to favor the culture of dominating societies. Indigenous activists, therefore, work to adapt the school and make it work to ensure cultural continuity. From formal curricula at all levels to classes in native arts and subsistence outside of schools, a common feature of contemporary indigenous activism is using the structure of formal education to teach traditional knowledge.

SELF-REPRESENTATION AND GLOBALIZED TOURISM

In the verandas of a bright and amply flowered patio in the center of Totonicapán a group of Belgian tourists settles in for a traditional lunch. A trio plays the marimba first for atmosphere and then as accompaniment. A group of six dancers, girls aged six to twelve, perform four folkloric dances. Although some interpretation is offered by a trilingual (K'iche', Spanish, English) guide, it is quite general, emphasizing that the dances represent traditional roles passed from mother to daughter. In essence, the dances speak for themselves. Dressed in the traditional handwoven red blouse and black ankle-length skirt, the girls began with two folkloric vignettes centered on domestic tasks, female fertility, and acknowledgment of the four cardinal points. When they exit the dance floor, passing between two lunch tables, they greet the tourist guests in K'iche'. For visitors familiar with Maya cosmology and gender, the dances are loaded with meaningful references. For those less familiar, the performances nonetheless featured indigenous culture enacted by indigenous dancers. Next is the Snake Dance (Figure 10.2), in which all six performers dance while shouldering one large stuffed-animal snake, pushing and pulling one another in a herky-jerky fashion (read by the anthropologist as an excellent metaphor for interpersonal relations in a culture that values both individual autonomy and group cooperation). The last dance begins with a coquettish entrance after which the girls rush the lunch tables and grab guests, compelling them to dance. Eventually, all dance together, generating a certain degree of optimism for the possibility of cross-cultural relations that respect difference while finding common humanity. Tourists then return to their seats for dessert; the girls gather their props and offer farewell (and "eat well") wishes in K'iche'. The guide announces that tips for the dancers and for the marimba combo are welcome.

10.2. The Snake Dance in Totonicapán, July 2007. (Photograph by author.)

In addition to presentation to the community, short folkloric forms are enacted for outsiders. Various Totonicapense folkloric groups regularly make presentations to foreign visitors within a sustainable, community-based tourism program. In some presentations folkloric dances are performed using the masks and outfits of traditional dance. The distinction may not be clear to tourists. However, at cultural festivals where I observed indigenous and nonindigenous dancers present on the same stage, the full *morería* outfit provided the ultimate authenticity trump card.

Presenting folkloric dances to tourists is a way to generate cash income but also to present a positive image of Maya culture to powerful outsiders who are potential allies. These visitors come to Totonicapán in the spirit of adventure and ecological tourism, and it is clear that they are interested in an authentic experience. What they get is local and personal, although adapted to their frames of reference. Those involved in organizing and presenting dances must balance tourists' expectations with dances of the field as they are. In this respect Miguel emphasizes again that the short form of the dance is of greatest utility. Tourist itineraries generally cannot accommodate several hours of traditional dancing. Additionally, a shortened, simplified presentation allows the visitor a sample of traditional dance with knowledgeable K'iche' guides to offer brief descriptions and answer questions. Moreover, the emphasis that folkloric dances place on authenticity certainly appeals to the tourist. Here, not only are Maya life and customs referenced, but they are danced by Maya performers in an indigenous Maya community.

Presenting folkloric forms to tourists obviously reflects globalization, but it also manifests a common indigenous strategy. From Waswogoning, a model Ojibwe village on the Lac du Flambeau reservation in northern Wisconsin, to Ainu (Japan) presentation of dances, various indigenous groups have worked to put tourism to work for economic as well as cultural ends. If such encounters are to serve representational goals, differences in language occasionally must be bridged. In the case of the sustainable tourism program in Totonicapán, dance serves as an excellent medium of cross-cultural communication in which there is a considerable shared message as well as content that is accessible to only parts of the audience. Moreover, the way in which dance is employed parallels strategies of intercultural communication described by Laura Graham (2002). Exploring a series of cases in which indigenous leaders had varying degrees of success in cross-language communication, Graham notes that at times indigenous language is a barrier and sometimes it is an asset. For audiences that crave authenticity, native language, even if it is marginally understood, is of great utility. Its form, rather than content, is what matters. On the other hand, at times, vital content is lost in poor or incomplete translation. Additionally, employing the language of the dominant group, even if well translated, can undermine the authenticity of the message. As such, indigenous spokespeople occasionally mix native and dominant languages in their presentations. In one case described by Graham (2002:213–214), a leader began and ended her speech with an untranslated greeting and farewell. In folkloric presentations offered to tourists in Totonicapán, a similar pattern of cross-cultural communication was manifested. The case above (from 2007) featured untranslated K'iche' greetings and farewells with dance serving as the medium of intercultural communication. Folkloric performances transcend language barriers through dance, effecting communication while avoiding some of the difficulties of language described by Graham. Moreover, such performances nicely manifested Shay's (2006) contention that dance is an unparalleled means of expression of ethnic identity, but it also reflected larger goals of cross-cultural interaction based on mutual respect.

10.3. First Steps. As the morero *looks on, visitors to the Morería Nima' K'iche' in regalia from the Dance of the Conquest* (left)*, the Dance of the Deer* (center)*, and the Dance of the Mexicans* (right) *attempt traditional dancing, Totonicapán, December 2008. The* morero *offered a brief interpretation of each dance and its paraphernalia before inviting guests to dress and dance. (Photograph by Carlos Robles.)*

In addition to folkloric dances, tourists to Totonicapán have a brief encounter with traditional dance. Many travel itineraries include a visit to the *morería*. After a brief description of principal dances and their masks and outfits, the *morero* solicits male and female volunteers to dress up as traditional dancers. Once the tourist guests are suited, the *morero* demonstrates the steps of their respected dances and invites them to perform. Photography is welcome and, often to the delight of travel companions, these temporary traditional dancers struggle to see through masks and execute the steps. My students who have participated in this activity report a mixture of fun and confusion. To be included is exciting, but the weight of the outfit and the visual limitations imposed by the mask are disorienting. As such, the visit to the *morería* reflects ideas developed by Philip Deloria (1998:144–145). When nonindigenous are invited to dance powwow, cultural and power relations are inverted, if only temporarily. Whites briefly must conform with Native norms of performance in a Native context. The process is slightly more globalized at the *moreria*. Here, the guests are more frequently international outsiders, differing in ethnicity in at least two dimensions. However, in both cases, nonindigenous visitors dance under indigenous direction. They "play Indian," but the Indianness is determined by indigenous people, and the creative license that often manifests stereotypes in other cases of nonindigenous dancing Indian is constrained.

This strategy is paralleled in visits to artisanal shops, when visitors are asked to attempt various parts of the process of weaving, carving, or potting. Degrading stereotypes of skilled indigenous art as primitive (read unskilled) folkcraft are challenged. Interested (and globally privileged) guests who sit at loom, bench, or wheel learn to respect the skill and time involved in the production of traditional *artesania*. Artisans certainly aim to increase sales at better prices. In addition to appreciation of the amount of skilled work that goes into producing a high-quality craft object, the personal connection to the artisan helps the buyer understand it as qualitatively different from impersonally manufactured objects that surround them in their lives at home. Both realizations raise the amount the visitor is willing to pay. Beyond sales, however, artisans also hope to create knowledgeable allies in the struggle against the degradation of Maya culture. Inequality of one sort is utilized to counter another. The esteem of a well-heeled visitor carries weight and challenges the belittlement of craft in a way that is not directly available to the artisan.

CONTESTATION OF IMAGES OF MAYANESS

Several months into my fieldwork, I know what to expect when I am invited to travel once again with la Vanguardia Indígena. This time the trip is to Amatitlán, a lake east of the capital that is a popular recreation destination among Guatemalans. The lake is beautiful. There are launches and rowboats to rent and fresh fried fish to enjoy. Souvenirs, including items produced in Totonicapán, are available for purchase.

On this day, in addition to the regular attractions, Amatitlán initiates its titular fair. La Vanguardia has been asked to participate in the parade that marks the beginning of festivities. As other spots the Vanguardia has visited, Amatitlán is a primarily Ladino place, and the sight of dancers in Dance of the Deer morería *outfits garners attention. Amatitlán is also at a lower elevation than Totonicapán and it is hot. Dancing as they parade through the streets in masks and heavy outfits is hard work. The parade ends with the Vanguardia procession dancing an excerpt of the Dance of the Deer on the main* feria *stage. As the dancing ends, a speaker who seems Ladino puts into specific language one of the messages conveyed by the Vanguardia: traditional dances are a part of Guatemalan culture and indigenous dancers are Guatemalans. After the performance, the dancers are tired and sweaty.*

This act of self-representation has to combat not only loaded preconceptions of the Highland Maya but also exhausting heat.

10.4. Deer Dancers on Parade. Members of the Vanguardia Indígena perform in the streets of Amatitlán, May 1995. (Photograph by author.)

In addition to tourists as ethnic Others, K'iche' dancers encounter countrymen who are not Maya. Occasionally these ethnic Others are neighbors. Occasionally they are found in places outside of Totonicapán. Elite Guatemalan Others are not often encountered directly, but their influence is seen in dance. Much in the way that Amalia Hernández drew on native dances, so does the Ballet Moderno y Folklórico de Guatemala appropriate indigenous dance and put it to nationalist purposes. At the local level this process is paralleled. Located in the K'iche area, Quetzaltenango (Guatemala's second-largest city) is home to Siguan Tinamit, a professional ballet folklórico company founded in 1970. Although K'iche' dancers may be familiar with the national company by reputation, Siguan Tinamit and the fame it has garnered through appropriated Highland Maya dance forms are well-known and occasionally resented. In the present era, salaried jobs are scarce and visas to travel abroad even scarcer. The reality that professional companies of nonindigenous dancers travel internationally through enactment of indigenous culture is understandably irksome. Additionally, semi-professional groups of nonindigenous dancers are a part of the landscape. Indigenous dancers circulate stories about these ethnic Others who promise cooperation and support in exchange for dance knowledge. Mutual exchange continues until the nonindigenous person learns dances. The teacher then later sees the form reproduced without credit or remuneration to their indigenous authors. This is not to say that all collaborations are exploitative. Rather, given Guatemala's weak legal system and persistent inequality, such appropriations are possible and frequent. As such, presentation of indigenous culture by nonindigenous Others represents both economic exploitation and cultural appropriation. Privileges that in theory are to be distributed democratically without regard to ethnicity in reality accrue to those of the middle or upper class and predominantly to the nonindigenous. Moreover, given the reach and prestige of professional touring companies, they disproportionately impact what outsiders imagine as Maya.

It is here that indigenous participation in folkloric dances most reflects Victor Montejo's notion of self-representation. The creation and circulation of images of indigenous life and indigenous people in Guatemala have largely been outside the control of Maya, who until relatively recently had little access to mass media. Indeed, in an era marked by rapid circulation of image and persistent social inequality, a group that cannot influence the way it is depicted is subject to stereotyping. Not surprisingly, what constitutes an Indian in the imagination of non-Mayas has been loaded with romantic as well as degrading and racist notions. Montejo (2002) (among other Maya intellectuals) argues that contemporary Maya must combat these negative images. Such notions not only justify abysmal social policy (including education aimed at erasing Maya languages) but also impose a costly psychological burden on Maya individuals. Accordingly, the struggle to counter stereotypes with more positive and accurate images of Mayaness is crucial. This is about more than "identity politics"; stereotypes offer ideological support to political and economic inequality as well as foment negative self-image. Put another way, in addition to economic consequences there are public health costs. In this context, dance, the unequaled form of ethnic representation (as Shay describes it), must be contested. To leave an entire genre in the hands of the ethnic Other is to guarantee the reiteration and continuation of inaccurate and likely racist constructions of Indianness.

Beyond staking claim to an area where they had previously been represented by Others, K'iche' masked dancing has also ventured into domains where Others present primarily themselves. Rhonda Taube (2006) details Maya participation in *convite* or *disfrace* dancing in Momostenango, a K'iche' town neighboring Totonicapán. A competitive form in which dancers don sport-mascot-like costumes representing icons of popular globalized U.S. culture, *convite* has been a place for nonindigenous Guatemalans to assert their modernity. Through knowing manipulations of the products of Hollywood, mestizo Guatemalans publicly claim and verify their global cultural literacy. Not to be outdone or to cede globalized modernity to Others without comment, indigenous Momostecos put on their own form of *disfrace*. As Taube nicely illustrates, this is more than simple mimicry or ethnic competition. Maya *disfrace* characters are morphed and adapted to create a characteristically Maya multivalence. A given character by its iconography presents readings that are at once global, modern, and worldly but also traditional and Mesoamerican. They are not one or the other but both—another way of asserting cultural continuity that is adaptable and suited to the contemporary world.

K'iche' *convite* and folkloric dancing assert these claims of simultaneously modern and traditional. In a broader sense, the message of indigenous participation in forms invented, or at least dominated, by ethnic Others is repeated in other contexts. For example, a recent conversation with a K'iche' weaver included the subject of computers. Although it would take some time to learn, the utility of digital technology was readily apparent; it could help record and protect the rhythms and patterns of the art. If we listen closely to what Highland Maya say about themselves, it is clear that modern and traditional are oppositional only for the outsider.

Our evening begins with the end of a February day that seems like the beginning of spring. Under a clear and sunny sky, the temperature earlier passed freezing and the snow and ice show signs of melting. We are on our way to Triton College for "An Evening of Mexican Soul." The community college serving the near-west suburbs has arranged an appearance by the Mexican Folkloric Dance Company of Chicago. This highly regarded troupe will dance to live music performed by the award-winning Sones de Mexico Ensemble of Chicago. It promises to be an enjoyable evening. On the way, we enjoy dinner at a Cuban restaurant in a suburb with working-class Italian roots that is now home to many recent Eastern European immigrants. The bits of Caribbean Spanish we overhear while eating are distinct from the Mexican Spanish we will hear later.

The first dance listed in the program is Raíz Viva ("Living Roots" or "Live Roots"), which "is a reenactment of a pre-Columbian ritual to the sun." Not to my surprise, indigenous culture is referenced at the beginning and at points throughout the performance. What does surprise is the music. Dressed in stylized pre-Columbian Aztec costumes, male and female performers dance to a tune that is vaguely familiar with a beat that is definitely rock. How interesting, I think. A group of Mexican musicians based in Chicago has incorporated a form of music that has deep roots in our Windy City. That the dance troupe has chosen the piece to accompany a dance referencing the Aztec past is even more intriguing. "We have this Aztec heritage, but we also can dance to rock beats," the performers seem to say. (We will learn that the troupe created new dances for a number of songs on an album produced by the band that accompanies them.) It all has a very transnational feel to it. The rooting of performers and audience in two places is a salient feature of the evening's music, dance, and discourse. Mexican culture is not simply replicated for immigrants to enjoy and for their children to learn, but rather an identity both Mexican and Chicagoan is constructed.

The performance moves to the more traditional, sampling music and dance from a variety of Mexican states. Shifting from Mexico and Chicago to Latin America as identity reference points, the band plays "Qué Bonita la Bandera" in honor of the flag of Puerto Rico. Other pieces focus on how to be Mexican in Chicago; this one stresses interethnic solidarity with other Latinos of different national origin. How complex and layered is identity in the United States of the twenty-first century.

During the intermission, among other remarks, the troupe director tells the audience how fortunate the community is to have such a musical ensemble. Many cities in Mexico cannot boast a band of its quality, one whose recent album has been nominated for both a Latin Grammy and a regular mainstream Grammy. As a native-born Chicagoan, I find myself included in the sense of pride that permeates the speech. That mixture of peoples and cultures that makes our city great is alive and well, I think. At other performances, I have sensed and even admired pride in the audience, but not experienced it as directly. Something else is present here. Is this part of the process of glocalization, by which an immigrant community embraces both the cultures of its homeland and the influences of its receiving community? Is it akin to the process by which other immigrant groups have established communities and assimilated as a part of "white ethnic" Chicago? Or does it more reflect the history of rural African American migrants from the Old South who built communities and culture that are fundamental to the city, that form and re-form Chicago as much as they assimilate to Chicago?

We find the music so appealing that we decide to buy the CD for sale in the lobby. Its cover features one of the musicians in cowboy boots and hat. He sits on a rooftop overlooking urban neighborhoods anchored by the Chicago skyline and plays a violin. On the back of the cover, the group walks away from the camera, carrying instrument cases across a snow-covered field. The Chicago skyline forms the horizon. Looking over the list of songs and matching it to the title ("Four Sticks") listed in the dance program, I discover why the tune was familiar. J. Page and R. Plant are listed as songwriters and the title now rings familiar, a Led Zeppelin song. In my youth, not uncommonly for white kids from the suburbs, I was a fan of the British rock band. I contemplate the flows of culture and people that brought us to this moment. These Englishmen were strongly influenced by Muddy Waters and Howlin' Wolf, African Americans who made their way to Chicago from rural Mississippi in the mid-twentieth century. Here, or not all that far from here, Waters and Wolf and other descendants of slaves played and recorded the blues on electrified instruments. Adapting this form of music adapted from African traditions, they and others formed a musical style unique to Chicago that became the foundation of rock-and-roll. Now Chicago Mexicans play a product of this Africa-to-Mississippi-to-Chicago-to-London process and dance to it. While writing a check to cover the purchase, I overhear one of the musicians respond to an older man in Spanish, "Why, yes, we are Mexican, from San Luis Potosí." "Yes," I think to myself, "but you are also Chicagoans."

The above performance reflects entrenched and expanding transnationalism. It also indicates the expressive adaptability of music and representational dance. What began as elite construction of nationalist identity that assumed assimilation of cultural diversity now expresses identity that is consciously and explicitly multiple. Again, characteristic of all forms explored in this book, contemporary immigrant folkloric dancing, created in and circulated among glocalities, references indigenous culture. As it departs from state-sponsored and earlier immigrant dancing, it converges with indigenous dancing. Both express an abiding contestation of the ideology of unitary and homogeneous identity. Dancers of both assert the integration of their local, ethnic, and nationalist attachments, blending traditional and modern in the process.

Considering reference to indigenous culture in folkloric dance introduces a knotty problem. A book that examines how indigenous peoples are represented in dance by themselves, by Latin American elites, and by Latino immigrants must certainly consider representations of Indianness by U.S. performers who are unambiguously nonindigenous. In the following chapters, we explore a form of appropriation of Indianness in dance that asserts something similar to and something quite different from than the performances described above. Common with immigrant folkloric dance, it expresses the idea that self can be constructed by reference to the indigenous Other. However, rather than challenging social hierarchy and the ideology of unitary identity (as powwow and transnational folkloric dance do), sports mascots and their supporters embrace both.

Part Five

Chiefs, Kings, Mascots, and Martyrs

Eleven

Dancing Indian in Sports: Origins and Development

I choose my seat in the home grandstands near the open end of Memorial Stadium. This choice is informed by what I have read about Chief Illiniwek. I hope to have a clear view of the performance, including the Chief's initial appearance. I contemplate sitting closer to midfield for a better sightline of the main part of the performance but decide my current spot is just fine. I sit among spectators who appear to include students, staff, and Champaign residents. Although the game against Syracuse (sans its "Saltine Warrior" Indian mascot for nearly thirty years) is not the best college football I have seen, I enjoy the experience very much. I am an Illinoisan and cheer for the state's flagship educational institution. Those with whom I share the stands are remarkably friendly and welcoming. Well aware that the team is not what it once was, Fighting Illini fans nonetheless support it enthusiastically and in good spirit. It is easy to understand how going to the university is so fondly experienced and remembered by so many.

The half ends and the sense of community felt in the stands is further enacted on the field. Before the famed marching band of the University of Illinois and Chief Illiniwek appear, the field fills from sideline to sideline and end zone to end zone with several high school marching bands. Stepping and playing (somewhat) in unison, uniformed in respective school colors, this mass of humanity makes individuality invisible.

It is not an undifferentiated mass of people, though specialization of individuals into functional subgroups reigns supreme. Players of particular instruments are organized into sections. Those who do not play but carry batons or flags (a particularly salient symbol of group identification) are displayed in unison. I agree for a moment with Spencer (1877); human societies really can be thought of as a complex but unified organism. It is a well-executed, if somewhat blunt, concrete manifestation of social solidarity and individual conformity to group purpose.

The field is cleared, and the University of Illinois band takes over. It lacks the human density of the mass of high school bands but more than compensates with its precision of movement and music. The music is crisp and tight and flags are waved in precise unison. I keep close watch on the end line for the appearance of Chief Illiniwek. I am very interested to see such a beloved and vigorously contested figure in performance. Just as described in the literature (King and Springwood 2001a; Chief Illiniwek Educational Foundation 2004), Chief Illiniwek emerges from the north end of the stadium to join the band that has marched in formation to meet him. I am not entirely prepared for my reaction. I expect to find the performance compelling, or comical, or even offensive. Instead, my reaction is mixed.

The audience in the home grandstands is riveted, which certainly has an impact on my encounter with the Chief. While I am not compelled to tears or chills, I feel as though I am witnessing something quite unusual. I am an outsider, but also drawn in by the atmosphere. I have the feeling one sometimes gets in an antique store. The Chief is anachronistic, which is distancing. However, just as does handwriting on an old postcard, his material presence closes temporal and social gaps. This part of my reaction must be similar to what gives Chief Illiniwek supporters such a strong sense of tradition.

Reflecting, I conclude that my cognitive dissonance comes from two sources. I had been recently and over a period of years attending representational dances done by indigenous people. Additionally, as a sports fan, I had previously encountered all sorts of halftime and intermission entertainment. What I currently witness references two cognitive frameworks, and neither accommodates the Chief well. Chief supporters are right. Although he may be termed a mascot, he is a bit different from other mascots I have encountered. The Chief is not Wisconsin's badger or Ohio State's buckeye. The performance is also unconnected to any indigenous dancing I have witnessed. The Chief's principal step is somewhat evocative of movement common in powwow dancing: ball of one foot to the ground twice, then the same with the other, in time with music. However, the rhythm is different from that of typical powwow music, and the step seems almost staccato. Moreover, the resonance and impact of a large powwow drum played by several singers at once are missing. The outfit is obviously well crafted and lovingly maintained but seems too large and not well suited to dance. The posture of the performer, particularly in his jutting chin, appears forced. I wonder if this is how the Chief embodies the pride and dignity that so many of his fans stress.

In any event, it is quite distinct from Native American powwow dancers and K'iche' traditional dancers, whose performances are less rehearsed and more in the moment. Additionally, while both K'iche' and powwow dances feature occasional individual performances, these are momentary breaks within a collective dancing. The Chief's dance is fundamentally a solo act.

After traversing the length of the field, the Chief dances to its center. It is during the midfield portion of the dance that the crowd is made an active part of the performance. The Chief salutes the grandstands with extended raised arms that are slightly open and with palms turned down. When he folds his arms, elevated in front of his chest, he is effectively demanding recognition. The crowd responds, "CHIEF," in deep, extended unison. Although a glance across the field into the visitors' sections reveals a milling, unorganized, and largely uninterested crowd of individuals, in the University of Illinois stands a sense of unity, interconnectedness, and social solidarity is palpable.

A curious article appeared in the November 12, 2008, *Chicago Tribune* (Twohey 2008). It was a short piece, located three pages into the front section; it could almost be called a blurb. Although he had made his last appearance as an official symbol of the University of Illinois about three months after the performance described above, Chief Illiniwek was dancing again. The eighty-year-old tradition of a buckskin and feather bonnet–clad student dancing as a mythical Indian chief had returned after a nearly two-year hiatus. Students, using their own resources, had a new costume made and rented space from the university for the performance.

As does most of the press coverage of the Chief Illiniwek controversy, the piece raises more questions than it answers. The article mentions only "cultural insensitivity" to explain why the university decided to end its use of Chief Illiniwek as an official symbol. Who and what had driven the institution to such a vague position are not explored. The motivations to revive the dancing Indian were similarly vague. Students had worked to return the Chief to campus for months during a historic presidential campaign, an increasingly unpopular war, and an unfolding financial crisis. A member of the event's organizing group (Students for Chief Illiniwek, or SFCI) reports, "[Chief Illiniwek] inspired me to be a complete man." Chief Illiniwek is of vital importance to some students in a way that is difficult for outsiders to understand.

The article does make clear that supporters of the Chief are adaptive and persistent. SFCI had realized that legislative and legal efforts to force the university to keep or readopt the Chief had run their course. This organized, yet not officially sanctioned, performance suggests that Chief supporters had accepted that the university was under no obligation to keep the Chief.

11.1. Chief Illiniwek Dances, September 2006. Above, *entering the field from the end zone.* Left, *dancing at midfield.* Below, *saluting the crowd. (Photographs by author.)*

The First Amendment does not compel the university to sanction student expression through a dancing Indian. Organized without university support, however, the performance almost certainly enjoys constitutional protection as exercise of free speech and assembly. A university spokesman indicated that the institution did not sponsor the event, but that the students would be allowed to hold it.

Presently I address the main question raised by the *Tribune* article: why does Chief Illiniwek, a well-known dancing Indian mascot/symbol, elicit both strong support and strong opposition? In considering this broad question, I explore Chief Illiniwek in terms of the power of representational dance to construct and contest ethnic identity. Moreover, common to other forms that I have explored, the secular ritual of dance is tied to myths. Revisiting themes covered earlier, I consider how Chief Illiniwek reflects social and political inequality in changing times.

It is somewhat inevitable that this book would consider a figure such as Chief Illiniwek. As I discussed in Part One, there is a certain benefit in seeing one's own society through a lens shaped by ethnographic experience. Keesing's (2000) "inside outsider" becomes an outside insider, and beliefs and practices of one's home society that went unnoticed come to the foreground. In the present case, after exploring traditional K'iche' Maya dance in Guatemala, I became interested in Native American powwow. Although important differences exist, both forms struggle for self-representation in a context of persistent inequality and appropriation of indigenous culture by Others. Presently, I continue to explore the culture and society of my home country through the outside-insider lens. In both Guatemala and the United States, indigenous political leaders (kings and chiefs) become symbolic Indians put to use by state-sponsored institutions. As nonindigenous Guatemalans sometimes claim Tekun Umam as their hero, some nonindigenous Illinoisans claim Chief Illiniwek as theirs.

Also examined earlier, when people dress as ethnic Others and perform public dances, the images of identity become contested. When a history of colonialism and a present of deep inequality mark relationships between the groups, the image constructed in dance takes on political dimensions. In Part Two, I described how both the Guatemalan state and K'iche' Maya dancers have deployed the same martyr of resistance to quite different ends. When whites reference Native people and culture, differences of power and histories of colonization enter the picture as well. In both cases the actual indigenous people referenced are neither powerless nor voiceless. On the contrary, in the United States as well as in Guatemala, indigenous responses may be muted and behind the scenes or overt and directly confrontational. Beyond these shared issues of appropriation of Native culture by powerful ethnic Others is the issue of representational dance and change. In my treatment of powwow, I explored changes in how indigenous people represent themselves in dance. As Native people have achieved greater participation in U.S. society on their own terms, they have attained greater latitude of self-representation. Self-representation, in turn, expands power and the ability to participate in civil society. Presently, I examine a similar shift. Here, however, it is a nonindigenous audience that contests real and perceived shifts in interethnic relations through support of a dance that constructs an imaginary Indian.

Given the predominance of sport in mainstream life, the appropriation of Native culture for athletic team names, mascots, and symbols is a socially and culturally significant topic. We may be unaware of the meaning of a place-name taken from an indigenous language but religiously follow a local athletic team named "Indian" or for a Native nation, and occasionally for a particular Native person. The recently retired Chief Illiniwek of the University of Illinois is a particularly salient white representation of Indianness linked to his dance. Chief Illiniwek, then, is broad U.S. cultural practice in microcosm. In this chapter I consider the origin and development of Chief Illiniwek in the context of imaginary Indians and Indianness in sport. The following chapter examines Chief Illiniwek as manifested in secular ritual and framed in myths of identification. I conclude Part Five by examining the controversy over the Chief as an example of both indigenous activism and how ethnic conflict sharpens attachment to symbols of ethnicity.

Philip Deloria (1998) notes that playing Indian—that is, dressing, crafting, dancing, and various forms of mimicry of Native peoples and cultures—has been at the core of mainstream identity from its earliest days. The tax protestors of the Boston Tea Party chose to dress as Indians, referencing notions of autonomy and freedom and distancing themselves from the European roots of their culture and identity. Whether in revolts against economic stratification following independence, in struggles with the impact of industrialization, or in the counterculture of the 1960s and the New Age movements that followed, mimicking Native people is a strong current in mainstream identity formation.

It is in sport that appropriation of Indianness in name, symbols, and act—playing Indian—is most salient, most readily available, and most controversial. From professional football's Redskins and Chiefs, to major league baseball's Indians and Braves, to countless educational institutions, sports teams are often identified as general or specific Native individuals or groups (when not named for animals or natural forces). As the present discussion most concerns the representation of Indianness in dance, I focus here on sport-connected performance that involves the actual embodiment of notions of Indian life, culture, and history. While the identification of institutions of higher learning with names and images of Indians was commonplace by the late nineteenth century (King and Springwood 2001a:45), halftime presentation of Indianness seems to have begun in the early National Football League. Moreover, the first performers were Native people themselves.

Jim Thorpe (Sac and Fox), considered one of the greatest multi-sport athletes of all time, coached the Oorang Indians of Ohio from 1922 to 1923. Springwood (2001) details the strange history of the Oorang Indians and the complex implications of indigenous people constructing Indianness in a way that met with audience expectations. The team included Native athletes of various tribal affiliations. In addition to playing football, the Native athletes performed a halftime show that included "war whoops," various animal tricks, and tomahawk, knife, and sharpshooting demonstrations (Springwood 2001:304). Whatever motivated Thorpe and his players, playing Indian at halftime became quite popular among nonindigenous sports fans in the subsequent years. No doubt this example of Native people "imitating non-Indian imitations of Indians" (Deloria 1998:123) influenced, if indirectly, the construction of an imaginary Indian at the University of Illinois four years later.

In 1926, a University of Illinois student (an Eagle Scout and experienced Indian hobbyist) dressed and danced as a Plains Indian at halftime of a football game (King and Springwood 2001a:47). In 1930, Stanford "officially adopted the 'Indian' name and caricature of a feathered Indian" (Springwood 2001:304). "Prince Lightfoot," complete with Plains-inspired regalia, began to appear and perform at Stanford football games in 1952 (Springwood 2001:305). In 1931, Syracuse created its mythical "Saltine Warrior," Chief Bill Orange (Fischer 1999:31). As was the case with Stanford's Prince Lightfoot, Chief Bill Orange did not become an embodied feature of Syracuse football until after the end of World War II, when images of Plains peoples predominated in film and on the increasingly available television (Fischer 1999:31). Students of Florida State University voted to name the institution's athletic teams in 1947 "Seminoles" (King and Springwood 2001b:130). The Florida State Seminole was subsequently manifested in a variety of imagined Indians performed by students, including "Sammy Seminole," "Chief Fullabull," and "Savage Sam," before arriving at its current incarnation, "Chief Osceola" (King and Springwood 2001b:138).

Interestingly enough, the same postwar period that spawned suburbanization, imagined as a new pioneering conquest of nature, also engendered a fascination with television and movie Indians. The era eventually brought increasing activism for legal and economic equality coupled with a more open examination of the meaning and nature of colonialism. Indigenous activism of the 1960s and 1970s pushed for greater political autonomy and respect for the sovereignty of Native nations as well as civil rights for Native individuals. Important victories were won on an array of fronts, including shifts in U.S. government policy away from paternalism and assimilation and toward Native self-determination and self-government. General public attitudes showed signs of improvement as in many respects Native ethnic status shifted from a negative to a positive identity (with improved yet stereotyped notions of Indianness).

The influence of "red power" was felt on some campuses more than others. In response to concerted Native criticism, Stanford retired Chief Lightfoot in 1972 (Springwood 2001:306) and Syracuse eliminated Chief Bill Orange in 1978 (Fischer 1999:37). These and other Chiefs, however, do not disappear quietly. They typically enjoyed support engendered in vigorous student and alumni counter-protests (Davis and Rau 2001; Fischer 1999:38; King 2001:291; Springwood 2001:306). Indeed, largely a result of coordinated efforts by students, alumni, trustees, and even state and federal legislators, Chief Illiniwek of the University of Illinois continued to perform as an official symbol into the 2006–2007 basketball season. As I described at the beginning of this chapter, the Chief, although not officially embraced by the university, continues to dance.

There are a number of facets to the Chief Illiniwek case that merit attention. He is the most controversial of dancing Indian mascots (or symbols) that have survived into the recent present. He is typical of other dancing Indians; although his name alludes to a specific people, in act and costume he represents a generic Indian—one Spindel (2000) and others point out is an amalgam of Boy Scout Indian hobbyism, film and literature romanticism, and decontextualized Plains cultural artifacts. Chief Illiniwek also enjoys a deeply loyal following. As such, I argue, exploring the Chief in detail is a way to explore white dancing Indian in a general sense. In short, he is both a special and a representative case.

The life history of this official honored symbol of the University of Illinois represents twentieth-century Indian play in microcosm. In the Midwest and at the University of Illinois of the 1920s, a number of trends intersected that shaped the creation of the Chief. College education was no longer only available to the wealthy, and although non-whites were largely excluded, higher education was becoming democratic. Much of the experience and material culture associated with college was in formation at the time of Chief Illiniwek's origin.

As the white middle class prospered and enjoyed real political muscle, the country centralized, expanded, and began to assert geopolitical influence. A period of democratization was one also noted for imperialism and militarism. Three wars in particular informed U.S.-indigenous relations and the formation of nationalism during the period. The Civil War ended slavery and established a strong, centralized state capable of controlling its own territory and intervening in the affairs of states beyond its borders. Rebellious southern states subdued, the military of the Union turned its attention to "pacification" of the Plains. With the Wounded Knee massacre of 1890, the "Indian Wars" ended and the United States was on the verge of completing its "manifest destiny" on the continent.

These post–Civil War Indian Wars coincided closely with the rise of mass media, including the proliferation of portable photographic equipment. Through newspapers, novels, and other media, the average citizen could read about and see images of Native people of the West. While print media provided textual and photographic representations of Native people of the Plains, traveling Wild West shows granted white audiences access to corporeal Native individuals.

Most famously developed by Buffalo Bill Cody, the Wild West show was an entertainment extravaganza, a secular ritual that constructed the story of the transcontinental triumph of U.S. settler society. Of course, enacting how the West was won required both cowboys and Indians. Native people were employed to represent battles and to embody a version of their cultures that appealed to white audiences. Not surprisingly, dance was a part of how Indians were constructed for Wild West show audiences. Such performances, because they confirmed the story of conquest embraced by the dominating society, were allowed. Consequently, in Wild West shows, dancing continued and was, contrary to official government policy, encouraged and remunerated. Moreover, it seems very likely that Native performers danced separate dances in their off hours, away from the gaze of the outsider audiences. Despite its development and circulation of the generic Indian of the white imagination, the Wild West show provided economic opportunity, a motivation for the continuation of dance, and context for intertribal connection (Ellis 2005:14; Nesper 2003:448–450).

Live performances, however, would eventually give way to recorded ones. Spindel (2000:115) argues that the Western movie was born as it became clear that filming and distributing moving images of Indian wars were more efficient and profitable than transporting troupes of actors and animals around the country. Indeed the transformation from live entertainment to recorded, mass-distributed images is another important trend in mainstream life at the time. As a result of these currents, by the 1920s, performers and audiences of Indianness shared a set of stereotyped ideas concerning what made an Indian an Indian.

Although the eastern prairie plains featured a number of settled-village farming peoples, images and description of nomadic peoples of the western

High Plains (with their formal warrior societies) generated responses of both romantic yearning and fearful disdain. The introduction of the horse and the firearm and the incorporation of Native economies into a global system of exchange had had profound transformative impacts on the indigenous peoples of the High Plains. Although the High Plains peoples of the eighteenth and nineteenth centuries represented societies in transition, the nomadic warrior on horseback became the generic Indian of time immemorial in the mainstream white imagination. As images of Plains peoples became available through mass media, they met perfectly with the needs of an expansive settler state. Fierce, brave warriors made for fine enemies. Although ideal for romantic imagining, nomadic High Plains culture was exotic enough that whites who otherwise might be sympathetic to the plight of indigenous people could convince themselves that Indian disappearance was fated anyway.

The mass media, however, revealed the savagery not only of the Other but of the self. The massacres at Sand Creek (1864) and Wounded Knee (1890) encompass and symbolize a period of state-orchestrated and state-tolerated brutality, which occasionally brought condemnation. The behavior recorded and reported at massacres of Native people, including the deliberate killing and mutilation of women and children, seemed neither Christian nor civilized. Although the mythical notion that Native people were predestined to disappear was often still embraced, solution of the "Indian problem" became contested. In this period of U.S. expansion, Native people themselves were not passive victims and deployed a range of strategies for dealing with the "white problem" (Nabokov 1999:172). With the waning efficacy of physical resistance, Native leaders turned to discourse through mass media to gain white allies (these strategies most notably exercised by Sitting Bull). Accordingly, the Indian Wars dramatically expanded settler dominance of the continent, but not without contestation of policy toward indigenous people by Natives themselves and within white society.

The third war I briefly reference here is World War I. At Champaign, the University of Illinois built a magnificent stadium to memorialize those students who had served and died during the Great War. The twentieth century would come to be known as the "American century" by virtue of the military and economic strength demonstrated by U.S. involvement in its first major international war. The cumulative effect of wars and expansion was a degree of militarization of U.S. society. Martial themes run through early twentieth-century life, from Boy Scouting with its salutes and hierarchy, to marching bands with uniforms and batons, to the relatively new, popular, and violent sport of American football.

The society and economy that made possible U.S. military strength were in a period of transition. The process by which the typical citizen would no longer be a small-town dweller employed in agriculture was well under way. This industrialization and its de-territorialization undermined connection to particular places and specific concrete communities. Rather individuals were becoming members of the "imagined political community" (Anderson 1983) of a large, powerful state. Moreover, institutions (of education and of work) would form an important portion of the social groups and networks inhabited by an increasingly mobile population. The extended kin groups and small face-to-face communities that had predominated in human societies until industrialization were becoming less and less a part of the social landscape of the United States. On college campuses, attachment to alma mater (an inevitable response given the above transformations) was often manifested at intercollegiate football games. Indeed, the success of the University of Illinois football team during the 1920s earned the University of Illinois a reputation for sports excellence (Spindel 2000:72).

Although U.S. society underwent profound changes in the fifty years preceding the debut of Chief Illiniwek, there was also a degree of continuity. Racism and race hierarchy predominated in social life. Non-whites existed as second-class citizens, and stereotyped mimicry of Others by whites was widely practiced and accepted (at least by whites). Despite forces that we now identify as "modernization" and "progress," Jim Crow ruled the South and white supremacy dominated mainstream culture throughout.

As Deloria (1998) points out, during shifts that call into question or at least require reorientation of self, whites have typically drawn on imagined Indianness to create and re-create satisfying and seemingly authentic sources of identification. In 1926 at the University of Illinois, social transformations and individuals steeped in the contemporary forms of playing Indian came together (King and Springwood 2001a:45). As a result, Chief Illiniwek would embody martial themes, institutional identification, and stereotyped images of Indianness.

Before addressing the creation of Chief Illiniwek directly, a brief description of the societies after which he is named is in order. Often misidentified as a "tribe," the Ilaniawaki (from which the state takes its name) was a loose political alliance of as many as twelve culturally and linguistically related peoples (Bauxar 1978:594). Formed in the mid-seventeenth century, the Ilaniawaki comprised the Kaskaskia, Tamaroa, Cahokia, Peoria, Michigamia, and Moingwena nations (Prochaska 2001:157). The Peoria and Kaskaskia eventually absorbed other groups and became the most subject to written description (Callender 1978:673). Alliance formation was a common strategy at the time, as the effects of intensified trade with Europeans and inter-European struggle for control of North America rippled from the east.

Typical of the adaptive strategies of the area, member groups of the Ilaniawaki (or Inoca, as they self-identified; Callender 1978:679) combined hunting and gathering with corn, bean, and squash low-intensity agriculture (Callender 1978:674). Social and productive tasks were organized through extended kin groups, and people lived in rectangular lodges (not tipis) organized into semi-permanent villages (Callender 1978:674). While raiding participation (and hunting ability) were important markers of adult male status, the elaborate horse-raiding complex of the High Plains was absent (Callender 1978:675–677). Male clothing included robes, calico shirts, leggings with garters, yarn belts, and beaded sashes. Rather than feathered war bonnets, Inoca men wore on their heads fabric turbans, headbands, and roaches of animal hair. Adornments featured silver ear and nose pieces, feathers, and feather pendants. Extensive face painting and tattooing were also common (Callender 1978:674, 677–679).

As was widespread practice (evidenced in several state names), European colonial maps identified regions of North America by the names of local Native nations. The French made Ilaniawaki[1] into Illinois; English speakers articulated French *nwa* as *noy*, thus giving the state its name. In a sort of second-phase appropriation, during the 1920s the group of loosely affiliated peoples that gave name to the state would be imagined as the Illini "tribe." Illini and Illiniwek also began life as symbols of institutional identification for the University of Illinois. Popular imaginative memory converted settled-village farmers into nomadic feathered warriors.

The imagined leader of this confederation, Chief Illiniwek, first appeared at halftime of a football game between the University of Illinois and the University of Pennsylvania in 1926 (King and Springwood 2001a:45). Embodied as a generic, Plains-inspired Indian, Chief Illiniwek shared a peace pipe with a William Penn impersonator (King and Springwood 2001a:46).[2] That a ritual of reconciliation is referenced implies conflict had recently ended. However, if the main theme here is the legitimacy of the colonial enterprise and friendly Native acceptance of Euro-American dominance (King and Springwood 2001a:47), martial themes were just beneath the surface. Chief Illiniwek appeared with the university's marching band (and he would eventually become a central part of the band's halftime presentation). The performance took place during the intermission of a football game (an elaborate metaphor of war) in a grand stadium dedicated to war dead.

Chief Illiniwek's creation involved collaboration among Euro-American men who put Indianness to work for personal and institutional purposes. Robert Zupke, the famed Illinois football coach, referenced the Native peoples of Illinois to instill a sense of tradition and loyalty that corresponded with contemporary notions of student athletics. "Illini is the name of a tribe of Indians and the word Illiniwek means the complete Indian man, the physical man, the intellectual man, and the spiritual man,"[3] he is reported to have orated at a pep rally (King and Springwood 2001a:45). Zupke also interpreted *Illiniwek* as "the complete human being—the strong, agile human body; the unfettered human intellect; the indomitable human spirit" (Honor the Chief n.d.a). The institutionalization of Zupke's ideas is the source of the enigmatic student quote ("[Chief Illiniwek] inspired me to be a complete man") in the newspaper article described at the beginning of this chapter.

The 1920s student who would materialize the complete Indian man himself was deeply steeped in the tradition of playing Indian. Lester Leutwiler, before dressing up as Chief Illiniwek, had organized a powwow for his senior project at Urbana High (King and Springwood 2001a:45). He had cultivated his interest in Indianness in the Boy Scouts, where he learned from Ralph Hubbard, the renowned Indian dance interpreter and crafter. Indeed, the intersection of Indian and martial themes was manifested in the Boy Scout organization itself. Militarism and playing Indian were comingled from the inception of U.S. scouting (Deloria 1998:95). Some within the Scouts had argued that boys suffered a separation from their natural selves resulting from industrialization and urbanization. They could be formed into better men by playing Indian. Others preferred the model of military discipline as the mode of enculturation exercised by the Scouts. By the time the author of Chief Illiniwek was a Boy Scout, patriotism and discipline had won over nature and Indian play (Deloria 1998:96). The vision of Indianness as an appropriate mode for the development of good strong American boys would remain within the Boy Scouts, but in a subservient role. Thus, Leutwiler, the first Chief Illiniwek, while learning to dance and dress like an Indian, did so within an organization that overtly served the needs of a state of growing military strength. The two currents continue to coexist, sometimes awkwardly, in the Boy Scouts to this day.

The hobby Indian tradition in scouting, as Deloria explores, has at times involved submission of whites to indigenous authority, if only temporarily, inverting the formal hierarchy of power (Deloria 1998:144–145). Indian hobbying occasionally draws authenticity from contact with actual Native people. In such context, members of the dominating society become marked as unknowing outsiders who must turn to indigenous people for guidance. As seems to be the case for the creators and re-creators of Chief Illiniwek, however, Native authority is limited to moments when University of Illinois students and officials visit Indian country to acquire material culture. Elements of movement and objects acquired, the power to re-create Indianness on campus rested firmly with students, bandleaders, and football coaches. The audience, in the way it demanded and consumed Indianness, shaped construction as well. As Spindel (2000:93) remarks, "[m]ost Americans preferred to have American Indian customs explained to them by other white Americans."

Indeed, in Chief Illiniwek we see facets of what Deloria identifies as "people" and "object" hobbyism (1998:135). In the former, Native *people* are the source of authenticity, and hobbyists, at least tacitly, acknowledge that cultures can change without "dying out." People hobbyism allows that actual human beings need not correspond to the image of generic Indian to be "real." In the latter "object hobbyism," artifacts rather than people become the emphasis, and authenticity is derived from objects. To object hobbyists, the social context of production and reproduction matters less than the objects and actions themselves. Divorced from the social relations that create and distribute cultural artifacts and knowledge within indigenous societies, the material culture of Chief Illiniwek manifests object hobbyism. The Chief becomes an exotic symbolic tapestry onto which audience and performer embroider their own conception of self and Other.

However, the creation of the Chief tradition reflects both people and object hobbyism. Although Zupke invested his team with an Indian identity indigenous to central Illinois, Leutwiler and subsequent Chief impersonators repeatedly and deliberately drew on Lakota (Plains) material culture and Lakota individuals to authenticate the Chief. The successor to Leutwiler, Webber Borchers, determined that Chief Illiniwek merited an "'authentic' costume made by 'traditional' Indians" (King and Springwood 2001a:46). To contract the assembly of such a garment, Borchers traveled not to Oklahoma to consult the descendants of member groups of the Inoca alliance but to the Pine Ridge reservation in South Dakota to arrange and supervise the fabrication of a costume by four Oglala women (King and Springwood 2001a:46). Some of the authenticity craved and purveyed by Borchers came of savagery. An elderly woman who worked on the costume was reported by Borchers to have been present after the Battle of Little Big Horn and "had helped mutilate the dead of Custer" (King and Springwood 2001a:47). Even though Native people were consulted and employed in the process, their purpose was to authenticate a costume, which was largely designed by Borchers. The emphasis was on the object of the costume, with people and place serving to confirm a notion of authenticity controlled firmly by a nonindigenous Indian dancer. Given the reality of poverty on Lakota reservations, it seems likely that the women employed to make the costume viewed the process more as a source of needed cash than as traditional production.

The new "authentic" costume debuted in November 1930 and another important object of authentic Indianness was soon added. Borchers briefly incorporated a horse into his performance, further referencing the Plains-inspired generic Indian. Not surprisingly, Borchers drew on his status as a member of ROTC to access and train his equine accompaniment. As in the Boy Scouts (Borchers, like his predecessor, was an Eagle Scout), military training and playing Indian coexisted in the construction of Chief Illiniwek (King and Springwood 2001a:49).

When a new costume was needed in 1982, the university again turned to the Lakota. This time, however, it was band director Gary Smith who traveled to Pine Ridge. Chief Illiniwek by the 1980s had become the business of university employees as well as students. Smith consulted with Oglala officials and reported that they were not displeased with Chief Illiniwek, as he was not a caricature of Native people (Spindel 2000:134). Eventually, Smith requested a new set of regalia for Chief Illiniwek. Although the time required would prohibit assembly of a new outfit, officials informed Smith that Frank Fools Crow, an elder of considerable renown, had Chief's regalia at hand. Fallen on hard times, Fools Crow was in need of money, and after negotiating with Smith he agreed to sell a buckskin suit to the university for $3,500 (Spindel 2000:135). Furthermore, with the support of alumni, Smith arranged for Fools Crow to visit the university for formal presentation of the new regalia at a football game. The ceremony—including an impromptu blood-brother ritual attempted by Webber Borcher and an emphysematous coughing attack by Fools Crow, which was taken by the audience as an Indian incantation—was cut short as the football teams took the field (Spindel 2000:136). Fools Crow, as later reported by other Oglala, found the performance of Chief Illiniwek "comical" but reserved comment to avoid offending his hosts (Spindel 2000:136). A new outfit and tacit approval of the tradition secured, Chief Illiniwek was at the beginning of a period of popularity that was fueled by slick iconography and effective marketing of licensed products (Spindel 2000:120–141).

While trips to visit "real" Indians are central to the lore of Chief Illiniwek, the filtering that Leutwiler and subsequent embodiers of Chief Illiniwek employed reflects preconceptions of Indians and notions of authenticity that stressed accurate mimicry of material culture rather than Native symbolic meaning of object and act. However, if "real" Indian material culture is the key, why not consult the Peoria of Oklahoma in the creation of the Chief? To both performers and audience, the Lakota must represent a more authentic Indianness than the Peoria relocated to Oklahoma.[4] Moreover, the mass-media encounter with Plains culture is reflected in the Chief and would be continued in the burgeoning Western film genre. Early audiences of Chief Illiniwek knew him to be true because they had seen photos and read descriptions of Plains peoples. Later audiences knew he was true because they saw like figures in film and on television.

Chief Illiniwek fully reflects the context of his creation. What became an "honored tradition" is rooted in a period of particular forms of white identity, militarized nationalism, social inequality, and playing Indian. The story could have ended with a note about how political activism started in the sixties led to change in the seventies. However, the University of Illinois was somewhat isolated from the social currents that compelled change at Syracuse and Stanford. As a result, the Chief continued into the present and has a dedicated following. Somewhere along the way the quaint became a tradition to be fiercely defended. How this happened is in no small part rooted in compelling ritual enactment of the Chief and satisfying mythology about the Chief.

NOTES

1. *Ilaniawaki* is a term itself of uncertain, and likely not Inoca, origin (Callender 1978:679).

2. The performance is evocative of the final scenes of the Guatemalan Dance of the Conquest described in Part Two. Here, Native acquiescence to European authority is the center of attention. In K'iche' performance, it is an afterthought.

3. Interestingly enough, the word *Illiniwek* is of uncertain origin and is not an Inoca term meaning "man" (Callender 1978:679).

4. When "real Illini" support for Chief Illiniwek was needed in the face of intertribal calls for his retirement, Chief supporters did turn to the Peoria of Oklahoma.

Twelve

Chief Illiniwek Enacted in Ritual and Myth

Through stylized action and concrete objects, a ritual makes real the more abstract concepts of religious belief. Myth, of course, is the common narrative form in which religious beliefs are articulated in stories. Accordingly, myth and ritual have a complex interrelationship. They are mutually dependent; myth motivates ritual and ritual constructs and teaches myth. Rituals, unlike most other cultural behaviors, must be done and done (with varying room for improvisation) in a prescribed manner. It is myths that explain why ritual is obligatory and often why it is done a certain way. Although a myth is narrative, a story, its realization in telling is behavioral as much as ritual. The two together transcend the ideational and material. A ritual makes a myth real, subject to the five senses. Myths are indeed commonly held because they are shared in ritual, and rituals are done because myth requires it to be so. Although noting that myth and ritual are inseparable, the communicative limitations of writing now demand that I separate them. First I address the halftime ritual at the University of Illinois, and then I consider myths and mythic themes expressed in Chief Illiniwek.

SECULAR RITUAL, PERSONHOOD, AND IDENTITY

Chief Illiniwek's performance engenders many of the elements of ritual. Although the Chief is not a supernatural figure, attitudes expressed about him both inside and outside of his performance suggest that he is something more than strictly mundane. We would be hard-pressed to find a Chief supporter admitting to ritual adoration of the imaginary Indian. However, U of I alumni frequently recount experience that generates a profound emotional response that carries physiological manifestation. Carol Spindel describes a regularity of responses claiming "chills to the spine" and "tears to the eye" (2000:120–141). More recent writers to the editor of the *Chicago Tribune* occasionally report that viewing the Chief is profoundly meaningful, prompting physiological response. When I attended the University of Illinois–Syracuse game, it was clear that the Chief's appearance and performance were the main event of halftime. Folks who gave only cursory attention to other aspects of the intermission were fairly riveted by the Chief. Although he may not be a deity, an animistic force, or the like, experiencing the Chief in action, and by extension the Chief himself, is extra-mundane. Moreover, many phenomena associated with ritual are present in the Chief and his dance. However, also clear is that attending a football game and engaging the Chief at halftime are something different from, say, the rite of the Eucharist or a vision quest. Moreover, for some indigenous dancers, religious practitioners, and activists, the Chief's performance is certainly profane, if not sacrilegious. Noting that the performance is *secular* ritual is, for these reasons, necessary.

The context of football is also important to note. While figures such as Chief Illiniwek are often labeled "*sports* mascots," they are quite often most associated (in origin and performance) with football. As I explored earlier, the initial presentation of Indianness at a sporting event was during halftime of a football game. Origins of the famous dancing Indians of Syracuse, Stanford, and Florida State Universities are all connected intimately to football. Football is the context of other, more obscure, imagined Indians as well. One of the more interesting manifestations, the "Indian Family" of Arkansas State University, has performed primarily before and during football games (Landreth 2001). The family, while representing little specific to the Osage from which ASU takes its team names, does manifest a variety of Indian types (Landreth 2001:47–51). "The Brave" is primitive and warlike, a savage (Landreth 2001:51–52). "The Chief" is "stoic and dignified" (2001:53). A female "Indian Princess" fulfills the helpful befriending maiden type. Both the Chief and the Princess accept white dominance. The Brave is the figure that most closely aligns with the metaphors of football. At the University of Illinois, Chief Illiniwek overtly is structurally most parallel to Chief of Arkansas State. However, Chief Illiniwek implies the Brave in its references to warring, bravery, and courage. Football and performed Indians have a close association in U.S. sport. The question is, why football in particular?

There is considerable symbolic overlap in playing Indian and playing football. It was while attending a U of I football game that it occurred to me that understanding how a symbolic Indian engenders such a powerful response involves locating its performance firmly in the context of football. The game of football and the dance of Chief Illiniwek are secular rituals: symbolic representations that performed together portray and construct common white notions about human and social nature.

Football in the United States is a game about war. Its terminology is dominated by war metaphors. From linebackers who "blitz," to quarterbacks who throw "bombs," to offensive and defensive linemen who struggle "in the trenches," the language of football is often the language of war (Ross 1971:36). Indeed, the language of the game occasionally becomes the language of war. During the Cold War, the documentation, codes, and communication devices necessary for the president to initiate a nuclear attack came to be known popularly as "the football."

Beyond what is spoken, the game itself, in the way it assembles its players and determines the winning team, is stylized, nonlethal combat. The successful team defends its own territory and invades the territory of the other. It scores points not by finessing the ball over, into, or through a net, but by moving it down the field and overcoming forcibly the defensive play of the opponent. A team wins by physically and bodily dominating the other team. Moreover, it is a game that symbolizes the kind of war states make. More than any other form of polity created by human beings, the state functions to create and control boundaries. It seeks to establish uniform political control over territory. Football is a game that rewards the team that seizes and protects territory. Within a given quarter of play each half of the field and its end zone are identified with one team. When a team successfully moves the ball across the midpoint in the field, they enter the territory of the other team. Points are scored when the ball under control of a team is moved into the end zone (or through the goalposts) at the far end of the opponent's half of the field. Although seizing territory is the object of the game, the border between the teams, the line of scrimmage (itself likely derived from *skirmish*), may not be violated until the moment that play initiates. Fair play makes the unannounced attack favored by actual states off limits in football. In effect, two groups line up in opposition to one another across a temporary border and struggle physically to gain or protect territory. Not surprisingly, military leaders and social commentators have acclaimed football as an ideal training ground for the leadership, self-sacrifice, discipline, and sublimation to authority necessary for a functioning state military.

As closely as it is associated with war, however, football is also an elaborate model for traditional mainstream notions of success. As Susan P. Montague and William Morais (1976) and William Arens (1975) describe, the same enacted ideals of hierarchy, discipline, and teamwork apply to business as well as to war. The team that wins is the team that prepares, works hard, and works together. As in the military and in the economy, tasks are highly specialized (Arens 1975:77). Football players are assigned positions based on skill and body form. In a given offensive play each has a specific assignment that must be carried out in close coordination with others. These tasks are controlled through hierarchy. Clear lines of authority are established and followed in winning football programs. It is not a metaphor of democratic cooperation derived from discourse and consensus but a game of action in which orders are given and (with limited opportunities of improvisation for some players) followed. As such, football can be a counterweight to the self-absorption that sometimes infects U.S. individualism (Montague and Morais 1976:50). It also expresses the strong, if tacit, value placed on conformity. In these somewhat contradictory messages of individual and group, star players receive the adoration of wide audiences while other players, crucial to the team, garner the esteem of teammates, coaches, and game aficionados. The game embodies adulation of both individual accomplishment and noble self-sacrifice within a setting of savage competition.

The symbolic violence that is part and parcel of football presents players and audience with distinctly U.S. ideas about the nature of social competition (Montague and Morais 1976:46). There are limits on how players may strike one another, but not on how hard they may do so. Although rules are established in the name of fair play, the unrestrained physicality of football reflects the mainstream ideal (not entirely shared by all) that competition is inherently good and vigorous competition is best. At the same time, while embracing a rather savage competition, the game generally does not dissolve into chaos. As such, it confirms the notion that ardent competition can be controlled and channeled to socially appropriate goals.

As it constructs the boundaries of violence and the limits of appropriate competition, so does football construct masculinity. It is one of the few U.S. sports in which there is no parallel sanctioned female competition. The football field is a male domain (Arens 1975). Women participate, with some rare and always extensively noted exceptions, at the edge of competition as cheerleaders. Embodiment of gender ideology is accomplished in act and artifact. Men, displaying their bodies in a way that stresses masculinity, hurl themselves at one another in unbridled competition. Women in short skirts offer support and are peripheral to the action on the field (Arens 1975:77). In the contested ideologies of gender and success, football manifests the "traditional" (Montague and Morais 1976:37).

Beyond the particulars of football, understanding the affective impact of ritual is key to understanding why Chief Illiniwek is compelling to his supporters. Anthropology, primarily initiated by the work of Victor Turner (1969:96–97), identifies one dimension of the emotional power of ritual with the term *communitas*. Associated with the liminal phase of rites of passage, *communitas* involves an intense sense of belonging and connection to social fellows. In *communitas* not only are our neighbors encountered differently but also time and place may seem suspended in a kind of eternal present. As human beings we need these moments socially and emotionally. Yearning (at least in rhetoric) for days gone by when neighbors knew one another and when communities were strong is a manifestation of this need. However, modernity, with its alienated production, demands of increasing production, and commodification (and hence scarcity) of time, makes *communitas* increasingly difficult to achieve. Some of us may retreat further into self-absorption, material acquisition, or the like, but Turner insists that one way or another we need moments of *communitas* just as we need the social structure that guides ordinary life (1969:139).

As scarce as it is in modern, complex society, *communitas* is rarely the normal state of social affairs. It is the ritual manifestation of *ideals* of social solidarity that are supposed to inform social discourse outside of ritual; it teaches us how to be human in human community (Turner 1969:134). We experience *communitas* in particular ritual settings and it becomes the example of how social discourse ought to be. Of course, within and between societies exactly how one should be human varies. The University of Illinois complex of secular rituals that combines football, marching bands, and the Chief expresses particularly U.S. ideas and tensions of personhood and society. These notions are not without contradiction and are occasionally contested. Secular ritual, common to much human ritual, does cognitive work on shared ideas that are central to a people but that are also complex and difficult.

A central contradiction expressed in the Chief Illiniwek secular ritual is found in the mainstream notion of self. Individualism, the primary orientation of self to self rather than of self to group, is the cornerstone of explicit U.S. ideas of personhood. In action, individuals are the principal makers of identity. We, acting within constitutionally protected freedoms, make our own choices ("decide for ourselves") and shape our own lives. We are expected to be "true" to ourselves, to "keep it real," and essentially to express our individual selves authentically. Complementing emphases on personal space and privacy further express and convince us that we are separate and distinct bodies in charge of our own present and future.

However, reflective of any people's struggle with the tensions created by organization of self-aware human beings into social groups, U.S. individualism does not always reign supreme. Alongside the rhetoric of freedom and choice are strong currents of conformity and submission to authority. We embrace the notion of self-expression in theory but are ambivalent about its actual exercise. From "get a haircut" to "get a job" to "love it or leave it" to "support the troops," social life in the United States is full of direct and indirect pressures to conform. Even our expressions of nonconformity tend to conformity. Hippies marked themselves with flowers and tie-dyed t-shirts, punk rockers with safety pins and tattered clothing, and early indie (independent label) music fans with flannel.

While contestation of culture, including notions of personhood and self, is to be expected in a large and complex society, it is clear that the notions of both freedom and conformity are tightly held by individuals and institutions despite (or because of) their inherent contradictions. It is said that in the United States, one is "free to be the same." In short, we convince ourselves that we wear the same clothing, speak and act like our colleagues, and closely follow shifting trends in fashion and consumption by virtue of personal choice. We are certain that our identities, although they reference all sorts of socially defined sets of symbols, are of our own making. This individualistic conformity is, when it works, highly effective. It realizes social control and conformity without overt coercion. After all, our actions and expressions, no matter how much they conform with others, result from our own choices. We have available a satisfying and socially shared explanation of our conformity that mutes the coercion inherent in human social organization.

In performance of the Chief Illiniwek secular ritual, conformity and submission to authority by the audience are stressed. When the Chief strikes his cross-armed, chin-raised pose of authority, students, clad in identical or nearly identical t-shirts, respond in unison, "CHIEF," with the effect of a subsonic rumble. It has a powerful impact, marking the moment as highly communitarian and uniquely distinct from mundane, particularized experience. After the game, audience members return to lives in pursuit of specialized knowledge or in performance in a specialized economy. This specialization and our ideology of self give the impression of individualism and the potential of social isolation. Yet, for those moved by the Chief and attached to the University of Illinois, there is also a community derived from conformity and shared attachment.

The performance of the Chief works directly on the contradictions of individualistic conformity by embodying the contradictions of the noble savage. An Other par excellence, the noble savage provides an antidote for the challenges of modern existence. The noble savage lives in an imagined past connected with nature, by means of simple technology, in a small face-to-face community. In other words, he is free of the contamination of modern alienated life and free of its demands. However, as Deloria (1998:20–21) points out, the construction presents fundamental contradictions, allowing for the imagination of Indians that are both good and bad. Unconstrained by "civilization," the savage is capable of all sorts of depravity in the collective imagination of settler societies. From cannibalism, to constant warfare, to free love, in the savage we locate the ultimate transgressions and what we fear, dislike, or desire in ourselves. Indeed, sedentary farming peoples have probably had similar notions of nomads who lived beyond farm and field since the earliest days of settled agriculture (Maybury-Lewis 2002:26–29). Early farmers were bound to place and agricultural production and vulnerable to attack. In state societies, peasant farmers also have to pay rents and tax to elites. Nomads are free of such obligations and ties and become ready symbols of freedom but also parables that verify the need for the firm social control exercised by states. Contemporary state-dwellers encounter similar restraints on their freedom; they live lives dependent on complex society and technology. The noble savage is dependent on nature but free of the alienation and obligation of modernity. Deloria (1998:157) attributes the longevity of the noble savage ideology to its inherent contradictions. It survives and is repeatedly put to work not despite its good Indian / bad Indian paradox but because of this fundamental contradiction. As Lévi-Strauss might put it, the noble savage is "good to think" for the citizens of modern settler societies.

Students, faculty, and some Illinoisans construct an important part of their individual identity through the university, and the Chief is a symbol of the institution manifested in individual human form. Part of explaining why the imaginary Indian is such a compelling symbol lies in embodiment of the noble savage. The Chief, by reference to the imagined autonomy of the savage—an individual unconstrained by "civilization"—presents a model of pure individual freedom. At the same time, the Chief is noble and this nobility holds the possibility that strictly autonomous individuals will not destroy one another in pursuit of pure self-interest. Together, nobility and savagery assert the possibility of conformity embedded in self-orientation, of articulation to group that does not sacrifice individual freedom.

Here again there is interesting symbolic overlap with football. As I explored above, football also works on the tension of individuality and conformity in mainstream society. It provides opportunities for individual expression through performance in only limited contexts. The quarterback can be a star; the linemen, less so. Most of the game is a lesson on the value of authority, coordination of behavior, and the supremacy of the group. It also enacts ideology of success and of competition that is rigorous but not socially corrosive. We stress the benefits of competition but deemphasize the reality that with victory of some comes defeat of others (Montague and Morais 1976:46).

The notion of meritocracy in aggregate practice determines a few winners and many also-rans. As a consequence, rigorous competition for limited social rewards results in social tension. Mainstream ideology, however, emphasizes the benefits of rigorous competition and victories of self while diminishing the untoward impacts of its many defeats. Wealth concentration exceeding that of the other core countries is justified and its consequences minimized. The Chief and football embody and enact notions of social competition that are savage but with noble outcomes.

Typical of any people, we assume that our ideas about ourselves are true of the human condition. The University of Illinois complex of secular rituals manifests ideas that audience members see as human nature in general. Asking why so much cognitive work is done at halftime begins to reveal how particular ideas about the human condition are believed universal by those who hold them. Moreover, the college experience is something beyond an academic endeavor. Clearly, many U of I alumni take more than a degree from Champaign. Accordingly, college manifests general human processes of socialization. As college students become graduates, they also become adults.

Turner developed the concept of *communitas* embedded in his work on rites of passage and liminality. Rites of passage, from the smallest-scale society to most complex large-scale ones, tend to mark social change of individuals and groups in three phases. After breaking from a currently held status, initiates occupy a margin or in-between period before emergence and reincorporation into society, occupying the new status. College is a period of transition from adolescence to adulthood, and social scientists (anthropologist Michael Moffatt [1989] in particular) have noted that we should think of the ideal college experience as one of liminality. The college student, no longer living with parents, is nonetheless not a completely independent adult either. College kids play college pranks yet gradually acquire more and more characteristics of adulthood. They are no longer children but not yet fully adult.

As noted above, particularly in the early twentieth century, one of the purposes of playing Indian was to raise strong, vital children. Modernity and its dependence on technology and incomprehensibly complex systems of production alienate children from nature and leave them rather unconnected to the kin groups where they have been typically socialized and enculturated. Given popular notions of indigenous culture, connecting children to Indians also connects them to their human nature. In playing Indian, children are encouraged to indulge their savagery and learn to channel it to socially approved ends. As children, early Chief embodiers and audiences were exposed to appropriated Indianness in the belief that the process would mold them into ideal citizens of the republic.

The land-grant residential college campus acquired a function of socialization as it became accessible to a wider segment of U.S. society. Students would acquire knowledge but also character. In effect, large public institutions came to be the locus of adolescent transition to adulthood. Indeed, the rhetoric of college until the social transformations of the 1960s stressed college as a maker of men and women. It acquired a conflicted legal status of in loco parentis and was seen as an appropriate place to teach academic lessons and also civic values. The notion that an educational institution can impart values and form character seems quaintly optimistic, but it remains a part of the culture of the U.S. college to the present day.

Accordingly, during halftime at the University of Illinois three social forces held as appropriate agents of socialization come together: football, playing Indian, and the college experience. Football and the Chief enact notions of savagery and nobility and play on their inherent contradictions. However, thinking of college as a liminal space and of college student as a liminal status suggests that we think of noble and savage not only as contradictory but also as transformative. The ideals often ascribed to the Chief are also the characteristics that are valued in citizen graduates. If college is an extended margin period in the shift from childhood to adulthood, in it are potentially savage, socially incomplete adolescents transformed into well-formed noble (and entitled) graduates. The Honor the Chief Society states it nicely: "The tradition of the Chief is a link to our great past, a tangible symbol of an intangible spirit, filled with qualities to which a person of any background can aspire: goodness, strength, bravery, truthfulness, courage, and dignity" (Honor the Chief n.d.b).

The secular ritual of the Chief is at least partly a rite of passage. Indeed, the student involved in the effort to resurrect the Chief reports that the imaginary Indian "inspired [him] to be a complete man" (Twohey 2008). The secular ritual presents and teaches these ideas, making liminal college students into dedicated University of Illinois and Chief Illiniwek loyalists.

Moments of social connection in ritual, however, have a thorny character. They tend to convince those who experience them of the undeniable truth of the concepts enacted. The Chief is profoundly meaningful (and undeniably good) to those who experience the palpable force of interconnected community that pervades Memorial Stadium before, during, and after football games. However, in the complex, multi-ethnic reality of contemporary U.S. society, diverse, varied, and localized conceptions of truth and community do not always articulate well to one another. Chief Illiniwek is a controversial and vigorously contested figure. Those who form an attachment to the Chief through the experience of his performance have at their disposal a variety of responses for critics. A complex and rich set of myths justifies (and even necessitates) the Chief's performance.

THE CHIEF AND MYTHS OF IDENTIFICATION

Myth is about forgetting and remembering and it does not reflect a highly systematized or rational process. It creates a meaningful and satisfying tapestry from what is available to the mythmaker and myth listener. The process is, as Lévi-Strauss conceptualizes it, one of bricolage (1966:16–35). Myth (and culture in general) is created in a way that is better characterized as handicraft than as formalized design. We human beings, as cultural artisans, create tapestries of tradition from what is available at hand. The pieces do not always fit perfectly, but what we craft is nonetheless beautiful and compelling to us. The music, dance, and material culture of Chief Illiniwek manifest bricolage well.[1] Both the preexisting cognitive framework and the symbolic objects and acts to represent the shared ideas come from disparate sources. What is available to midwestern bricoleurs of Indianness is Plains-influenced clothing, including the feathered war bonnet, beaded buckskin shirt, and tasseled buckskin pants. Hollywood film provides a general rhythm and melodic form of music that says "Indian" to mainstream society. Beyond artifact and act, the stories that inform symbolic representations are products of bricolage. The bricolage of myth assembles fragments of stories and cements them with themes that are at hand to performer and audience. In the present case, to tell this story of an Indian chief is to tell the story of a noble savage. As such, the story cannot be told without referencing a particularly salient white story about Indians: the myth of the "vanishing American." Of course, the theme of manifest destiny is predominant and abundant on the crafter's workbench and is readily incorporated. The bricoleur of myth also weaves the tapestry with threads that elicit a particular emotional response. The myth of Chief Illiniwek is to be experienced with nostalgia.

As I explored earlier, Deloria (1998) notes that ideas about Indianness are a constant source of material for the construction of U.S. identity. Indigenous cultures (or at least colonial imaginings of them) were the source material predominantly at hand for the making of nationalist identity for the new republic. Thus begins a process of identity bricolage fraught with contradictions and informed rather constantly by the notion of Indians as noble savages, pure and purely free.

While I have been stressing how the bricoleur works with what is available, what is absent from the workshop of myth and identity is just as important. British colonists and later post-independence settlers rarely engaged indigenous Americans as full human beings. Contemporary formal education generally omits rigorous history, ethnography, or sociology of past and present indigenous peoples and their cultures. In everyday social life, white midwesterners encounter Indians in sports and entertainment but rarely Native Americans in social discourse. This mixture of mythmaking ingredients, dominated by imaginary Indianness and without serious engagement of Native people as complex and fully human, has profoundly shaped the bricolage that is Chief Illiniwek. (It has also, no doubt, deeply influenced the content and tenor of the conflict over the Chief.) As such, the performance of Chief Illiniwek is a concrete manifestation of various myths and mythic themes, including the myth of the vanishing American, the myth of Indian self-conquest, and the myth of manifest destiny. It draws on, pronounces, creates, and re-creates these myths in general and specific forms.

Similar to the case of Tekun Umam as a Guatemalan state symbol, Chief Illiniwek as an institutional symbol draws heavily on the mythic theme of the noble savage. In postcolonial settler society, to the imagined free but dangerous Other is added another dimension. A key element of the noble savage mythology in its modernist composition is the location of its imagined world in the past or on the edge of fading into the past. Deeply engrained in the folk theory about Native peoples is the notion that encroaching modernity inevitably changes or destroys (and destruction and change are often facilely equated) indigenous societies. Cultures and lifeways that are different from those of the dominating society are deemed incompatible with the challenges of contemporary life and economy. Despite indigenous strategies of resistance and survival, even as Native populations expand, and in ignorance of vigorous twenty-first-century "global indigenism" (Niezen 2003), cultural homogeneity is always just around the corner in the popular imagination. That scholars, poets, novelists, and just about every other kind of writer have been inaccurately predicting the demise of Native peoples for generations does little to dissuade those who hold this ideology tightly. The story of the vanishing American is a myth precisely because its logic makes refutation difficult. Disappearance is axiomatic, taken as a given, if not now or tomorrow then sometime in the future. Moreover, common to many myths, it makes human social processes into natural or divine ones.

Deloria, identifying this complex as the "ideology of the vanishing Indian" (1998:64), notes that the myth originates with the onset of the forced removal policy of the early nineteenth-century United States. This co-occurrence is functional. As Native peoples were forced from their homelands by virtue of government policy that enjoyed widespread support, the myth served to assuage popular and institutional guilt over what was without legal or moral grounds. Viewed through the lens of the myth, the disappearance of Native peoples was not a result of deliberate government policy and social action but part of a natural and inevitable process. The Trail of Tears and numerous other forced removal marches happened not because whites coveted Native-controlled resources, but because Indian ways and Indians themselves were incompatible with "progress." That Indians are marched off beyond the horizon was taken as evidence that they have indeed vanished, and the myth took on a self-serving circularity. It justified otherwise illegal and immoral action and then took the result of such action as proof that it is part of a natural process outside of human control.

The white population, by virtue of this inevitability, is the predestined inheritor of the land of the vanishing American. Indeed, the vanishing American is a main pillar upon which rests the grander myth of manifest destiny. The nineteenth-century ideological predecessors of Ronald Reagan did not have the luxury to post facto declare the continent a "raw, untamed wilderness," as the fortieth president declared in the inaugural address upon his second term. In the early republic, manifest destiny had to be made by forced removal of Native peoples from productive lands. Human-designed and -orchestrated exercise of power became a natural process. Confinement to reservations followed, and vanishing would be furthered not by removal from homelands but by removal of culture and language from individuals and groups. Late twentieth-century devotees of manifest destiny would claim not that Indian disappearance was inevitable but that Native populations never really existed in any significance from the beginning. Either way, European occupation of the continent and white control of its natural resources are predetermined. Just like the story of the first Thanksgiving, the idea of the vanishing American is a national myth. The first Thanksgiving scripts the acquiescence of Indians to colonization. The vanishing American and manifest destiny legitimize the wealth, privilege, and political power derived from territory and resources once controlled by Native peoples.

One of the most interesting facets of the vanishing American myth is the plethora of local variants it has spawned. The vanishing American has vanished nobly or ignobly from a wide range of landscapes. Very often, subsequent settler populations are keen to build local myths of identification around their vanished Indians. Ambivalent white adoration of fictional vanishing Indians (most famously *The Last of the Mohicans*) and of actual figures, including Sitting Bull, Geronimo, Cochise, and Black Hawk, is a mainstay of local imaginings of the past.

Chief Illiniwek, although not an actual specific historical figure, fits squarely in this tradition. Moreover, a widely circulated myth associated with him manifests an interesting subtype of the vanishing American. A theme we might call "Indian self-conquest" is told and retold in the story of Starved Rock. As I explored above, the Inoca formed an impermanent alliance of corn-farming peoples. The constituent groups of Inoca did not feature the elaborate warrior societies of the Plains peoples (whose societies themselves had undergone intense transformations as a result of the incorporation of the horse). While as interesting as any group, the allied peoples after whom the state is named are not suited to a dramatic myth of identification that University of Illinois loyalists crave, create, and re-create. Nor is the rather sad story of Illinois "removal" suitable for a myth of positive identity reinforcement.

With the defeat of the French by the British in 1763, the political landscape of North America changed significantly. A shift in the upper Midwest, from encounters with traders, missionaries, and the militaries of remote empires to invasion by settlers of the new republic, was set in motion. By the early nineteenth century a familiar pattern emerged with Native populations in decline as settler populations increased. Native responses ranged from violent confrontation, to millenarian movements, to flight, to acquiescence. Treaties were signed and their promises of security on small portions of original homelands were violated. Despite their support of the colonists in the Revolutionary War (Bauxar 1978:596), Inoca peoples were subject to pervasive encroachments into their territories beginning in 1783 (Stone and Chaput 1978:607). Seeing little hope under such circumstances, the Kaskaskia in 1803 signed the Treaty at Vincennes and ceded territory for two reservations (Prochaska 2001:158). In the same year that Illinois became a state (1818), the Peoria, already living in Missouri, entered the Treaty of Edwardsville (Prochaska 2001:158). Inoca left Illinois not through death in battle but by signing treaties in the face of overwhelming social and cultural dislocation.

In 1830, the Indian Removal Act became U.S. law, establishing a policy by which the federal government would negotiate treaties with Native peoples so that they would relocate west of the Mississippi. In response, the Kaskaskia entered a treaty again in 1832, leaving Illinois to settle with Peoria already located in Kansas. Not all Native peoples complied with the removal policy. In spring of the same year, Black Hawk and a group of around 1,100 Native people (warriors and their families) resisted removal by crossing the Mississippi River (from present-day Iowa into Illinois). They had been removed earlier but maintained annual pilgrimages to ancestral gravesites (Bauxar 1978:598). This action precipitated violence that escalated into a two-and-one-half-month confrontation between Black Hawk's group and regular military and irregular militia forces (Jung 2007:65–92). Black Hawk's War, as it is known, was marked by massacres of Native people (including women, the young, and the old) carried out by undisciplined militiamen (Jung 2007:7). Native physical resistance to removal in Illinois declined dramatically with the defeat of Black Hawk (Jung 2007:185). Although the confrontation is remembered as "Black Hawk's War," it is more reminiscent of violent ethnic conflict than of a struggle between formal military forces. At present, Black Hawk is appropriated and memorialized as the name of an Illinois state park and as the name and emblem (a disembodied head in profile) of Chicago's National Hockey League team.

In theory, under the Indian Removal Act, Native people had the right to remain and become citizens of the states that now encompassed their ancestral homelands. In practice, the options available to Native nations facing removal were limited. It was clear that the Indians were to go; one way or another removal would be effected. Treaty negotiations were marked by bribery and coercion, and when treaties were not negotiated or signed treaties contested, removal was forced. The period saw most infamously the Cherokee Trail of Tears (1838), more locally to Illinois the Potawatomi Trail of Death (1838), and more anonymously many other forced marches. Often ill-provisioned, poorly organized, and occasionally violently attacked by settlers, these multiple trails of tears resulted in thousands of deaths and initiated a period of grave hardship for many Native nations. Economic, political, social, and spiritual upheavals followed removal. Food production strategies well adapted to local ecologies were not suited to the new, often inhospitable, and unfamiliar environments of relocation. Peoples whose articulation to the spiritual dimension through particular sacred places on particular landscapes faced not only material hardship but religious crises as well. Moreover, their new and latest "permanent" reservations were often located in territory claimed or occupied by other Native peoples (either from time immemorial or by earlier flight or forced removal).

The policy of removal, by the standards of its own era, was problematic. In *Worcester v. Georgia* (1832), the Supreme Court threw into doubt its legality. Moreover, while popular, the policy did not enjoy universal support among whites. The *Worcester* case itself involved a Georgia law designed to restrict the activities of white clergy who were assisting the Cherokee and other Native groups in their resistance to removal (Wilkins 2002:51). White activism was prevalent enough that the Georgia legislature took steps to curtail it. Nonetheless, backed by strong popular support and restrained in only a limited sense by the judiciary, the Jackson and subsequent administrations promoted and executed the removal of thousands of Native people from their ancestral homelands. By today's standards, removal would likely be deemed a genocidal policy and certainly has much in common in ideology, justification, and practice with ethnic cleansing.

The Southeast became largely free of Native populations (with important exceptions of Florida Seminoles, Eastern Cherokees, and Mississippi Choctaws whose ongoing presence resulted from Native resistance). What is now Oklahoma became peopled by and named for Native nations of what is now the "Old South." The process that removed Inoca peoples from their Illinois homelands culminated in 1854 when the Peoria and Kaskaskia formally joined with other surviving peoples of the Illinois confederacy, the Wea and Piankesaw (Peoria Tribe of Indians 2007). Eventually, in 1867, the confederated Peoria relocated to Indian Territory and are federally recognized today as the Peoria Indian Tribe of Oklahoma.

In the mythology of Chief Illiniwek, the story of Starved Rock is the preferred explanation for the absence of Indians from the state. Through this salient story, Chief Illiniwek becomes the leader of a great and noble but vanished people. Located within an Illinois state park identified by the same name, Starved Rock is a 125-foot sandstone butte overlooking the Illinois River. According to popular Illinois lore, sometime in the late 1760s the last members of the Illinois confederacy holed up in a defensive position atop Starved Rock. Their enemies were not Frenchmen or Englishmen, but Potawatomi, another Native people.

A Peoria man had been implicated in the murder of Potawatomi Chief Pontiac, and his loyal followers demanded revenge, or so goes the story. Rather than surrender and without adequate food or water, the last of the Illinois died in battle or of hunger. They died nobly, facing other savages. It turns out that the Indians conquered themselves.

Spindel (2000:58–59) identifies a number of implausible elements of the story of Starved Rock. The rock formation itself is too small to hold large number of warriors, let alone an entire population. As important, it is not a particularly good defensive position; it affords no route of escape. There is more archaeological evidence of European occupation than of a catastrophic battle between Native peoples. The ethnohistoric record indicates large settlements of Inoca peoples further south in Illinois in and after 1770. Additionally, there were sufficient numbers of Peoria and Kaskaskia to warrant removal treaties nearly 150 years later. Not surprisingly, historians have doubted the account for some time. Emily Blasingham, in her 1956 account "The Depopulation of the Illinois Indians," notes that "[s]everal modern historians, with whom we agree, regard these accounts of the extermination of the Illinois as folklore, lacking corroboration from any known historical facts. Such an 'extermination' is dramatic, but in the realm of fancy, rather than fact. In fact, the history of the Illinois continues for several years" (Blasingham 1956:212–213). Callender (1978:678) notes that other works written in 1920 and 1947 describe a paucity of evidence and identify the story as "myth." Bauxar contends that there was a confrontation between Native groups at Starved Rock, but that an untenable position "forced the Peoria to withdraw" (Bauxar 1978:596). A cataclysmic battle at Starved Rock resulting in the deaths of all of the remaining Illinois never took place. Yet on a recent guided tour of the park, the story was repeated when we arrived at the Starved Rock formation.

To her credit, the guide took pains to identify the story as legend. However, its reiteration "as legend has it" was typical mythmaking in the way it referenced certain undeniable realities while omitting others. The territory that is now Illinois was certainly peopled before Europeans arrived. Also certain is that intergroup or interpolity collective violence (as raiding or as warfare) was an important feature of the early colonial period. Moreover, conflicts near or at Starved Rock pepper the ethnohistoric record from 1722 to 1751 (Blasingham 1956:203–207). Left unsaid in telling the myth of Starved Rock is the cause of conflict between Peoria and Potawatomi that led to Pontiac's murder and the subsequent war of revenge. The audience is left to draw its own conclusions, which for some must be that Indians fight Indians because they are Indians. Stories like this reinforce in the mainstream imagination the notion that savage warfare is part of the nature of Native peoples. The myth of Starved Rock is taken as evidence for and serves to reinforce such imaginings. In leaving largely unsaid the cause of the conflict, the story makes an important choice that places it squarely in the category of myth of identification. Although not spoken, the implication is clear. European political control of the territory was necessary to pacify and civilize warlike Indians.

In "Blood of the Leviathan: Western Contact and Warfare in Amazonia" (1990), Brian Ferguson examines a number of problems in the rendition of the history of "tribal warfare." First, while pre-Columbian warfare certainly existed before European arrival, it is knowable in a sense bound by the limits of archaeology. Ferguson points out that descriptions of tribal warfare written by missionaries and earlier colonial officials are highly compromised (1990:238). Both political subjugation and religious conversion are more easily justified when the subject people are "warlike."

Beyond the problems of when and how descriptions of warfare were produced, Ferguson identifies numerous facets of colonization that both remove restraints on and generate incentive for interpersonal and collective violence. Rather than "pacification" of warlike peoples, the impact of European intrusion is better termed "warrification" (Ferguson 1990:239). Ferguson is careful to avoid portraying precolonial territories and societies as free of violence, stressing instead factors that must be considered in the analysis of conflict in the colonial era. Three main forces drive warrification: European direction of warfare, demographic disruption, and the introduction of manufactured tools.

Warrification occurred perhaps most obviously when European powers, in competition to expand colonial holdings, enlisted Native groups as military allies. Infectious diseases of Old World origin disrupted groups demographically, generating social and political instability that, combined with other factors, fostered the conditions for collective and interpersonal violence. Whether fleeing advancing European incursions or the effects of the diseases brought by Europeans, desperate people were forced out of their homelands (collectively or individually) and into the territory of their neighbors (Ferguson 1990:242).

Additionally, articulation of Native economies to global trade introduced new products and tools and generated resource competition within and between Native societies. The Western manufactured tool most directly responsible for increasing warfare, of course, is the firearm. Not only are those in possession of guns less restricted from attacking others, but those without firearms are strongly compelled to acquire them. The introduction of guns profoundly shaped conflict among Native peoples. Beyond tactical changes, balances of power were undermined, competition was exacerbated, and conflict became deadlier (Ferguson 1990:247). Although not as directly violent as firearms, metal tools nonetheless are part of the picture of warrification. While reducing the amount of time required to complete tasks, metal tools also accelerated resource depletion. As people became dependent on manufactured tools and the resources they exploited became scarce, increased competition within societies and between societies occurred (Ferguson 1990:244).

All of the factors identified by Ferguson apply in the upper Midwest (Bauxar 1978; Callender 1978; Stone and Chaput 1978). Increasingly intermeshed in the fur trade, the Haudenosaunee (Iroquois Confederacy of Onondaga, Mohawk, Seneca, Cayuga, Oneida, and eventually Tuscarora) expanded into the territories of its neighbors in pursuit of beaver populations, which were in decline by the 1640s. To maintain their supply of manufactured metal tools (upon which their economies now depended), groups fully committed to the fur trade and needed supplies of pelts that outstripped local animal populations. In the case of the Haudenosaunee, an aboriginal diplomatic strategy that combined alliance formation with the threat of military force was adapted and employed to seize and control productive lands. This expansion had a cascading effect across the continent, as groups in pursuit of resources or fleeing violence encroached on neighboring territories.

Well beyond the traditional Haudenosaunee homelands in upstate New York, violent encounters between Iroquois and Illinois are recorded as early as 1656 (Blasingham 1956:195). In addition to the destabilizing effects of the booming fur trade, Native nations were drawn into alliances with European powers. Native groups sought protection and secured trading arrangements. Europeans desired Native-produced trade goods and European states needed warriors in their struggle for control of the continent. In addition to guns and other manufactured tools, trade with Europeans exposed Native populations to deadly infectious diseases, of Old World origin to which they had little immune response. The peoples of the upper Midwest suffered repeated outbreaks of smallpox and other diseases, and their populations declined significantly as a result during the later seventeenth and eighteenth centuries.

As was the case with many of the Algonkian groups of the upper Midwest, the Inoca formed trade and military ties with the French. Conflict with the

Haudenosaunee (Iroquois) and other British-allied Native polities must, therefore, be understood as partly reflecting geopolitical struggles, not simply as fighting between "traditional enemies." Indeed, Bauxar describes relationships between the Anishinaabé (Ottawa, Ojibwe, Potawatomi) and Inoca before this period as "traditionally good" (1978:600). Although initially motivated by trade with the French, when the Inoca went to war against other indigenous groups, it was often under French guidance. When attacked by other Native groups, it was often because of their French alliance. These arrangements resulted in cooperation with the European power that would lose control of Illinois territory. By the early 1750s, French influence in the upper Midwest was in decline and anti-French movements within Native nations fractured alliances. After 1763, the French would no longer be a significant force in the Midwest. Indeed, it is in a context of shifting geopolitics and accompanying intergroup political uncertainty and instability that the Peoria and Potawatomi entered violent conflict. The time of the mythical fight of the last of the Illini was a warrified one. Pontiac was killed in revenge for his stabbing of a Peoria leader during an argument in 1766. The dispute concerned the military campaign that Pontiac had led against the English after they defeated the French and implemented unfavorable trade and settlement policies. Violence, in escalating reciprocation, would be carried out by groups allied under Pontiac against the Inoca groups as a whole (Bauxar 1978).

The formation of the Inoca alliance and any inter–Native nation warfare must be understood through the lens of warrification. This is not to say that violence and warfare were absent from the upper Midwest before intensification of trade, geopolitical machinations of the French and British, and outright European invasion. However, warrification is left out of the Starved Rock myth, favoring the image of inherently warlike Indian savages attacking one another by virtue of nothing more than their nature. Taking the larger context of violence into account reveals a picture of people and peoples experiencing rapid, profoundly disruptive demographic, political, and economic transformations that placed them in struggles for survival individually with members of their own societies and collectively with other Native polities. The question is why this context is left out of the myth of Starved Rock that is associated with Chief Illiniwek.

As I have stressed, effective myths of identification reference certain past realities while ignoring or denying others. They do this in order to foster the creation and maintenance of satisfying views of the collective self in the present. Here, remembering violence between Native peoples has a certain foundation in history but also references deeply held stereotypes of Indians as potential savages. However, a more nuanced treatment of the context reveals not savagery but rather human responses to difficult circumstances.

That European imperialism created the circumstances for increasing violence undermines both the image of Native savagery and the notion of Europeans and Euro-Americans as agents of civilization and pacification. Moreover, the story masks the less noble reality of Indian removal policy. It is more romantic and more satisfying to imagine Illiniwek Indians fighting to the death atop Starved Rock (before independence) than to confront removal (a U.S. policy). The Trail of Tears, as we Illinoisans prefer to remember it, happened somewhere else. For realization in the form of Chief Illiniwek, the myth of Indian self-conquest is central in affirming the Chief's warlike potential and for distancing white performers and audiences from the role of their cultural and political forefathers in the genocidal dimensions of conquest and colonialism.

The Chief must also be an exotic Other, and the humanization of Native responses to colonization offered by Ferguson diminishes their Otherness. It is not difficult to imagine recourse to violence if facing a world in complete disarray, where survival is at stake. Simply beginning to grasp this helps us see Native people less as Others and more as human beings. Social and cultural distance is deemphasized and empathy and sympathy become possible. However, the formation of identity that is central to Chief Illiniwek's performance requires a figure that is clearly a distant, racialized Other.

The myth of Starved Rock, known widely to University of Illinois students and cited by Chief supporters, avoids these realities and provides a pure, vanished, and noble savage. According to a dedicated Chief supporter interviewed by Spindel, the Illini confederacy is of "a bygone era that very few white people ever saw. It internally destroyed itself through several different mechanisms" (Spindel 2000:21). It is a concise articulation of both the vanishing American myth and the myth of Indian self-conquest. The student continues, arguing that because their culture had changed by the time of white settlement, the Illini are unknown. Another student asserts: "There is no one today who can claim that they are descendents of the Illini. They were wiped out in conflicts with other tribes. There are no direct descendents of the Illini remaining" (Spindel 2000:23). In its "Brief History of the Chief" (2004), the Chief Illiniwek Educational Foundation contends, "No one of Illiniwek lineage is known to exist today." Indian self-conquest is affirmed and the existence of the contemporary Peoria in Oklahoma is denied.

Reiteration of the myth of Starved Rock and its connection to Chief Illiniwek extends beyond campus. In a letter to the *Chicago Tribune* in support of retaining Chief Illiniwek, Jeffrey Duncan claims that the Illini "no longer exist because of the campaign against them by the Great Lakes tribes in 1769. The last of the Illini were exterminated at what is now called Starved Rock by the Ottawa, Potawatomi, Kickapoo, Chippewa, Fox, Sac and others" (Duncan 1998). Duncan continues, articulating the myth of Indian self-conquest in a way that not only denies the role of European and Euro-American colonialism but implies contemporary Native American culpability. "I have heard Native Americans speak passionately of the disgrace they feel because of how the Illini are portrayed. I find it ironic that they are the descendants of tribes that eliminated the Illini" (Duncan 1998).

Another editorialist in support of the Chief, although not mentioning Starved Rock specifically, does draw on the myth of Indian self-conquest. "Part of that history is the fact that the Illini were driven into what was to become Illinois and then almost entirely exterminated by other Indians, chiefly the Iroquois" (Wise 2003). Iroquois, this time, are the culprits, rather than Potawatomi. No less than respected national columnist George Will reiterates the myth of Indian self-conquest, asserting that the "Illini confederation of about a half-dozen tribes . . . were virtually annihilated in the 1760s by rival tribes" (Will 2006). In this vein, so argues the Chief Illiniwek Educational Foundation, "When Lewis and Clark made way through the Illinois territory, they missed the peak of Native life, a life disintegrated and dissected by Iroquois imperialism and bloody intertribal warfare" (2004). The "imperialism" in the foundation's mythmaking is of Native origin. There is no mention of the role of intensified trade with Europe and alliance with European powers in "Iroquois imperialism." Moreover, "the peak of Native life" is evocative of Deloria's (1998:135) description of object authenticity that presupposes a past of pure culture. (To its credit, the Chief Illiniwek Educational Foundation website did include a link to the official website of the Peoria Tribe of Indians of Oklahoma.)

Either through ignorance or by application of a rigid, essentialized notion of authenticity, the continuity of Native people of Illinois is denied. Moreover, Indians themselves are portrayed as the agents of death of indigenous culture. None of the above arguments even mentions the role of French and British imperialism in the warrification of North America. It is superb construction of a myth of identification, denying culpability of the collective self and emphasizing the exoticness of the Other, off of whom self is reflected. The myth justifies embodiment of Chief Illiniwek, asserting his authenticity by virtue of his unknowability.

The story of Starved Rock is unique to Illinois, but the vanishing Indian is common mainstream mythology. The notion that indigenous people do not exist (because they do not conform with the essentialized notions of the dominating population) or will soon disappear is common across the Americas. The ideology surrounding the appropriation of Tekun Umam as a symbol of the Guatemalan state also presupposes the disappearance of the Maya. Additionally, in both cases the appropriate response to the presentation of the Indian hero is nostalgia. As I explored earlier, Renato Rosaldo (1989) articulates the concept of "imperialist nostalgia" to describe how colonial officials, missionaries, and anthropologists have tended to remember a past that they helped destroy or profoundly change. There is ambivalence inherent in such nostalagia. We yearn for a romanticized, purer past, but we also need to justify the present that supplanted it. Chief Illiniwek is certainly experienced with nostalgia, particularly for alumni who recall college life along with the imagined Illini past. The myths of Starved Rock and of the vanishing American enhance remembering, making imperialist nostalgia into guiltless nostalgia. With these myths available we need not concern ourselves with the role of our state and our ancestors in the destruction of a way of life. Rather the disappearance of indigenous culture is a result of an inevitable process or fighting among Native peoples. During the period when overt contestation of these constructions was absent, enjoying the performance of Chief Illiniwek was like eating one's cake and having it too.

In the end the Chief is "us" of the mainstream United States. He represents conflicted ideas about self, contradictory perceptions of the nation-state, and paradoxical notions of human nature. Framing Chief Illiniwek as a figure of myth and as an object of secular ritual explains his formative impact on many University of Illinois students. Social solidarity and attachment to community and institution are effectively enacted in the ritual of dancing at halftime. In terms of myth, Chief Illiniwek manifests imperialist nostalgia, references a story of conquest that minimizes white culpability in the ethnic cleansing of Illinois, and reinforces the vanishing Indian ideology and its partner, manifest destiny. However, myth and ritual do not fully explain the profound dedication of some Chief supporters. Certainly the myths are compelling stories of a postcolonial society, but why must they be told through the Chief? On the other hand, what is it about the performance that motivated a sustained campaign to retire the Chief? These questions I explore in the next chapter.

NOTE

1. Barbara Myerhoff employs the concept in her ethnography *Number Our Days* (1978). Her application of bricolage to frame the belief of practices of a community of elderly Jewish Californians moves it from consideration of the primitive Other to the modern self.

Thirteen

Chief Illiniwek Contested

The Peoria tribe of Indians of Oklahoma request the University of Illinois to cease the use of Chief Illiniwek as a mascot.

Whereas, the Peoria Tribe of Indians of Oklahoma is a federally recognized tribe of Indians;

Whereas, the Business Committee of the Peoria Tribe of Indians of Oklahoma is authorized to enact resolutions and act on behalf of the Peoria tribe;

Whereas, the Peoria Tribe of Indians are descendants of the Kaskaskia, Peoria, Piankeshaw and Wea Tribes, a group of tribes known as Illiniwek, or Illini or Illinois nations, whose members were removed from their homes and forced to move first to Missouri, then to Kansas and finally to the northeastern part of the Indian Territory now Oklahoma;

And whereas, the image portrayed by Chief Illiniwek does not accurately represent or honor the heritage of the Peoria Tribe of Indians of Oklahoma and it is a degrading racial stereotype that reflects negatively on all American Indian people;

Now, therefore, be it resolved that the Peoria Tribe of Indians does not endorse nor sanction the characterization of Chief Illiniwek as a mascot for the University of Illinois, and be it finally resolved the Peoria Tribe of Indians of Oklahoma request the leadership Board of Trustees of the

> University of Illinois to recognize the demeaning nature of the characterization of Chief Illiniwek and cease the use of this mascot.
>
> —OFFICIAL POSITION ADOPTED BY THE PEORIA TRIBE OF INDIANS, APRIL 2001

The process leading to the production of this remarkable document was a long one, involving local indigenous and nonindigenous activism and national intertribal and interethnic cooperation.[1] It was not a direct path but in many ways exemplifies indigenous movements of the early twenty-first century. Moreover, that a tribal government would feel compelled to issue a formal statement about a dancing mythical Indian indicates something of how Chief supporters reacted to Native activism.

As was the case with the appropriation of Tekun Umam in Guatemala, the use of symbolic Indians in the United States does not go unnoticed to living indigenous people. By the late 1980s, Native activists were publicly criticizing Chief Illiniwek. During a period when the university administration seemed incapable of giving indigenous criticism serious consideration, opposition to the Chief increased and became well organized. Eventually a movement emerged to retire Chief Illiniwek in performance and image. Just as official response to criticism of the Chief was unsatisfactory to indigenous activists, so was retirement unacceptable to Chief supporters. Larger segments of the institution and its home community were drawn into the conflict on both sides. The campaign to retire the Chief became a national effort, involving considerable intertribal and interethnic cooperation.

In terms of image self-representation, Native people confront a deeply rooted tradition of appropriation. In *Playing Indian* (1998), Deloria notes two contradictions that repeatedly emerge in the history of white appropriation of Indianness. First, "authentic" identities become necessary to deal with societal changes that expose gaps between the ideal and the real. The consolidation of power and land in the early republic threatened the ideal of a nation of equal yeoman farmers (1998:69). Early industrialization undermined the concept of autonomous, skilled craft production (1998:60). In the late 1940s and 1950s, democratic ideals that justified great expense in blood and treasure conflicted with ongoing realities of white supremacy and discrimination (1998:134). Other contradictions are more permanent and existential. Playing imaginary Indians inevitably confronts actual indigenous people. Real, complex living individuals and nations never comply perfectly with the preconceptions that whites carry (and embrace) (1998:70). Moreover, the civil rights movements of the 1960s initiated sustained overt indigenous political activism. By the late 1980s many indigenous activists had been engaged in lengthy and serious consideration of the impact of representations of Indianness by Others. Not only would Chief Illiniwek and his supporters encounter actual living indigenous people, but they would confront politically active ones.

In 1989 Charlene Teters (Spokane), a Native graduate student of art at the University of Illinois, took her children to see an intercollegiate basketball game. When Chief Illiniwek made his halftime appearance, Teters and her children were shocked and humiliated. Although U of I colleagues advised her not to confront the university about the Chief, Teters was compelled as a mother to raise her concerns. Other Native students had begun to confront the Chief as stereotyped misrepresentation, but it was the public discourse by a Native mother that brought the issue to the public consciousness. However, many non-Native students, Champaign community members, and university officials, including members of the board of trustees, were shocked and astounded that anyone could find anything wrong with the Chief.

Jay Rosenstein's film *In Whose Honor* (1997) features Teters predominantly. Its broadcast on public television further publicized the issue, generating support and putting Chief fans on the defensive. Maintaining that the Chief was authentic and that his performance respected and honored Native Americans, the university elected to dismiss growing complaints of racism and misrepresentation. As the institution dug in its heels, opposition to the Chief stiffened and coalesced around the goal to retire him, as had been the fate of Stanford's Indian and Syracuse's Saltine Warrior. Various intertribal organizations adopted positions in favor of retiring the Chief (as did many non-Native groups, including the United Methodist Church and the American Anthropological Association). Although initially offering tacit support of the Chief, the Peoria of Oklahoma adopted the official position listed above. The university, backed by strong support from students, alumni, and many Illinoisans who never attended college at the Champaign-Urbana campus, continued to embrace the Chief as the institution's official symbol. The beginning of the end came when the National Collegiate Athletic Association (NCAA), responding to pressure from an array of bodies, including some of its member colleges and universities, listed Chief Illiniwek among the mascots it deemed "hostile and abusive" (although the name Fighting Illini would be allowed). Under the policy, Indian mascots could remain if the university in question secured approval from the respective Native government. Outside of consent similar to that negotiated by Florida State University, continuance of symbolic Indians meant forfeiting the right to host NCAA post-season contests. Likely because of its earlier stance and response to Native activism, the University of Illinois was unable to obtain permission to continue the Chief. Not long after it had to surrender rights to host the post-season tennis playoffs, the university ended Chief Illiniwek's tenure as official symbol in spring 2007.

The campaign to retire the Chief reflects a more general indigenous social activism. At root, being marginal in the creation of self-image marks and perpetuates lack of political power. Whether imagined as savage, primitive, noble but vanished, or any such combination, there is little room for actual, fully human individuals and nations to live and thrive. Savage Indians must be conquered and pacified, primitive Indians modernized and assimilated, and vanished or vanishing Indians pitied. In this way, meaningful participation in the creation of Indianness (self-representation of image) is tied directly to power (self-representation in politics). Indigenous activists understand this intimately. Degrading images foment and justify attitudes and policies that lead to degradation. Even when the image seems to be positive and to honor, the fact that its construction occurs with little or no Native input is a clear sign of political weakness and marginality. By personal and shared communal experience Native people understand well that democracy in the United States has a history of imposing heavy burdens on or simply neglecting those with little political voice. Accordingly, combating stereotypes, influencing the construction of Indianness, or engaging in image creation outside of direct white influence is more about addressing social ills than it is about "political correctness."[2]

The role of the Peoria and other tribal governments in the campaign to retire Chief Illiniwek reflects self-representation in another sense. When the Lakota tribal government requested that Chief Illiniwek's regalia be returned, the discourse began to sound like that between the Greek and British governments in their dispute over antiquities held in England. The position taken by the Peoria, similarly, is an official request regarding the representation of a people, made by one governing body to another. These acts are more like those of a polity than of an ethnic interest group. The campaign, therefore, is expression of identity politics, but also of Native self-government. It seeks control over the representation of Native people in image through the collective self-representation of Native sovereignty. However individual Native opinion may vary on the mascot issue, there is strong consensus supporting Native nation sovereignty.

STRENGTHENED IDENTIFICATION WITH THE CONTESTED CHIEF

Earlier, I argued that some of the effects common in human ritual help generate uncanny dedication to the Chief. Here, I contend that once said dedication is acquired, it becomes necessary to defend it. Moreover, a common effect of human conflict—increasing identification among insiders and increasing definition of outsiders—is clear in the present case. The secular ritual of the Chief initiates in-group membership, and defending the Chief reinforces it. In the process, true believers are separated from the rest.

The myth of the vanishing American is most directly challenged by the persistence of indigenous people and their cultural distinctiveness. As such, actual corporeal Native people are a source of cognitive dissonance for those who embrace Chief Illiniwek. The resulting conflict has internal and external dimensions, both involving fundamental difficulties of white identity. That which is taken for granted, uncontested, and unspoken (colonial history and contemporary privilege) is brought to the surface and subjected to debate. In referencing the past through the Chief it becomes necessary to justify conquest and colonialism overtly. For nonindigenous Illinoisans, the history of Native landscapes that came to form the state goes largely unspoken and unexamined. Elementary and secondary education textbooks only briefly cover Native history (and then almost always in a general sense with a tendency to focus on the Plains). Embracing the Chief means confronting history or constructing myth. In the process, myths that before were uncontested are now subjected to scrutiny. What is made more public—a particular Illinois history and a general U.S. history of removal policy—is unpleasant and seems uncomfortably like ethnic cleansing. It contradicts sharply with popular conceptions of the "American character." The presence of Native people erodes the ability of whites to locate Indians in the past. Native presence also undermines folk history that occasionally mourns genocide and ethnocide but frames them as problems of mistreatment that are temporally remote from present and socially distant from self.

The unwitting discovery of contemporary Native Americans with an unexpected political voice poses a challenge of internal dissonance for those who have experienced and embraced the Chief. If it stopped with passing mention of removal, Chief loyalists might be able to reinternalize the problem. For many nonindigenous Americans, the uncomfortable reality of discrimination against Native Americans persists, but things are better now, and there is little one person can do. Vocal, sophisticated indigenous activism, however, makes forgetting the issue impossible. Starting in the late 1980s, not only must the myth be asserted, it also must be defended regularly. For dedicated Chief supporters, contestation reinforces the need for the Chief. The myths—that warlike peoples destroyed each other and the disappearance of Native nations and their cultures was inevitable—are much preferable to the more complex history. In effect, performance of the Chief, in the context of rigorous and sustained criticism, is reassertion of the myths.

The need to defend the Chief has roots also in the nature of institutions of higher education. Just as the University of Illinois student community is a collection of individuals marked by impermanence, so the Chief as its symbol is less transcendent than he at first seems. In the context of vigorous social conflict, the Chief becomes more obviously a patchwork. Before the movement to retire the Chief, he was a powerful symbol of Illinois history, a source for unique Illinois identity. However, rather than accurate representation, critics revealed the Chief as a mixture of forms and notions largely of nonindigenous and non-Inoca origin. In the context of these realities, we might expect students to abandon their expectation that the university be a source of community or at least to question the Chief as a symbol of meaningful identification with community. After all, a university is an educational institution more than a community with a connection to deep, authentic past. Some, it is clear, arrive at just such a conclusion. They study, earn a degree, and move on. For others, however, the untidy nature of the bricolage that is the Chief requires defense rather than abandonment. The charge that a meaningful and satisfying symbol is essentially "made up" is met with impassioned counter-protest. Chief loyalists are indeed strongly attached to their bricolage and to the institution it represents. The unraveling of the symbols requires its protection and reweaving. The impermanence of college community requires stronger attachment and identification of membership.

"I'm beginning not to like Indians."

So commented former "Saltine Warrior" Andy Burns in response to accusations that the imaginary Indian he portrayed at Syracuse University was racist (Fisher 2001:37). Before affirming his dislike of Native Americans, Burns contended: "I treat the Saltine Warrior as an honor. It's not racism at all." Syracuse nonetheless eliminated the Saltine Warrior as a symbol of the university in 1978 (Fisher 2001:38). The (perhaps unintentional) candor of Burns occurs rarely, but the process by which he changed from honoring to disliking is present at the University of Illinois.

The reaction to the movement to retire the Chief from the beginning has, at times, been less than civil (Rosenstein 2001:243). Charlene Teters was the target of racist epithets, spitting, and other indignities (Spindel 2000:142). Her family and other families were also subject to threats and intimidation. Thirteen-year-old Wayne Crue, an adopted Shoshone-Bannock living in Champaign, endured racial epithets and taunting about his long, braided hair after publicly criticizing Chief Illiniwek. The stress causing academic and health problems, Crue and his adopted parents decided to remove him from Champaign and its school system to the Leech Lake Reservation in Minnesota (Kaiser and McSherry Breslin 2001). King and Springwood (2001a:63) report a sign predominantly displayed by a group of football revelers in the Memorial Stadium parking area that proclaimed, "Save the Chief, Kill the Indians." As recently as 2007 a student active in the retire-the-Chief movement was the target of a Web posting that suggested that she be subjected to physical violence. A student and supporter of Chief Illiniwek had something different than honor to offer to an indigenous classmate: "I say we throw a tomohawk [*sic*] into her face" (Associated Press 2007). Behavior of this type contradicted the university's position that Chief Illiniwek did not foster a "hostile and abusive" environment as argued by the NCAA, and made it increasingly unlikely that the Chief would be saved.

A hotly contested issue like Chief Illiniwek forms clear in-group and out-group identities. As identification strengthens, the conflict can become the lens for all issues. Over time, the Illiniwek controversy has created a sense of the world as divided into two kinds of people: Chief supporters and Chief critics. One t-shirt states of Chief Illiniwek adoration, "It's a U of I thing." Indeed, it is increasingly difficult to understand the Chief in a positive way from anywhere but a dedicated supporter's perspective. Moreover, the slogan further reinforces the Chief as essential to being an Illini. It implies that being part of the U of I is supporting the Chief. "It's a U of I thing" also reveals issues of race and power. Its construction is commonly used in expressions of minority identity. "It's a Black thing" says that the dominating society is unable and unwilling to understand the African American perspective. One must live in it to understand it. Accordingly, the primarily white college students who don the t-shirt imply that they are an oppressed minority. Taking care to distinguish perception from social reality, the slogan is a commentary on the changing (and for some threatening) nature of race relations. Power and privilege that in the past went unchallenged are now openly discussed and criticized. People previously marginalized now demand changes in the behavior of mainstream insiders.

The pressure to change puts at stake two elements of primary U.S. identity: race and institution. In the conflict over Chief Illiniwek, non-whites (and white allies) pressure whites to change how they represent non-whites. The University of Illinois is to lose a unique symbol and associated rituals. For some it is too much; the world must seem turned upside down. Both the positive value of the Chief and the privilege to represent ethnic Others are under attack. Both are vigorously reasserted in response, although not explicitly identified in the rhetoric. Chief supporters do not frame their activism as the protection of white privilege to define the culture and identity of ethnic Others. Nor do they speak of identification with the university out of a need for community through conformity in an anonymous large-scale society. Here, as is the case in general, the culture of identity is tacit, difficult for the insider to express in everyday language.

Compelling ritual enactment of identity combined with identification heightened in social conflict makes Chief Illiniwek a primary symbol of identity for some. To dedicated Chief loyalists (such as the students who have worked to resurrect him) the absence of the Chief would require a significant reorientation of identity. Clifford Geertz argues, changing and adjusting cognitive models threaten our ability to understand and bring order to our world (1973:162–169). Our cultures provide us cognitive maps to understand ourselves and our experiences. Without the culture, human life becomes "a mere chaos of pointless acts" (Geertz 1973:46). In this case, the Chief is the central symbol in a cluster of signs, beliefs, artifacts, and behaviors that guide and express identification with the university and reinforce an unequal social order. Given the human need for cognitive structure, if one is unable to imagine a satisfying and meaningful result of change—a workable substitute set of beliefs, acts, and objects in the future—then change represents chaos. Confronting cognitive chaos of identity, people become desperate and tend to engage in a variety of normative and non-normative behaviors. They may work to revitalize belief and structures subject to change. Or they may engage in self-destruction, abandon community and culture, or lash out. In the present case, some supporters work to rescue the symbol, others act out against those who oppose Chief Illiniwek.

There is profound irony in the effort to retire and the counter-effort to preserve the Chief. In essence, one group demands that another group change. This sort of cross-ethnic encounter, whereby the way that one group attempts to influence the way another group identifies itself, is reminiscent of colonialism. Whether it be conversion of landholding from extended kin group to individual, formal religious conversion, or boarding school education aimed at erasing Native languages, indigenous groups of the United States have suffered numerous attempts by colonizing Others to fundamentally change them. In the case of Chief Illiniwek, of course, the relative political power of the groups is inverted; the marginalized demand change in the culture of a mainstream institution. This inversion, and the fact that anti-mascot campaigns have been occasionally effective, drives some mascot supporters to attach themselves more fiercely to their imagined Indian. Unlike colonialism, however, mascot opponents demand change in only a specific practice, not an entire way of life. Inequality in power is challenged but not fundamentally changed.

Accordingly, the conflict brings into high relief ethnic privilege. White Illinois high school graduates who attend other colleges need not regularly defend the privilege that comes vis-à-vis their whiteness (and only rarely in relation to indigenous classmates). Chief supporters, however, must deal with and often choose to defend white privilege. They must also contend with the common belief (or even fear) that such privilege is waning. A clear option in defending a social position of privilege is to assert its power. In effect, claiming that the Chief honors Native Americans asserts the privilege to decide what image of another people is honorable. Continuing to argue that such a portrayal is honoring, even when many of the honored call it offensive, is a reiteration of social power. Honor becomes a sort of gift that the recipient does not want and yet cannot refuse. Needless to say, such gifts are not made among people of equal social standing. Chief Illiniwek's reiteration affirms power; his retirement affirms the loss of power. The change is not so much the actual erosion of white privilege but clear evidence that it is now subject to contestation. For those experiencing the conflict from the inside, the distinctions of social change are difficult. Having privilege contested is as threatening as losing it; ethnic equality is as menacing as inversion of power.

The dispute is uncomfortable for everyone. Prochaska (2001) contends that many University of Illinois faculty would rather the Chief just go away. It is not only students and the working class who benefit from the colonial past. Ultimately, academics are insiders in a mainstream institution founded by a settler society. The university figuratively and literally rests on what was Native territory. While referencing the past through the Chief necessitates justification of conquest for some students, alumni, politicians, and so forth, for scholars, people who by definition are charged with challenging and unpacking myths, the presence of the Chief carries an added dimension of difficulty. Not only does he (and particularly the protest against him) unmask privilege of colonial origin, but the defense mechanism deployed by Chief supporters is not as available to faculty. A cursory reading of history exposes the myths of self-conquest and the vanishing American as fanciful and self-serving. A passing knowledge of the present social, economic, and health ills suffered disproportionately by Native Americans only makes supporting the Chief more difficult for academics. Moreover, the weight of opinion in favor of the Chief pits professors against many of their students and often places them at odds with their employer. It should come as no surprise that most would rather the Chief just go away.

DIVERGENT NOTIONS OF HONOR, LEADERSHIP, AND PERSONHOOD

Nearly a year after I saw Chief Illiniwek dance at the University of Illinois, I am sitting again in bleachers. This time it is in Tulsa and the arena of performance is indoors. I am here for the annual Powwow of Champions, organized by the Intertribal Indian Club of Tulsa. Grand entry on Friday, the first night of the powwow, elicits a response that will recur regularly throughout the weekend. Six men of a Native color guard lead the entry parade bearing flags of the United States, a national veterans' group, and a Native veterans' group. It strikes me that their regalia is quite similar to Chief Illiniwek's outfit. Buckskin pants, like the Chief's, are tasseled. Five of the six wear chest pieces that are nearly identical to that worn by the Chief. Perhaps most evocative of the Chief, all wear feather bonnets. The formal placement of the flags at the edge of the arena is a moment of solemnity and power. In comparison, the intertribal dancing that follows is relaxed and convivial. Interestingly enough, the war veterans who paraded and retired the flags have taken off their headdresses for the intertribal dance. The war bonnet is apparently inappropriate for intertribal dancing. Moreover, these Native veterans are part of a parade that features a wide variety of Native dancers. In contrast, Chief Illiniwek dances in his war bonnet and is not structured by a diverse set of performances of Native dance.

This impression recurs during the various parts of the program that feature Fancy dancing. I recall (as I often do when attending powwow) the claim that Chief Illiniwek performs Fancy Dance. At the Powwow of Champions, the divergence between powwow Fancy dancing and Chief Illiniwek is particularly clear. The differences in music and step that I mentioned earlier are reiterated. However, the use of regalia similar to that of Chief Illiniwek highlights an issue of material culture. It occurs to me that while the form does allow a degree of expressive freedom—it is here that an emcee explains that Fancy dancers can do anything as long as it's on the beat—the conventions of dress restrict one from using the regalia of a color guard. To people who regularly attend powwows, the Chief's performance might be akin to seeing a decorated combat veteran perform a theatrical dance while in formal uniform—medals, insignia, and all.

Prochaska contends that those contesting the Chief in effect "talk past one another" (2001:170). The miscommunication implied by this assessment is rooted in differing cultural assumptions, some of them rather tacit, about the related areas of leadership, honor, and personhood. In total, divergence in these areas results in contradictory conceptual frameworks about what constitutes an appropriate portrayal of a Native person in dance.

The ceremony and dance described above manifest a conception of leadership that stresses performance of service to community as the means to formal political title. Chief Illiniwek, with his folded-arm salute, constructs a notion of leadership that stresses obedience to a position of authority. This second notion fits well with the construction of leadership and hierarchy in U.S. football, but not well with the common Native American emphasis on consensus achieved through discourse within councils of leaders. The assertion embodied by Chief Illiniwek that there would be one Inoca leader and that followers would be obliged to salute him in subservient unison is not well attested in the ethnographic or ethnohistoric record. The Chief, therefore, enacts an idea of political power that diverges from Native American political practice in the present and the past. To supporters, however, the performance

13.1. Regalia in Dance. Above, *Chief Illiniwek performs at University of Illinois (2006).* Below, *members of Native veterans' group participate in intertribal dancing at the IICOT Powwow of Champions (2007). The dancers below have retired the feather bonnets that they wore as flag bearers earlier. (Photographs by author.)*

enacts a key scenario that scripts ideal-type authority and loyalty. That is, it provides a way to think about authority and loyalty and a guide to construct them in multiple domains on and beyond campus.

In addition to the differing notions of leadership, there are divergent ideas about appropriate dress for Native leaders. Just as his outfit does not reflect the dress of the people Chief Illiniwek purports to represent, its mere presence in dance is problematic. The object authenticity that I explored earlier is the source of this particular difficulty. Its Lakota origin makes the outfit authentic to Chief supporters. However, the use of such regalia by actual Plains Native people diverges from Chief Illiniwek's performance. As I described above, the feather bonnet in particular is meant for someone who, by virtue of military service, has attained a position of prestige and leadership. While it is appropriate for the solemnity of bearing flags and remembering veterans, it is not appropriate for representational dance, whether casual or competitive. To the Native viewer (or to anyone who has regularly attended powwows), Chief Illiniwek's dance, complete with its leaping splits, manifests a profound misunderstanding of context. Chief supporters, on the other hand, find the dance authentic because they are guided by a conception of authenticity that stresses objects divorced from context.

The deep rumbling response of "CHIEF" to Illiniwek's cross-armed salute also reveals conflicting notions of honor. As I explored in my treatment of powwow, honor is the conferment of positive social esteem (or prestige) on some person or group by social fellows. Powwow, as I described, embeds honoring of individuals for service to community in a complex cycle of reciprocity enacted in and beyond the dance arena. The community, tribe, or intertribal audience honors the individual through songs and gifts. The notions of service and what constitutes service are reinforced in what is honored and in the discourse about the honoree. In turn, the honoree distributes gifts to members of the audience; the one singled out for honor singles out ones who have assisted in the service that is recognized. That there is no such reciprocity implied in the exchange of salute and response in the Chief Illiniwek ritual (nor context for Indians to honor whites) is only part of how honoring diverges. Powwow honorees receive the honor offered with humility, someone else speaking to their deeds. Because the Chief intentionally constructs pride as he constructs honor, humility is absent from the posture or step of the dance. The erect position, jutting chin, high-folded arms, and stern facial expression do little to enact humility. Accordingly, to someone who has experienced or observed Native honoring, the Chief's behavior is dramatically non-normative. On the other hand, to Chief supporters the performance is a good, although idealized, model of pride in self and institution, another key scenario that scripts actual social behavior for mainstream students and alumni.

Talking past one another in the conflict over the Chief is rooted also in divergent notions of personhood. This is most clearly manifested in the problematic claim that the Chief's performance is Fancy Dance. The dilemma goes beyond how Chief Illiniwek diverges from Fancy Dance in step, music, and dress. The real difficulty lies in context. As I stressed in Part Three, powwow constructs a notion of personhood marked by multiplicity. In dance and in a variety of positions attached to dance, powwow offers Native individuals a wide array of expressive choice. Within the style of Fancy Dance, individuals choose and construct regalia that follows a general pattern but allows individuality in colors and insignia. Moreover, Fancy dancing is part of a larger semantic domain of powwow dance. It has both male and female forms. Fancy Dance's modern athletic features are set against more staid Traditional and Straight dancing. Its allusion to warfare is set against dances that stress healing and procreation. The modern, athletic, male warrior is but one expression of Native identity in dance at a powwow, and Fancy dancing makes no claim to be the only way one can be a Native person. Where powwow manifests multiplicity of identity, Chief Illiniwek emphasizes singularity. He is the only Indian present, and consistent with the context of football, he is a masculine warrior. In effect, only one Indian is needed, because his purpose is to define Other against which self is reflected and constructed. This singularity, combined with the rhetoric of authenticity and the mythology of vanished culture, narrowly defines Indianness.

Moreover, the mainstream notion of self as largely unified and singular exacerbates the misunderstanding. The unmarked nature of white identity shapes how those who inhabit it think about identity in general. It is easy to imagine human identity as singular when the "regular" way of being is one's own. Ethnic Others from this perspective become facilely sorted as authentically different or inauthentic by virtue of perceived assimilation. Native people, to the contrary, whether consciously or not, must live within a multiplicity of identity. As is the case for ethnic minorities, the culture and social organization of the majority Other must be occasionally accommodated. As personhood is a tacit dimension of culture, understanding how it might shape the perception of a cultural Other is illusive. Social scientists who have investigated identity have failed to make clear how the assertion of singular Indianness is particularly irksome to people whose conceptions of personhood often stress individual autonomy and multiple ways of being human. For Chief critics, not only does a powerful ethnic Other attempt to define Indian, but the image of Indianness asserted is one-dimensional.

In addition to divergence in assumptions about personhood, difference in social position relative to stereotyped representations makes common ground difficult to attain. The ways that the Chief is constructed, given the larger context of appropriation of Native culture, do seem rather mild. Chief supporters stress that Illiniwek—unlike, for example, Chief Wahoo of the Cleveland major league baseball team—does not belittle or ridicule Native Americans.

Nor does the Chief depict Indians as overtly savage or bloodthirsty. As far as imaginary Indians go, the Chief seems among the least offensive. However, performance of the Chief does fully indulge in noble Plains-inspired Indian stereotype. Critics point out various inaccuracies; supporters respond, asserting the respectful character of the Chief. Given the obvious influence of cinema on the Chief—from regalia, to posture, to music—it is useful to consider the Chief accordingly. No doubt Chief Illiniwek is not evocative of the kind of savage killer promulgated by John Ford's racist (yet lauded) 1956 film *The Searchers* (or any number of pictures of the era). Nor does he seem influenced by the hapless victims of white expansion found in later films.

He is, however, an articulation of a romanticized noble Indian of white creation. He is noble in at least two senses. He embodies the nobility of separation as the manifestation of an authentic, pure Indian uncontaminated by whiteness. Additionally, he represents nobility of power as he references notions of Indian war leaders as expressions of unrestricted freedom—of pure autonomy. Because the Chief as a symbol references idealized notions of Indianness that are, in the minds of the audience, positive, the performance as a whole is cast as respectful. Given the power of ritual in moments of *communitas* to convince participants of the fundamental, universal truth of its message, Chief supporters are bewildered when those not similarly compelled by the performance label it "racist." When considering the stereotypes available for the bricolage of the Chief, dancers and audiences have selected some of the least negative material.

Convincing Chief supporters, however, that what they view as positive gifts of honor to Native Americans are little more than stereotypes is an uphill battle. Persuading them that positive stereotypes are confining and harmful is exceedingly difficult. That said, stereotypes of nobility are incompatible with social reality. They poorly frame any human society or individual. Human lives, histories, and community are more complex than suggested by the pure and noble Chief. In the context of mythical death of the Chief and his followers at Starved Rock, performance implies that only dead Indians are authentic Indians. Given the ambiguity of authenticity—with its essentialized notion of culture and its ignorance of change—these positive stereotypes provide little material for the construction of meaningful identities. That positive stereotypes are embedded in a set of ideologies that are confining and demeaning to actual, complex, living Native American individuals and communities is difficult for Chief supporters to grasp. They, after all, experience American society from a position of unmarked ethnic identity.

Whiteness, while fraught with its own ambiguities and contradictions, is not subject to the regular contestation endured by indigenous identities. Whites need not ponder the negotiation of modernity the way "Watt Scraper" does when he concludes that traveling the river of life in both a speedboat and a canoe has one going in circles (Nabokov 1999:462–464). Nor need whites confront the issue of shifting between diverse communities and cultures as poet Linda Hogan does when she contemplates amphibians. Indeed, the notion that someone could be inauthentic in his whiteness is, to say the least, odd. Whiteness is either, by virtue of its attachment to modernity, inherently inauthentic or, by virtue of its domination of the mainstream, simply "normal." The problem, of course, is that the very source of difference between white and indigenous is the tacit nature of the predominant identity. Being white is being "regular," "nothing," or "just plain American"—the null setting. That positive stereotypes are confining is difficult to comprehend for people not similarly confined. Given the challenges of identity formation in adolescence and adolescent lack of experience, it may be a tall order for students to understand how society and identity are experienced differently from the position of indigenous (or minority) status. On the other hand, considering the prestige attached to the title and the implication of experience and wisdom associated with appointment, trustees of a major research university ought to have been aware of such issues.

In the end, the resistance to change (or even to take criticism seriously) of the Chief was confirmation to Native activists of the need to retire him. It is stark evidence that portrayals of Native culture by white Others continue to almost certainly involve the deployment of highly stereotyped notions of Indianness, whether savage or noble. As I argued above, the Chief's performance is, after all, primarily about white identity, society, and folk history. It is hard to imagine that a white audience (at its present level of awareness) would find satisfying a complex, ethnographically accurate depiction of life among settled village horticulturalists or of the multifaceted nature of contemporary indigenous identities. The whole point of the Chief is to present an Indian constructed by whites to serve as an Other for the reflection of whiteness.

Although the campaign to retire Chief Illiniwek is evidence of increasing Native political voice and power, it is an incomplete victory for indigenous self-representation. Through Students for Chief Illiniwek (SFCI), the imaginary Indian is dancing again, albeit unofficially. SFCI reports that the November 2008 performance was attended by "over 10,000 excited members of the Illini nation" (Students for Chief Illiniwek n.d.). SFCI mounted a second Last Dance in October 2009 (Young 2009) and a third in October 2010 (Goldenstein 2010). All signs point to future Last Dance events.

As such, the notion that all Native people are Plains Indians will be enacted through a compelling secular ritual in front of receptive audiences. The folklore of Starved Rock will be circulated, and the associated myths of the vanishing American and of Indian self-conquest, reinforced. Moreover, it is clear that for some, the effort to retire the Chief only made the dancing Indian more compelling and turned latent ethnocentrism into overt bigotry. Although students will no longer experience the secular ritual of Chief Illiniwek by simply attending certain athletic events, he will occasionally be present. The initiated will have the opportunity to intensify identity through a calendric ritual. The uninitiated can convert vague anxiety about waning white privilege to represent cultural Others into focused animosity toward indigenous activists who work at self-representation. These performances confirm the dedication to the Chief and, in turn, the power of representational dance to instill and perpetuate compelling notions of identity.

Beyond dedicated students and alumni, the terms of Chief Illiniwek's retirement also indicate a partial victory for Native activism. The university will continue to identify its athletic teams as the Fighting Illini, referring to war veterans but also to a group of farming indigenous peoples who were not particularly militarized.

Throughout this book, I have explored the construction of identity in a variety of representational dance genres. Uniting the forms explored is the use of images of indigenous culture and people in the material and behavioral dimensions of dance. Some forms are danced by people who are indigenous themselves, embodying a public affirmation of identity. Other types feature performers who may identify as indigenous, but only in moments of dance. I have occasionally referenced one dance genre to highlight dimensions of another, but comparisons have been limited. In the next chapter I set dances next to one another, comparing them across a number of dimensions.

NOTES

1. The following paragraphs describing the effort to retire Chief Illiniwek draw on Garippo (2000), Harjo (2002, 2006), Merrion (2006), Milbert (2005), Rosenstein (1997, 2001), and Spindel (2000).

2. Political correctness refers here to a restriction of speech or self-expression that is offensive to a marginalized ethnic Other.

Part Six

Conclusion

Fourteen

Dance in Comparison

We gather once again in the courtyard of a household participating in Totonicapán's sustainable tourism project. At over 8,000 feet above sea level, the air is cool and the sunlight intense. Students visiting Guatemala during winter break sit at two tables under a veranda, enjoying lunch and live marimba music. A roof of alternating opaque and translucent corrugated panels provides both shade and sunlight. The view is well illuminated, the air cool and comfortable. Vines adorn the columns of the veranda and the roof that covers the patio. Flowering plants line the wall that separates this house from the next. Overall it is a pleasant atmosphere, achieved by making the most of limited resources.

Some of the students have remarked that the trip so far has been a unique experience. One comments that he could not imagine getting so far off the beaten path otherwise. Yet the moment and the space have certain transnational dimensions. Of our group of ten, five are native speakers of Spanish. They include sons and daughters of Mexican immigrants and a Puerto Rican woman, a citizen from a place that is part of the United States, yet not a state. The college that brought this group together is in the state whose senator, the son of a white woman and a Kenyan man, was elected president weeks earlier. The multiple places and identities represented by the group are extended by the current social setting. Our guide for the day is a mestiza Guatemalan; the hosts and the musicians, K'iche' Maya.

As we finish our meal, young women dressed in distinctive, handmade red blouses and black skirts, iconic of Totonicapán, enter the home, cross the patio, and prepare to dance. Once music is coordinated with the marimba trio, the young women begin their performance. The set comprises three short folkloric dances. The first is dedicated to the four cardinal directions, represented in the way the dancers arrange themselves in space and by the red, black, white, and yellow candles that they hold. The second dance is dedicated to the K'iche' woman's perraje *(a multipurpose textile), although part of the performance reiterates the cosmology expressed in the first. Two long rectangular textiles, a dancer at each end, are extended and crossed over one another. The dancers space themselves to create a symmetric, right-angle cross. By dancing in rotation, they imply a cross within a circle, referencing a Maya ordering of space. The third is a social dance in which some of the students, at the dancers' request, participate. This closing dance enacts the ideal that we all share a common humanity. This third message, perhaps not of the temporal depth of those expressed in the first two dances, has been repeated often by K'iche' and Kaqchikel people we have met on the trip. Beyond the multiple identities present and interacting, in this moment dancers also intersect. K'iche' Maya women perform folkloric dances for an audience that includes the daughter of Mexican immigrants who performs folkloric dances in suburban Chicago. At the moment she is on the floor dancing with an indigenous Guatemalan woman. I wonder if Amalia Hernández (or the state officials who sponsored Ballet Folklórico de México) ever imagined such a convergence.*

So far I have examined four distinct forms of dances that reference indigenous cultures. I occasionally have compared them with one another only to make particular points about a specific form. In this chapter, I revisit and expand earlier comparisons, gathering dances and dancers in the imaginary space of the written word. The first dance floor brings together Native American powwow dancers and K'iche' Maya traditional dancers and their "field" forms. Next, I consider theatricalized folkloric dances together, noting how they vary from their parallel field forms. Finally, I address official—that is, sponsored by states or by institutions—dances featuring little involvement of indigenous people in composition or execution. In particular, on our imaginary dance floor I bring together state-sponsored folkloric dancing and sport mascot dancing to explore their similarities. Because these forms sometimes are the subject of controversy, I dedicate Chapter 15 to the tacit social and cultural dimensions that drive conflicts over insistent self-representation on the one hand and Other-representation on the other.

14.1. Dance of the Perraje. K'iche' dancers perform for international visitors, December 2008. (Photograph by author.)

DANCES OF THE FIELD: K'ICHE' TRADITIONAL DANCE AND POWWOW DANCE COMPARED

I enter our hall of imaginary dance floors comparing Native American powwow with K'iche' traditional dance. Broadly and simply speaking, there are three forces at work that shape the differences and similarities between the forms. First, the aboriginal culture and sociopolitical organization at the time of European invasion shaped dancing and dance institutions that would be put to work in response to fundamental changes. Variability and commonality in the imperial and state powers that have imposed themselves on the respective indigenous societies also have played a role. How colonizer and colonized responded to one another created particular struggles and colonial dances that have shaped current dance traditions. Taking these macro-social forces into account, I compare powwow and K'iche' traditional dancing in terms of their material, behavioral, and ideational dimensions.

The material dimension of our comparison involves primarily the paraphernalia used by dancers. On the surface, powwow regalia and K'iche' vestments hold little in common. Velvet clothing, tin crowns, and wood masks, all key elements of K'iche' traditional dance outfits, are absent for powwow regalia. Sacred eagle feathers, roaches, and bustles, common elements in powwow regalia, are absent from K'iche' dance outfits. However, looking beyond the obvious, some similarities emerge. Feathers and attention to the combination of color and aesthetics that emphasize brilliance and movement are common to both.

The cultural distinctiveness of the peoples in question is reflected in their respective contemporary dance forms. Capes and tall headdresses are common in images of pre-Columbian Maya dancers. The basic form is quite reminiscent of dance regalia of pre-Hispanic origin, if we look past changes in materials of construction. Similarly, roaches and bustles appear throughout invasion-era depictions of Native peoples of the Woodlands and Plains regions. Again, materials have changed over time, but forms of outfits express adaptation with continuity. Accordingly, these are not simply matters of different styles in the present, but of aboriginal forms that have adapted over time to the materials available and the needs of the people who dance.

Moreover, in both powwow and K'iche' traditional dance, vestments are symbolically loaded. Most obvious, to wear regalia is to claim and demonstrate Native identity. That is, in both cases regalia is recognized by insiders and outsiders as fundamentally indigenous. Beyond their ability to assert indigenous identity, the material culture of dance carries meanings that become available only through participation or informed observation. Key symbols, including colors and their arrangement, are embedded in the paraphernalia of both traditions. Given how recently the Guatemalan state engaged in genocidal policy, K'iche' dance vestments continue to hide their meanings. Although, with time and stability in state action, it is not unexpected that K'iche' traditional dancers will use dance to directly instruct outsiders about their culture (as in the performance I described in the opening of this chapter).

Ownership is another important difference in the material culture of these "field dances." Powwow dancers own their regalia, while K'iche' dancers rent it from a *morería*. The expression of individuality within tradition, therefore, varies. The individuality of powwow regalia is immediately clear. Combination of color and the arrangement and placement of designs and symbols all vary considerably. K'iche' dancers are restrained by the character they dance and by the corresponding stock of the *morería*. However, they carefully select masks for quality and expression and clothing for combinations of colors to suit their tastes and interpretation of the character.

This difference in the degree to which individual expression is manifested in regalia may be attributed to causes beyond divergent ownership practice. First, as Native American powwow is not as directly narrative—dancers do not fill roles in a story—it does not necessitate regalia that references a specific character. That is, dancers enact a more general notion of male or female, hunter or healer, rather than a particular figure, in a particular story. Additionally, Highland Maya groups have had to meet the challenges of social control for large, dense populations since well before the European invasion, and dance that emphasizes sublimation of individual to role promotes (or at least symbolically embodies) social control.

Moreover, the role of community (although certainly not closed or monolithic) in resistance first to Spanish, then to state forces of genocide and assimilation, has been crucial in K'iche' cultural survival. Accordingly, dance that expresses individual conformity to role corresponds well with social structure through the aboriginal and colonial periods and into the present. Plains and Woodlands peoples, with generally smaller populations and more fluid settlement patterns (in aboriginal times and in adapting to the challenges of survival imposed by colonialism), give greater room in dance for individual expression. Both certainly value individuals who enact the shared traditions of the group but with divergent emphasis on how closely individuals must follow convention, powwow providing a bit more space for self-expression.

The genres also feature formal conferral of honor as a part of the larger context of performance. Highland Maya *ferias* and Native American powwows both assign "royal" status to young women. The *feria* each year names and confers the indigenous queen (*reina indígena*) to serve a twelve-month term. Like the powwow princess, the *reina indígena* has multiple public appearance obligations and is selected as the young woman who best enacts shared community values about gender and continuity of culture. As Roberts (2005:152), among others, points out, the beauty pageant, a product of the early days of mass media in the wealthy core countries, has gone global. Accordingly, it should be no surprise to find it in Guatemala and among indigenous groups and communities within Guatemala. Striking, perhaps, is the parallel between indigenous contests and their nonindigenous counterparts. The indigenous competitions eschew physicality and sexuality in favor of service to group and pride in culture and ethnic identity. For example the bathing suit competition, present in mainstream pageants in both Guatemala and the United States, is absent from *reina indígena* and powwow princess contests. Moreover, what constitutes talent varies significantly. Public speaking and traditional female production (e.g., weaving in the highlands and potting in the U.S. Southwest) are elevated in the indigenous contests where the mass-media-derived pageant stresses activities that a well-to-do woman might employ to entertain guests.

In effect, the indigenous pageants reject or invert almost every value expressed in the mainstream versions. Female economic contribution is valued, female sexuality is deemphasized, and distinctive culture is esteemed. In the process, standards of beauty, which are often part and parcel of ethnic bigotry and racism, are made irrelevant in the assignment of honorary office and social esteem to young women.

Although both genres informally and formally value individual expression supportive of culture and community, other manifestations of individual behavior present difficulties. Highland Maya and Native American communities face the common challenge of alcoholism. However, in terms of the presence and use of alcohol, K'iche' traditional dancing and powwow are nearly perfect opposites. Drinking at the Guatemalan *feria* is pervasive. Beer and liquor advertising is ubiquitous and the temporary restaurants that set up for the festivities offer and sell both. It is a period of intense socializing and activity, and even folks who do not normally drink imbibe. Beyond the local community, along with vendors and ride operators, the traveling group of *feria* people that I observed during fieldwork in 1994 and 1995 included its own *bolo*, or "drunk." Moreover, from offerings made to the spirits of the masks and at local altars to consumption during performance, alcohol use is a fundamental part of executing a traditional dance. *Kuux*, an unlicensed liquor made from fruit, is the libation preferred by dancers and the offering preferred by masks and their spirits.

Drinking at *feria* and at other times in the year is not without consequence. As is the case in many communities suffering from pervasive material poverty, alcoholism is a serious health problem in the Maya Highlands. Evidence of high rates of drinking ranges from staggering panhandlers, to people passed out in the gutter, to building fronts painted with the Alcoholics Anonymous symbol and schedules of meetings. Indeed, the pervasive use of alcohol in traditional dance can affect the *morero* (the person who runs the regalia rental shop) as well as the dancers themselves. In handling and cleaning the sweaty outfits that are returned to the shop, the *morero* is exposed to contagions that increase the taste for alcohol. To prevent drink from becoming a master, the *morero* must ritually cleanse and make offerings regularly with a traditional K'iche' religious practitioner (a *sacerdote maya* in Spanish or *ajq'ij* in K'iche'). Such belief and practice provide a cause for alcoholism and a ritual structure to treat it.

Powwow seeks a much more direct way to control the effects of alcohol. Drugs and alcohol are expressly forbidden at powwow and I have never encountered any evidence of drinking while attending. Where *feria* is a place for drinking and is dangerous for those struggling to control alcoholism, powwow is a safe place for the individual working to maintain sobriety. Indeed, the combination of positive self-representation with the absence of drinking and drunkenness is therapeutic for a recovering alcoholic. Moreover, it enacts a strong connection among sobriety, social solidarity, and the assignment of positive social esteem through honoring. Powwow works to prevent alcoholism as well as providing a context supportive of its treatment.

Beyond the health of individuals, there are political dimensions to powwow's ban on alcohol. A particularly ugly stereotype confronting Native people is that of the "drunken Indian." In the context of this stereotype, all the work that a powwow does to reshape the image of the Indian is potentially undone by one display of public drunkenness. Moreover, the use of alcohol as a tool of colonization and colonialism north of the Rio Grande is well documented. From intoxicating Native people into signing unfavorable land cession treaties to indebting them through sales of liquor, alcohol is associated with some of the worst dimensions of intercourse with white society. Powwow in its negation of alcohol, therefore, plays a role in the process of decolonization. Alcohol is a powerful symbol of colonialism and of negative practices introduced to Native societies by the colonizer. To ban it from context where Native culture is valorized is both healthful and politically astute.

Although only K'iche' dance involves consumption of liquor to achieve an altered state, both forms manifest physicality that is quite distinct from everyday existence. K'iche' dance and powwow dance are work; dancers move in often-heavy outfits, raising heart rate and body temperature. Physical stress of this sort, carried out over several hours, is known to trigger parasympathetic nervous system response, including the release of endorphins. The sense of well-being and physical exhaustion shared among dancers is therapeutic and socially binding.[1]

Additionally, articulation of dance and dancers to the sacred is common to the two genres. Both forms of dance initiate with prayer, both load certain objects with sacred power, and both combine fun and solemnity. Before the beginning of the first performance, dancers in Momostenango make offerings at a Maya altar outside of town, at the municipal government building, and at the Catholic church in the center of the town. Indeed, ritual avoidances by dancers, ritual cleansing of masks and clothing, and ritual offerings to various spiritual entities are key parts of preparation for K'iche' traditional dance. Powwow also initiates dancing with prayers and affords a great deal of ritual respect for regalia. Such spiritual loading of dance is not common in the other forms that I explored subsequently. Moreover, where fun and solemnity mix here, in the other forms consistent (or "professional") execution that minimizes difference from performance to performance is a more common ideal in "dance of the field" genres.

Origin and evolution of dancing form evince clear similarity. Both powwow and K'iche' traditional dance involve dance steps that are rooted in the aboriginal or primordial past. The common soft-then-hard step of powwow is reminiscent of the first steps of human beings on the earth (DesJarlait 1997:117). K'iche' steps that tend toward toe pointing and minimal lifting of the foot from the ground, are similar to depictions of dance in the pre-Columbian codices and inscriptions.[2] Again, this is not to say that present dance reflects an unchanged practice, a fossilized "survival," but rather a form of movement repeatedly adapted to contemporary purposes. As in the case of regalia, dance physicality is expression in the present of the past.

Powwow and K'iche' traditional dance do differ significantly in how they construct gender. Broadly speaking, women participate more directly in powwow. Male K'iche' traditional dancers are supported by female kin who do not dance but do participate in the rituals surrounding performance. As I described in Part Three, powwow expresses gender complementarity directly in dance categories. A variety of factors likely contribute to this difference. The greater gender equality present in mainstream society may play a role. Women's Fancy Dance, at least as reported by one emcee, was influenced by the Women's Movement. Moreover, matrilineal social organization is more common in Native North America, where patrilineality has dominated the social organization of Mesoamerican societies. Generally, in matrilineal societies women have greater participation in public life and in formal politics. Political centralization is another factor that often contributes to gender inequality. That is, societies with greater concentration of political power tend to be male-dominated, and pre-Columbian Highland Maya polities were centralized. Native American societies, particularly in the Plains and Woodlands, tend toward less centralized political organization. While male dominance was certainly not absent from the cultures of the Plains, the presence of matrilineal societies and the diffusion of political power in general likely mitigated inequality.

We now move to the ideational dimensions of dance in terms of themes of narrative, cosmology, and identity. Both genres tell "back stories" about the origin or action of their respective dances. More specifically, themes of war and hunting are recurring in powwow and K'iche' traditional dance. Male powwow dances[3] are primarily about either warring and hunting or honoring warriors. Even the Grass Dance, with strong themes of healing, has roots in war societies and references warring. Most famously, the K'iche' Dance of the Deer references hunting. Other highly salient dance-dramas, the Dance of the Conquest, the Dance of the Moors and the Christians, and the Rabinal Achí, all hinge on military conflict.[4] Although both express themes, traditional dance is more directly narrative. Dancers hold the roles of characters and dances tell a story. Each category of powwow dance has a theme and elaborate origin stories, but dancers express themselves more than as parts in a play. This difference is paralleled in regalia and may reflect differences in settlement pattern and economy, aboriginal patterns of articulation of individual to group, and survival strategies developed in response to colonization.

Interestingly enough, both genres express Native cosmology in dance. If the circle is a summarizing symbol shared across many Native American societies, the importance of the cross within a square or circle is common across indigenous Mesoamerican cultures. In both powwow and K'iche' traditional dance, participants map an idealized orientation of the cosmos onto the actual dance arena. Powwow dances concentric circles, defining life's path and articulating sacred and secular. Traditional dances often mark crosses within square or rectangular dance arenas. Dancers acknowledge the four cardinal directions as well as the axis mundi formed by the intersection of the lines connecting the corners of the world. Both Native American and K'iche' Maya dancers traverse space and time through dance that follows fundamental, culturally distinctive cosmoglyphs. In their attention to cosmology, the two forms explored here differ profoundly from the theatricalized forms explored below. No doubt the thin line between ritual and theater fosters the incorporation of indigenous worldview into dance at such a primary level. Powwow and K'iche' traditional dance transcend the specialization that in much of the social life of complex societies separates theater from ritual.

Both forms work on interethnic relations and the challenges of nationalism. Powwow, in its overt discourse, particularly in the commentary and humor of the emcee, addresses Native and white relations. Ethnicity is a common theme across a variety of K'iche' traditional dances as well. However, by dressing up as Mexicans or sixteenth-century warriors, dancers tend to mask some of the commentary by distancing it in time or space. Beyond ethnic to national identity, powwow and K'iche' traditional dance both argue for a place within the larger society that does not require surrender of a culturally distinct identity. Indeed, both use flags in ways that embrace national identity while rejecting state ideology that defines it narrowly and homogenously. Contesting nationalism and national identity in this way is a performative articulation of the goal of political autonomy within existing states commonly sought by indigenous movements.

As these indigenous dance forms move forward, it is clear that self-representation and cultural continuity will be predominant themes in their construction of identity. That powwow emphasizes self-representation to Others more overtly reflects differences in population proportions between the United States and Guatemala. While Native people comprise a small (but consistently underestimated) percentage of the U.S. population, Maya may make up more than 60 percent of the Guatemalan citizenry. Additionally, and partly as a consequence of demographic differences, Native American nations were subject to state hegemony from an earlier date and by a more powerful state. The Highland Maya groups of Guatemala experienced in the 1980s what Plains peoples endured in the late nineteenth century: application of state military force in an effort to control or eliminate Native peoples. Both states failed in their attempts to forcefully incorporate Native people and completely erase their cultures. As a result, both states carry (often in denial) the stain of attempted genocide.

Similar history has led to the creation of similar myths of identification. Obvious parallels are found in the Guatemalan story of the conquest and the U.S. story of the first Thanksgiving. Both deal with the origin of settler states. As is the case across the Americas, such narratives confront the reality that the current homeland was once someone else's homeland. While the Guatemalan story is marked with violent conflict and the Thanksgiving story with harmonious cooperation, both legitimize colonization and the subsequent establishment of the independent state. Guatemalan Indians resist but are defeated and converted. American Indians assist European colonists. At the end of both national origin myths, the indigenous peoples accept colonization. After the legitimate foundation of current state and society is established, important differences mark these official stories of national origin. Most importantly, the Thanksgiving story does not elevate a Native leader to the status of national hero. The Indians at the first Thanksgiving finish their symbolic work with the legitimization of mainstream society and then disappear. Unlike Tekun Umam, the Native people who helped the pilgrims are seldom named and do not become employed as fonts of authentic identity. As I explored earlier, it is the Plains warrior who picks up the role of noble savage carried by Tekun Umam in the conquest story.

Such myths, backed with power and satisfying to wide segments of society, tend to persist. However, in both present cases, the end of the Cold War has provided an opportunity for indigenous people to expand self-representation and to challenge real social order and the myths that buttress it. At present, indigenous critics contest both stories. As Maya activists have worked to recover Tekun Umam, so have Native Americans presented counter-hegemonic views of Thanksgiving. In both cases, indigenous opinion is complex and varied. Many wonder if anything of value can be recovered from symbols that have been put to so much ideological work harmful to indigenous people and culture. Some Native Americans find positives in the story and holiday, despite its justification of colonization (Keeler 2000). Others consider Thanksgiving a day of mourning (Wilkins 2002:104). Some Highland Maya find the story of Tekun Umam hopelessly racist. Others maintain a version of the K'iche' leader that rejects his noble savagery and celebrates his martyrdom and continued spiritual presence.

Dance is a form of self-representation that post–Cold War–era Highland Maya and Native Americans have embraced. That said, a key area where self-representation in powwow and K'iche' traditional dance diverges is in the expression of pan-ethnic (pan-indigenous) political identity. With its strong emphasis on things "intertribal," the expression of the cultural, social, and political connections that give cohesion to "Native American" is a central theme of powwow. The articulation of Maya is not as overt or direct in tradi-

Table 14.1. K'iche' traditional dance and Native American powwow dance compared

		K'iche' Traditional Dance	*Native American Powwow*
Material Culture	Form of paraphernalia	• Masks • Capes • Tall headdresses	• Roaches • Bustles • Eagle feathers
	Symbolic loading	Abstract, multivalent	Abstract, multivalent
	Ownership of paraphernalia	• Communal, in the *morería* • Regalia conforms to character	• Individual • Regalia allows robust individual expression
Behavioral Culture	Honoring	*Reina indigena* embodies ideals of culture and gender that eschew overt sexuality	Powwow princess embodies ideals of culture and gender that eschew overt sexuality
	Identity	Dance marks indigenous identity	Dance marks indigenous identity
	Alcohol	Present and widely consumed	Absent through formal prohibition
	Ritual	Sacred and theatrical comingle	Sacred and secular comingle
	Gender	Complementary roles in mounting a production	Complementary dance forms in performance
Ideational Culture	Continuity	• Step and regalia similar to depictions in pre-Columbian art • Origin in extensive pre-Columbian dramatic ritual dancing	• Step anchored in primordial past • Origin in hunting and warring dances of aboriginal past
	Cosmology	Key symbol of cross within square or circle	Key symbol of concentric circles
	Nationalism	• Inclusive pluralism • Patriotism contested through symbols of the state	• Inclusive pluralism • Patriotism contested through symbols of the state • Patriotism affirmed through military service
	Myths of identification held by Others	Official story of Maya resistance followed by acquiescence and assimilation	Thanksgiving story of Native cooperation and acquiescence followed by disappearance
	Pan-ethnicity	Peripheral	Central

tional K'iche' dance, where the emphasis remains strongly local. Powwow is, as I describe in the next section, similar to folkloric dance with respect to the enactment of pan-ethnicity.

FOLKLORIC DANCES AND THEIR INSPIRATION

As the crow flies, Tejutla, in the Department of San Marcos, is the closest town that I will visit with the Vanguardia Indígena. Although the community is not far from Totonicapán in space, this visit offers the most unanticipated set of experiences. The last ninety minutes of the bus ride, after we leave the department capital of San Marcos and pass through San Pedro Sacatepéquez, covers thirty-five kilometers of rutted road to the sleepy town of Tejutla. To my perception, it has many of the marks of an indigenous town. It is in the highlands, it is remote, and it is connected to the national transportation infrastructure by a poorly maintained road. However, some of the K'iche' Maya dancers inform me that, because of an intensive program of cultural assimilation carried out by the government in the 1980s, the town is now Ladino, in the center at least. We indeed encounter very few Maya people during our stay, although Tejutla is within the Mam Maya ancestral homeland.

Beyond this surprising intersection of ethnicity and geography, the event at which the Vanguardia performs offers the unanticipated as well. (Although in hindsight I come to realize that these new and unexpected experiences were connected by a general pattern of identity construction in flux.) The evening's music and dance performances are in honor of Señorita Espiga de Trigo (Miss Ear of Wheat). From the beginning, the event has the feel of something I might encounter at a county fair in my home state of Illinois. These are not people of maize, as the Maya often self-identify, but rather folks celebrating a product that, while important to the local economy, has little cosmological or cultural importance. The indoor theater space is adequate for the festivities. The sound is not perfect, but music and discourse are audible. The lighting illuminates, but photography is difficult. A modest audience attends.

On the stage come together what I later will understand as self-representation and Other-representation. The K'iche' Maya dancers of the Vanguardia Indígena represent their own community and culture to an audience filled with ethnic Others. They adapt bits of traditional dance to the theatrical setting and perform folkloric dances expressing local Totonicapense identity rather than general Indianness. Women wear clothing that they might don for a wedding or confirmation, not costumes specifically designed for dance. The performers from the host community enact a variety of Others in dances, and as the evening progresses, these dances strike me as odder and odder. Early in the program, dressed in uniform and generic Indian dress, young men and women of Tejutla perform a few standard folkloric dances, indigenous life painted as romantic and quaint. Juxtaposed with the dances of the Vanguardia Indígena, this performance highlights for me how the same basic form (folkloric dance) is put to varied uses.

Late in the program, a piece set to contemporary electronic pop music involves Other-representation that becomes complex and personal. Young men dressed in lime-green jackets take the stage and perform to early hip-hop music akin to MC Hammer. A form invented by African Americans, hip-hop in the mid-1990s had already established a wide audience and has become an international marker of pop culture from the United States. The dancing is energetic and well rehearsed. However, in it I sense a strained attempt to stake a claim on modernity, a cultural form of the United States symbolizing sophistication. Nonetheless, from the perspective of this gringo, what they enact seems neither Guatemalan nor American, but a cultural quilt-work with awkward and untidy seams.

At the end of the evening, one of the four young men approaches me and asks that I photograph him with his dance colleagues. I explain that because of the low level of light I am not sure how the picture will turn out. He says that is not important, and he and his friends seem uninterested in having a copy of the final product. Being photographed is what is most important. I am reminded of the occasion in Totonicapán when a non-Maya grandfather noted to me the fair skin of his granddaughter. I felt that he was attempting to connect to me, but in a way that also sought to distance himself from his indigenous neighbors. Years later, looking at the grainy and dark photograph of young Guatemala men in confident hip-hop posture, I am still struck by the complexity of identity it contains.

Above I compared two forms of dance that affirm the indigenous status of performers. On this next dance floor, identity becomes more complex. Folkloric performers have included elites (or creoles), immigrants (or mestizos, particularly in sending countries), and indigenous people. Accordingly, I discuss folkloric dance as a transnational form, stressing how it diverges, complements, and even reiterates the in-the-field forms of powwow and traditional dance. First I compare and contrast K'iche' traditional dance with folkloric dance in general, as they are most clearly parallel forms. Second, I place together on the imaginary dance floor powwow dance and immigrant folkloric dance, as they deal with similar challenges.

I return to the Guatemalan dichotomy of *tradicional* and *folklórico*. In presentation of images of indigenous people, past and present, *baile folklórico* and *baile tradicional* are most closely tied. Indeed, folkloric dance draws on and represents traditional dance and traditional dancers. By considering how traditional and folkloric dances differ in terms of material culture (paraphernalia), behavioral culture (performers and performance), and ideational culture (meanings presented in performance), I hope to illuminate important features of both genres.

Masks, augmented by wigs and elaborate headdresses, are almost universal in traditional dance. These items are key to distinguishing characters

14.2. Complex and Complicated Identity. Performers at the Miss Ear of Wheat festival in Tejutla dance hip-hop, July 1995. (Photograph by author.)

within a dance-drama and often allude to indigenous religion and ritual. While masks are seldom absent from traditional dance, they rarely appear in folkloric dance. Members of rural indigenous communities often know one another fairly well. In places where folks enjoy a good deal of face-to-face interaction, masks serve to sublimate a known person to ritual and dramatic roles. In large-scale, complex societies, where anonymity prevails, masks are not as necessary.

Vesture and props employed in traditional dance are heavily loaded with abstract and multivalent symbols. The oscillating piping that decorates garments represents duality and the necessity in life to find balance between opposites. Symmetric crosses within squares appear repeatedly, symbolizing Native cosmology. Mirrors sewn onto regalia imply, as they have for centuries in Mesoamerica, prognostication and divinatory rituals. The colors of a particular outfit, which at first may seem mismatched and random, overall balance strong and weak hues.

The emphasis on vestments that present multiple and abstract symbols and on fairly cumbersome masks and headdresses further deemphasizes dancing in *baile tradicional*. Heavy masks and outfits provide performers with little freedom of movement, obscure the vision, and offer little ventilation. To the contrary, costumes in folkloric dance are more concerned with eye-catching aesthetics than with symbolic loading. Folkloric costumes also are more dedicated to a "realistic," if somewhat polished, depiction of the past. Moreover, they are functional, giving dancers greater freedom to move. Overall, folkloric costumes reflect the priorities of modern dance; they are pleasing to the eye and accentuate the movements, abilities, and bodies of athletic dancers.

Beyond differences in material culture, K'iche' traditional dance and folkloric dance diverge in action and enactment. There is clear influence of traditional dances of various Mesoamerican groups on the Mexican and Guatemalan folkloric repertoire. As I discussed earlier, given the presence of both folkloric and traditional dancing in K'iche' communities, it is likely that folkloric dance has influenced traditional dance as well. Accordingly, my discussion focuses not on issues of choreography, but on variance in how gender is enacted in dance, how people learn dance, and whether dance should be considered ritual or drama (if such a distinction is possible).

In Highland Maya traditional dance, performers are predominantly male. While young girls appear in the Dance of the Conquest as K'iche' princesses, all of the main characters (including female parts) in La Conquista and in other traditional dances are played by men. The Margarita in the Dance of the Mexicans and the Little Old Woman in the Dance of the Deer, for example, are played by men in women's garb. On the occasion when male and female players do appear together, one is masked, the other is not (Figure 14.3). This is not to say that women do not participate in the production of traditional dance. They help dancers into their masks and costumes, an awkward and time-consuming task. They provide important assistance, including provision of food and drink during performances that last for several hours. Women and children are present throughout the dance, permanent members of audiences that tend to ebb and flow. This distribution of tasks in traditional dance reflects a wider Maya pattern of sexual division of labor in which male and female roles, while well defined, complement one another. Men's work and men are incomplete without women's work and women. Complementary gender division of labor, in turn, reflects a general Mesoamerican pattern of dualism, a cultural thread that runs through ethnopsychology, ethnomedicine, and cosmology.

In folkloric dance, male and female onstage presence is more symmetric. Male-female pairing is common, and even in dances not directly related to courtship and marriage, there tend to be equal or near-equal numbers of male and female performers. While dualism is implied at times, conventions of modern dance and modern social relations best explain gender equality in folkloric dance. In complex industrial and post-industrial societies, gender roles are regularly contested and re-created. Not surprisingly, when presented by nonindigenous troupes, folkloric dance constructs ideal gender relations of primitive or natural Others. Gender danced then becomes gender of a simpler, more ordered time. Social relations in complex anonymous (modern) society can seem disordered and unstable. Depicting the courtship dance of a bucolic people provides a model of "natural" gender relations against which actual relations can be contemplated.

K'iche' transnational dance performances in Totonicapán present an evolving gender division of dance labor. The folkloric norm of placing both male and female dancers on the same stage was initially embraced. The performances of Totonicapán's Vanguardia Indígena that I observed in 1994 and 1995 involved male and female dancers. Recently, however, folkloric performances in Toto have featured female groups of dancers. Indeed, all seven of the performances for international visitors observed over a four-year period have featured dance groups comprising young women *exclusively*. This represents an interesting expression and inversion. Highland Maya gender roles in relation to colonial structures have assigned women the task of protecting and continuing culture through dress, language, and enculturation of children. Male roles stress engagement of the Other and the outside world. For example, indigenous men have long adopted dress similar enough to the ethnic Other to foster work for wages outside of Maya social settings. The goals of self-representation, however, complicate this strategy. That the role of conservator of culture is female makes women ideal enactors of culture in dance. As a result, when interaction with outsiders is to communicate unique identity and to fulfill the guests' expectation of authenticity, Maya women are best for the task. Folkloric dancing for visitors, viewed from this perspective, parallels Walter Little's (2004) conclusions regarding female Kaqchikel vendors in transnational tourist markets. Tourists who seek "Maya" prefer women in traditional clothing. Globalization complicates the gender assignment of intercultural discourse, although the basic structure of gender complementarity remains. K'iche' traditional dance continues to be the domain of male dancers; folkloric dance becomes its female complement. In effect, at least as performers for international guests, K'iche' Totonicapenses have indigenized folkloric dance, changing its gender composition to better fit the Highland Maya model of classification while at the same time accommodating the expectations of visitors.

In addition to who dances, K'iche' traditional dance and folkloric dance vary in how dancers acquire their skill. As has been much of life in indigenous communities, traditional dance training is firmly embedded in kinship structures. Parents and other senior kin teach children to dance, who grow up and teach their children to dance. Preparation for execution of a particular dance

14.3. Gender and Dress in Dance. Above, *girls without masks portray the daughters of the Rey K'iche', enacted by a masked male dancer at center. Before beginning the play, dancers participate in the parade in honor of Saint James, Apostle, July 1995, San Cristóbal,* Totonicapán. Below, *folkoric dancers at Taste of Chicago, July 2006. (Photographs by author.)*

involves review of texts to ensure proper recitation of lines and review of the general structure and plot. A good deal of time and effort goes toward ritual treatment of masks and purification through ritual avoidance of certain activities. All of this happens within dance groups that are bound by overlapping ties of community and family.

Folkloric dance is taught by employing models from formal education. Integrated into curricula and as part of extracurricular activities, it carries out some of the enculturation (and en-identification) previously embedded in family. Folkloric dancers have the opportunity to attend any number of clinics and schools that are advertised on the Internet. Even in real space, there is a certain transnational dimension to training, with professional dance companies offering classes within the home country and abroad. For example, Quad-Cities Ballet Folklórico has hosted professional dancers from Veracruz who give classes to young performers (Speer 2004). Kin functions of enculturation, typical of modern complex society, are partly carried out by institutions (schools). This education of heritage through dance is about forming good children as well as passing tradition. Discourse at Hispanofest frequently stresses how folkloric performance is a positive alternative for school-aged kids. Tradition is opposed to gang membership and other dangers of life in the United States. Training of this sort reflects the high specialization of modern, complex society and its emphasis on formal organizations as mechanisms to achieve goals. In this case, school and dance in school are put to the purpose of re-creating and maintaining distinctive and positive identity.

One of the most obvious differences in performance between folkloric and traditional dance is a product of these differing modes of instruction. Folkloric dances are highly polished, with little evidence of variance from text. In such performances, dancing is central; heavily choreographed forms are followed closely by athletic dancers. Traditional dances, on the contrary, are highly improvised. In fact, dancing itself is sometimes rather peripheral, subservient to drama, plot, and ritual. Moreover, dancers typically ingest considerable quantities of alcohol as a part of performance, and a good deal of horseplay may occur. The demand for accurate replication, control, and predictability typical of market-dominated society is evident in folkloric dance and absent from traditional dance.

The differing emphasis on accurate replication also reflects divergent purposes. Folkloric dance is primarily theater. Although it does work on important and illusive features of identity, it is not ritual in the classic, access-the-supernatural sense. Performance of traditional dance is often sacred ritual as well as drama. As I mentioned earlier, dancers prepare themselves and their masks through ritual offering and purification. Moreover, elements of the performance itself access the supernatural. Performing with ritually treated masks is said to invoke the spirits of certain principal characters who are at once historic figures and deities.

In object and action, folkloric dance and traditional dance vary in ways that are consistent with their histories, contexts of production, and purpose of enactment. The ideational dimension—that is, the meanings presented in dance—manifest a similar pattern. Here I address how cosmology, mythology, and identity are constructed in dance. Both K'iche' traditional dance and folkloric dance reference cosmology (the ordering of time and space). Traditional dance also enacts mythology (stories that explain time and space). The forms diverge in two fundamental ways: in degree of multivalence and in directness of symbolization. Just as folkloric dance is less directly ritual than traditional dance, its references to cosmology are overt and monovalent. Folkloric dance frequently references the four cardinal directions, but does so explicitly, through the title of the dance or in its description in written programs or announcements during performance. Traditional dance embeds such references within forms that are overtly about something else. Moreover, it deploys symbols that are loaded with multiple meanings. Two figures from the Dance of the Conquest covered in Part Two illustrate the point. Tekun Umam overtly is a martyr to K'iche' and Guatemalan independence. The character in his green color also references life force, central in the Maya (and Mesoamerican) color-direction cosmology, and the pre-Columbian divinity Q'ukumatz. The red of Ajitz (a simple "witch" to outsiders) references east in the same cosmology, one of the colors of sacred corn, and at least two deities of pre-Columbian origin. Indeed, in their presentation of indigenous religion, folkloric dance, and traditional dance are in near-perfect inversion of one another. In portraying pre-Columbian practices, folkloric dance is explicit, striving to realistically depict a bygone era. The pre-Columbian in traditional dance is abstractly presented, coded and hidden from outsiders. One must come to the performance with fairly extensive knowledge of the particular drama and of Mesoamerican traditions to understand the allusions made in mask, regalia, and actions.

Many of the differences in traditional and folkloric dance can be better understood if we compare the challenges that their respective dancers confront. While they vary substantially in form, both deal with issues of meaning and identity. That is to say, both present images that people use to build ideas about themselves, their present and their past. Difference in form and connection in purpose reflect the differing challenges faced by dancers and audiences.

European invasion initially brought greatly diminished political autonomy to the Native peoples of the Americas. Weakened control or outright loss of land and marginal access to productive resources resulted in a long and continuing period of persistent material poverty. Indigenous people have faced and continue to face outright destruction, coercive assimilation, and political marginality and oppression. While the colonial period ended for the nonindigenous in the late eighteenth or early nineteenth century, for the indigenous peoples of the Americas colonialism is an ongoing reality that continues into the new millennium. Guatemala is independent of Spain; however, the K'iche' and the other Mayas continue to lack robust political autonomy and experience inconsistent protection of human and cultural rights. Traditional dance, born of colonialism, continues to deal with colonialism. Dances present strategies of interaction with powerful Others, models of behavior, and coded and hidden content of cultural continuity.

The Dance of the Conquest nicely exemplifies and helps explain this masking of meanings. Introduced by Spanish clergy to aid in the Christianization of Indians, La Conquista overtly presents the subordination of Maya to Christian religion and Spanish and other, later outside political orders. Its more covert allusions to the *Popul Wuj* and Mesoamerican cosmology and worldview suggest religious belief and practice that combine Christian and aboriginal and imply that the current political order is temporary. *Indígenas* who perform the dance can give the appearance of compliance with the policies of the colonizer, while sharing among themselves the meanings and symbols that are essential to cultural continuity. On the other hand, folkloric dance outwardly and explicitly refers to the ancient practices and exotic beliefs, not to preserve and hide them but to create a sense of heritage that is unique, compelling, and deeply rooted. The whole point is to reference something exotic, not to feign assimilation.

While the challenges for immigrants are not colonial, living in the United States does pose a triple threat to identity. It is a large, anonymous, and potentially alienating society for the native-born (to say nothing of the newcomer). Moreover, a general inability or unwillingness to recognize complex ethnic diversity presents further difficulties. Marketing strategies present Latino "brands" and images that sublimate a good deal of diversity. Everything south of the border becomes the same in the mass-media imagination. Moreover, persistent negative stereotypes, mostly latent until the current immigration "debate," are again overt, common in the discourse of AM talk radio and cable news networks. The mass media, as such, purvey contradictory and uncomfortable images of Latinos. On the one hand, the imaginary abstract political identity of Latino is reified, homogenized, and made hip. On the other, immigrants from Latin America are imaged as poor, job-hogging criminals. Folkloric dance is one of many ways that transnationals, immigrants and their children, deal with an array of challenges to identity and meaning. It asserts the particulars of ethnicity in a climate that favors broad abstract categories of identity. There are so many Latino groups of such great variety performing in all sorts of venues because the threats of anonymity, meaninglessness, and marginalization are pervasive and continuous.

In Chapter 10, I described the emergence of folkloric performances by K'iche' dancers in transnational settings. In effect, the two forms compared presently in our imaginary dance hall coexist in social reality. The advantage K'iche' dancers have over other performers of folkloric forms is proximity to one of its key sources. Traditional dance performances provide a font of ideas for folkloric dances. One salient example of this is the occasional use of *morería* regalia and masks for shorter theatricalized presentations. Beyond the flow of influences, the obvious question is, why do K'iche' Maya present both forms? If we continue with the basic hypothesis established here—that dance forms vary according to needs of and constraints on the dancers and audiences—it follows that Maya face overlapping challenges related to both ongoing colonialism and globalization.

Scott (1990:183–201) suggests that the coding of cultural content in such performances protects and stores it for more overt expression on a better day, when the calculus of social action changes to make overt resistance more likely to succeed. Otzoy (1999:164), in calling for the incorporation of the Maya danced versions of the conquest story into a reworked official conquest story, suggests just such a changing political landscape. That K'iche' Mayas dance parallel forms speaks further to change and to evolving, multifaceted self-representation.

A key difference between K'iche' traditional and folkloric dance is the reference to other communities and to generalized Maya culture. Part of this likely is because of the influence of the professional companies that work to present a variety of dances from various communities. The genre becomes salient across Maya towns. Nonetheless, folkloric vignettes, although danced by K'iche', express a more general pan-Maya awareness than traditional ritual dances, which tend to reflect local histories and views. Tourists add another dimension. In transnational settings, performance implies these more abstract levels of identity. The audience is made up of international Others from wealthy core countries. The corresponding abstract levels for identity are Guatemalan, indigenous Maya, and peripheral. Placing side by side these individuals of multilayered identity emphasizes and makes real the strata that articulate structurally. In this case, the encounter activates abstract levels of identity: white-person-from-wealthy-core-country and indigenous-person-from-poor-periphery-country. To all present, contemplation of normally abstract identification beyond local, everyday experience is encouraged and enhanced.

Given that long ritualized traditional and short theatrical folkloric forms have coexisted for at least fifty years in Totonicapán, it seems imprudent to predict that the first will disappear to be replaced by the other. The shift is not simply from ritual to theater (Turner 2001). At this point it is clear that both forms are important enough to enough members of the community that they continue, the arc of change better conceived of as from ritual to ritual *and* theater. Together, they provide a set of semiotic identity complexes that allow performers and audiences to share and distribute symbols that express cultural continuity through age-old tradition, but also to assert self-representation through a newer form more suited to multi-situated interethnic relations that are marked by power and economic inequality.

In folkloric dance, indigenous K'iche' dancers reach a wider audience, representing their own culture. They also reference a more abstract level of Maya identity that, as constructed by outside Others, emphasizes general Indianness. In entering this realm, dancers and organizers challenge the notion of Indianness constructed by Others but also work in an area where indigenous people have connected to one another. While traditional dance continues to reference the local K'iche', folkloric dancing references both the local and the transnational. It offers possibilities of further connection to other Maya groups and to indigenous groups beyond Guatemala. In some ways, then, K'iche' folkloric dance does what powwow does, referencing pan-ethnic identity and occasionally playing to multi-ethnic audiences. In the next section, by comparing powwow with folkloric dance on our imaginary dance floor, I work to highlight similarity and differences.

FOLKLORIC AND POWWOW DANCES: PAN-ETHNICITY AND INFLUENCING OTHERS

The next comparison visited in this chapter considers Latino folkloric dancing in the United States and Native American powwow. Unlike the other imaginary dance venues where forms from disparate places are compared, here the make-believe stage has a basis in social reality. In common, Latino folkloric and powwow dancers both live within a state dominated by ethnic Others. Moreover, Latino and Native American are both political pan-ethnic identity categories that are at least partially structural complements to white. Accordingly, the present comparison will emphasize how powwow and folkloric dancing respond to the challenges of being part of a pan-ethnic group that itself is nonetheless a minority. Common to both is the work of self-representation to self and to powerful and privileged ethnic Others. In the endeavor, common forms (shared dance styles or a set of dance vignettes) are put to multiple purposes. As I have covered both forms in the preceding sections, I condense the following discussion to consideration of, first, material and behavioral culture and, second, ideational culture.

An obvious divergence between folkloric and powwow dance is in dress and choreography. Folkloric dance expresses uniformity: dancers typically wear the same outfits (with male and female variants) of matching color and closely coordinate bodily movement. Theatricalization and also a degree of abstraction of identity are the roots of this idealization of the social life. Folkloric dancers enact a version of themselves (or their countrymen) remote from the social context of performance in space. When folkloric dance draws on the indigenous peoples of homeland, unique identity is referenced through Others (or an internalized otherness). Uniformity, then, reflects the tendency explored throughout this book to see the Other as homogeneous. It also manifests a common (mis)conception of contemporary Native peoples and the ancients as dedicated (if not slavish) enactors of their cultures. We imagine them as unpolluted by the messy individualism of modern life, and such imagined Indians become good symbols for the struggle to maintain identity in an immense and anonymous society. For immigrant dancers, life in the United States challenges stable and known identity. For immigrant parents, the influence of the mainstream on children is obvious and at times threatening. Enacting strong dedication to cultural tradition responds to the chaos of constructing a social identity in the receiving country's social life for new arrivals and parents of Latino children born in the United States.

Powwow does also express a degree of uniformity in material and behavioral culture. However, it allows a greater deal of individual expression than folkloric dance. Dancers have choices in category, and these, to a degree, parallel the variety of vignettes available to folkloric dancers. Both powwow and folkloric dance have more traditional and more modern from which to choose. However, while powwow dancers perform together and respond to one another, they do not closely coordinate their dancing. Regalia, similarly, while reflecting general standards for each category, allows for a great deal of self-expression in variety of color and iconography. This distinction reflects differences in both minority experience and particularly Native American notions of self. Depending on region, Native Americans, as original inhabitants, have dealt with the white Other for a longer span of time and from their Native homeland. Cultural survival is an ongoing struggle that is part of life from cradle to grave rather than a challenge presented by the immediacy of migration from one state to another. Powwow dance therefore expresses Native conventions of individual autonomy within connection to culture and group rather than constructing social stability through close coordination of dancers.

This is not to say that powwow neglects the embodiment of coordination of individuals to group purpose. As I explored in Part Three, grand entry sorts individuals in parade-like fashion and communicates a clear message about specialization and personhood. Additionally, contest powwows occasionally present team dance competitions. An informal survey of powwow programs reveals that team competitions occur, but not as frequently as do individual dance competitions. The 2009 Gathering of Nations (the largest powwow) included a "Sisters Team Dance Special" (Gathering of Nations Powwow 2009). The Intertribal Indian Club of Tulsa Powwow of Champions, however, has not included team dancing in recent years. Nina de Shane notes that "Team Dances [were] the latest additions at Six Nations" powwows (de Shane 1991:383). The 2010 Grand River program lists powwow dance contests, Smoke Dance contests, and Iroquois social dancing, but it does not mention team dancing (Grand River Powwow 2010). Although it is typically not a regular or main event—the Gathering of Nations Powwow (2009) lists its 2009 team dance event under "special contests"—team dancing seems to be growing in popularity presently. A review of powwow programs and video reveals an interesting mix of similarity and difference when compared with coordinated dancing in the folkloric genre. Team competitions tend to maintain gender classification while sublimating dance categories. For example, in one case, a team of traditional Shawl dancers competed against a team of Jingle Dress dancers. The dancers were all female, but the dance forms varied by team. Such articulation affirms the importance of gender in powwow dance categories but emphasizes the diversity of female identity rather than the coordination of men and women. Moreover, team events present a complex take on personhood and group. The team is formed of dancers who express individualism in their regalia and selection of dance style but who dance in close coordination with others. As a whole, it is a great opportunity to contemplate the tensions of personal autonomy and community. As folkloric dancing, team powwow dancing communicates a message about individual sublimation to tradition. Powwow team dancing adds messages that affirm the diversity of personhood.

At first glance, powwow and Latino folkloric dance are similar in their expression of gender. Men and women dance in both forms, but powwow is a bit more complex in the gendering of participation. In grand entry, men and women are sorted into categories; they are in the arena together but dance separately. In intertribal dancing, men and women, elders and children, all dance and socialize together. Rounds and other courtship-inspired dances coordinate men and women relative to one another in space (a field form often paralleled in folkloric dance). In competitive dance, men and women occupy the dance arena at separate times (and powwow looks more like gendering in K'iche' traditional dance). These differences are informed by divergence in purpose. Theatricalized folkloric dance constructs gender to assert distinctive cultural identities. It symbolizes unique culture that is imagined to have stable and clearly defined statuses and roles (unlike modernity). The enactment constructs identity, but for actual Latina women, gender is more complex. Dancing may present ideas about gender, but it simplifies gendered social reality. For powwow dancers, gender is enacted less to express unique ethnic identity and more to work on the complexity of gender relations in actual social groups. As in its expression of other social relations, powwow expresses multiplicity of gender.

Despite these differences, how one becomes a powwow dancer or a Latino folkloric dancer has an interesting similarity. Websites and videos are available to assist the newcomer to either form. Latino folkloric dancers can also attend schools and classes organized by professional touring companies or can read how-to self-instruction materials. Nonetheless, a current of self-teaching, learning from attending performances, and learning by doing is common to both forms. This stems from a popular sense of need for self-representation between both groups. In other words, they are both cultural expressions from the grassroots rather than orchestrated by institutionalized and formal education (the kind sponsored by states).

Both forms also present a variety of expression. The folkloric repertoire of vignettes includes representations of the pre-Columbian, the colonial, and the present. A group can make multiple claims on culture and promote a notion of identity that is complex, both modern and traditional. Powwow in dance categories provides a similar set of styles that are deployed to express Native identity that is complex with continuity from past to present. Both forms grant their participants and audiences an ethnic lingua franca that can be adapted to local purposes. The culture and history of a particular Native nation can be expressed in powwow; the distinctive homeland (including regions with states) can be constructed through the selection of vignette and by reference to specific indigenous groups in folkloric dance. The familiarity of the general form among audiences and performers who share and live within broad, abstract pan-ethnic identities fosters communication and cooperation while allowing expression of the kind of identity (local and unique) that human beings find satisfying. A Lakota dancer attending a Potawatomi powwow understands the basic forms and may be intrigued by the distinct ways that such ideal forms are enacted. A Bolivian dancer gets the basic ideas expressed in a Mexican performance because they share the same basic vocabulary of theatricalized form. In the process, the paradox of politically unified though culturally diverse is resolved. We dance the same dance, but in our own way.

Similar to their enactment of gender, powwow and folkloric dance express both commonality and divergence in dancing cosmology. Both make reference to Native orientation of the world, one in a direct, singular way, the other in multiple ways. If gender relations danced in folklore are meant to represent a temporally and culturally distinct set of (idealized) social relations, folkloric enactment of Native cosmology represents a generalized Native religion. Folkloric dance frequently refers in performance and in accompanying programs to the Mesoamerican orientation of the four cardinal directions. It is directly danced and overtly described. As in its gendering of dance, folkloric dance enacts cosmology to enhance self-authenticity through Other-representation. Indeed, an immigrant folkloric dancer from Mexico found my question about whether spirits were summoned by performance (a common occurrence in K'iche' traditional dance) rather unexpected. Folkloric reference to religion is representation of the beliefs and practices of ethnic Others.

Powwow also references cosmology and worldview. At times, religion is the subject of direct discourse meant to inform both Native and non-Native components of the audience (the former often defines particular Native culture within the category Native American). Powwow diverges in representation of cosmology from folkloric dance by its use of tacit and unspoken communication. The arrangement of the arena with its concentric circles is less the subject of direct discourse and more an unspoken discourse of cosmology enacted. Again, as with gender, powwow educates outsiders of varying levels while also making key symbols concrete for insiders. It influences Others while constructing cultural continuity for insiders.

A similar pattern applies to the broader questions of the articulation of people and communities to their natural environment. Both forms reference this in overt discourse. Folkloric dance in performance and the written program references the notion of Native people as "natural." Powwow also implies a connection of people to the natural world in explicit ways. Discourse references nature in general and activates a salient notion (sometimes a stereotype) about Native Americans. However, indigenous paraphernalia articulates the individual to the group and humankind to the natural order through symbols and concepts particular to Native nations.

It is when we compare the ethnic politics of powwow and immigrant folkloric dancing that the genres seem most similar. Although the ethnicity of the dancers varies, both forms work on similar problems. Immigrants and their descendants deploy folkloric dances to build political ties within a pan-ethnic category of Latino but also to express something distinctive about particular identities and cultures that make up the larger, abstract category. Powwow dancers and organizers build intertribal cooperation within the pan-ethnic category of Native American while also representing the specific Native identities and cultures. Latinos and Native Americans share the experience of living within a society dominated by ethnic Others, and political strength comes from finding commonality with people of similar culture and experience. Satisfying and unique identity, however, is rooted in particular and local

Table 14.2. Native American powwow and immigrant folkloric dance compared

		Native American Powwow	*Immigrant Folkloric Dance*
Material and Behavioral Culture	Dress	• Varies by style and gender • Individual expression	• Varies by gender • Uniform within performance
	Symbolic loading	Abstract, multivalent	Representative, monovalent
	Gender	• Dancing together (social dances) • Dancing simultaneously (intertribal dances) • Dancing separately (competitive dancing by category)	Men and women dance together, often depicting the courtship of the rural Other
	Training	• Embedded in kinship • Internet and video instruction available	• Traveling companies that offer instruction • Internet and video instruction available
Ideational Culture	Ritual	Sacred and secular comingle	Sacred depicted, not accessed
	Cosmology	Key symbol of concentric circles informs movement of dancers and construction of dance space	Cosmology overtly referenced, but key symbols are not central to performance
	Pan-Ethnicity	• Dance works to influence the image of Native American among ethnic Others • Dance works to build intertribal cooperation • Set of common styles adapted locally	• Dance works to influence the image of Latino among ethnic Others • Dance works to build interethnic Latino cooperation • Set of common themes and vignettes adapted to reference specific homeland

shared history and culture. Both forms find allies for cooperation but also for reflection and overt construction of unique identity. Moreover, the need to self-represent through pan-ethnic political cooperation derives, at least partly, from the stereotypes, misrepresentation, and misunderstanding prevalent in mainstream society. Cooperation among diverse groups drives intertribal powwows and Latino ethnic festivals. It is enacted symbolically in dance. Both powwow and folkloric dancing work to influence the perception of Others in the mainstream, carrying out self-representation of image in dance, building alliances for greater self-representation in politics. Beyond similarities are divergences. Both self-represent to outsiders and to self. Powwow retains a degree of multivalence. Folkloric dance is theatrical with elements of secular ritual. Powwow is theater as well as secular and sacred multivalent ritual.

OTHER-REPRESENTATION, POWER, AND NOSTALGIA

In late August 2006, the covers of two different newspapers featured similar photographs. Kalihwisaks: "She Looks for News," *the official newspaper of the Wisconsin Oneida, presented two images of Smoke dancers performing during halftime of a Green Bay Packers pre-season scrimmage. The title of the one-paragraph article accompanying the photographs declares, "Smoke dancers take Lambeau field" (Kaquatosh 2006). The article notes that the halftime show, presented by Oneida people, included powwow dances as well. Two weeks later, under the caption "Chief's Last Dance?," a full-color image of Chief Illiniwek, captured in his iconic splits-jump, stretched across the bottom third of the front page of the* Chicago Sun Times. *In common with the images of the Oneida dancers, the Chief was photographed at halftime of a football game. The* Sun Times *article referencing the photograph (Newbart 2006) describes in some detail the events leading up to the end of Chief Illiniwek as an official symbol of the University of Illinois. It focuses on NCAA policy and the response of university officials and Chief supporters. No mention of Native people occurs until the final two of twenty-two paragraphs.*

The performances and their descriptions differ in a number of ways, most obviously in the ethnicity of the dancers. Chief Illiniwek's performer is white, manifesting Other-representation; the Smoke dancers are Native, manifesting self-representation. More subtle differences are evident as well. The Chief is male and singular. The Oneida halftime show includes male and female performers and other Native dancers. In addition to mention of Smoke dances, a young boy in Grass Dance regalia is visible in the background of one of the photographs. Native culture and identity on display here are both male and female, multiplicity of powwow played out at halftime.

The newspapers vary as well. As Oneida performers represent themselves in dance, so is Kalihwisaks *self-representation in media. There is a sense of pride as the article notes the 60,000 spectators who witnessed the dancing. In contrast, the language of the* Sun Times *has the tone of objective journalism, but the article leaves out crucial information. What motivated the previous seventeen years' efforts to retire the Chief is not specified. The* Sun Times *may not be an official newspaper of mainstream Illinois, but like other coverage of mascot controversy, it does not capture the depth or complexity of Native concerns. Nor does it explore why an educational institution and its students and alumni would dedicate considerable time and resources to protect a sports symbol/mascot.*

I picked up the copy of Kalihwisaks *while on a visit to the Oneida Nation museum outside of Green Bay, Wisconsin. Two weeks later when I saw Chief Illiniwek on the cover of the* Sun Times, *I felt a vague sense of opportunity lost. The Packers had, perhaps unknowingly, evoked the spirit of the Oorang Indians, turning halftime over to a group of Native people who represented themselves in performance. Audience and performers alike, in the current manifestation of Native dance, benefit from time and social persistence. Oneida dancers, performing in a society that has come closer to its ideals of equality, need not enact Nesper's "authentic fakes" (2003:458–459). They are not compelled to "imitate white imitations of Indians" to the degree or in the way that Jim Thorpe and his Oorang Indians were.*

How then, I wondered, setting the newspapers side by side, did the Packers achieve what the University of Illinois could not? The weight of tradition, of course, makes Chief Illiniwek appealing, and turning the performance of his dance over to Peoria people, who would change it significantly, becomes difficult. However, the same span of time that makes tradition also makes the Chief the subject of criticism. He was created during a period when "authentic fakes" reigned supreme in the representations of Native people. Moreover, partly by historical accident, the relationships between institutions and Native groups are divergent. Wisconsin is for the Oneida what Oklahoma is for the Peoria: home, but home after removal. Nonetheless, it is clear that there are a good many Green Bay Packers fans among the Native peoples of Wisconsin. It seems also true that the Packers organization understands this and recognizes value in a positive relationship with the Oneida community that neighbors Green Bay. The University of Illinois has perceived Native people quite differently. The state was ethnically cleansed of Native people well before the university was founded. The Peoria are not neighbors but sources of cognitive dissonance. The lore of the Chief reinforces the notion that they vanished. The large majority of Native students who enroll at the University of Illinois, by virtue of the same removal policy, are from out of state even if their ancestors lived in what is now the state. As a result, Native activists come from remote communities. Peoria people who are college football fans likely support the University of Oklahoma. Institution and constituent indigenous individuals are not connected at University of Illinois as are the Packers and the Oneida. It is no wonder that a solution involving indigenous self-representation was never seriously considered.

In the final imaginary staging of dance, I consider Other-representation directly. The dancers in this last act are selected and sorted by class and ethnicity. In the first comparison, I consider Latino folkloric dancing and Indian mascot dancing with a particular focus on college students. In the second, I consider institutional adoption of symbolic Indians across national boundaries.

In Chapter 9, I remarked on the connection of Latino folkloric groups with institutions of education in the United States. Indeed, establishment of folkloric dancing at all levels of education was one of the goals of Chicano student activism in the late 1960s (Shay 2006:81). When we emphasize the context of education of folkloric dance, commonalities with symbolic Indians in sport emerge. In both cases, student activities (sports and performance) involve the embodiment of Indianness for public audiences. At the U.S. college, transitions of identity are common experiences for students of all backgrounds. Careers are chosen, adolescents become adults, and attachments to new sets of people and even to an institution are formed. In the process, students reconcile identity uncertainty, as college has some of the properties of the liminal phase of rites of passage. Moreover, beyond campus awaits a large and anonymous society. For white students, unmarked and tacit ethnicity is a cognitive challenge, and symbolic Indians offer an authentic and unique connection to community and institution.

Latino students face the same alienation and anonymous society, but from a different social position than their Anglo classmates. That white is unmarked means that Latino is marked. Additionally, social inequality makes Latino subject to construction by Others and burdens it with oversimplifications. Latino, by bringing together people of various heritages, becomes a source of political power. However, Latino pan-ethnicity requires work to foster political cooperation and establish more concrete identification within an abstract level of social classification. Folkloric dance offers a means for college students to self-represent and challenge stereotypes. Occasional enactment of Indianness in such performances accesses sets of symbols that proclaim authentic and unique identities. This is not to say that the two forms are identical. Certainly, folkloric dances are different from mascot performances. The first and most obvious difference is that Latinos typically do not enjoy the power and privilege of the white university students who have portrayed Chief Illiniwek. Moreover, there are obvious differences in material and behavioral construction of Indianness in the two forms. To organize these differences, I employ Deloria's classification of playing Indian as either "object" or "people" (1998:135).

We return to Chief Illiniwek, where object authenticity is the governing ideology of construction. Chief supporters emphasize the regalia and its origin. How such dress is used by Native people in public performance does not enter the discourse or influence the dance. Emphasis on objects over actors and context of enactment is clear in how the Chief's dance is termed. The insistence that the Chief perform Native American Fancy Dance betrays a lack of familiarity with actual Native dancers and dancing. The outfit as object and the dance name as label serve to authenticate preconceptions of Indianness. They reflect not Native influence on performance but defense of creative appropriation. What makes so striking the image on the cover of the *Chicago Sun Times* (and others like it) is the fundamental decontextualization of its central cultural artifact. A feather bonnet, normally reserved for honored warriors on solemn occasions, adorns a performer in mid-leap, legs split wide.

Although problematic at times in its representations of Indianness, Latino folkloric dance approximates Deloria's people authenticity. In written programs, oral discourse, and performance, it is clear that folkloric dance attempts to represent actual forms and music. Common to many presentations, the folkloric version of the Deer Dance, although distinct in dress, does have an in-the-field complement that stresses similar themes. Moreover, folkloric Deer dancers do not employ the headscarf of a daykeeper or the staff of a *cofradía* officeholder as an object to authenticate the Indianness of the performance. Folkloric enactment of the Deer Dance may irk indigenous dancers, but it does not divorce potentially sacred objects from their context. Nonetheless, to some this seems like outright appropriation. However, it is also clear that many folkloric dancers consider Native people and histories as part of their own heritage, more than Indian Others who have vanished.

While folkloric dance is distinct from symbolic Indians in sport, it is not perfect. Precise mimesis does not address the essential problem. That is, authenticity of act is still not people authenticity. Nonindigenous representations of indigenous culture must be evaluated partly for accuracy, but also in terms of the stereotypes and harm that they may promote. This requires input in a variety of ways from those whose cultures are portrayed. It also requires that the input from field dancers is received by social actors in dance companies who are willing to listen and able to influence performance. In an ideal world, sports teams would follow the model of the Green Bay Packers and premier folkloric companies would collaborate on an equal basis with indigenous dancers of the field. Ideally, all would enjoy equitable access to travel and income derived from sponsorship and international presentation. However, this is not reality, and some basic steps are suggested. First, indigenous authorship should be acknowledged and compensated. Second, premier companies (and their sponsors) should avoid viewing indigenous culture as a commodity ripe for appropriation. For semi-professional and amateur groups, in addition to constructing positive self-image, greater awareness of living indigenous peoples and their struggles can be accomplished in training and performance. Indeed,

Latino dancers in the United States, because they have experienced society from a minority position, are potential advocates for indigenous cultural and human rights. What is to be avoided is the fanciful imagination of the indigenous past accompanied by ignorance and indifference to the indigenous present that Rostas (2009:191–208) found among some "Mexica" dancers in Mexico City.

INSTITUTIONS AND AUTHENTIC INDIANS

> For all Guatemalans, the figure of our courageous warrior TECUN UMAN should represent: (a) a lesson in patriotism; (b) an example of authentic nationalism; (c) a symbol of national identity; (d) an example of the defense of freedom, foundation for national unity; (e) champion of sovereignty; (f) the honor and courage of the Guatemalan soldier; (g) principle of dignity for the Guatemalan Army.
>
> FROM A PAMPHLET PRODUCED AND DISTRIBUTED BY THE GUATEMALAN MILITARY (CITED IN OTZOY 1999:133)

> [T]he complete human being—the strong, agile human body, the unfettered human intellect, the indomitable human spirit.
>
> UNIVERSITY OF ILLINOIS HEAD FOOTBALL COACH ROBERT ZUPPKE (1913–1941), DESCRIBING THE MEANING OF "ILLINIWEK" TO HIS PLAYERS (CITED IN GARIPPO 2000:VIII)

> He is a tangible symbol of an intangible spirit filled with qualities a person of any background can aspire to: goodness, strength, bravery, truthfulness, courage, and dignity.
>
> THE CHIEF ILLINIWEK EDUCATIONAL FOUNDATION

> Spirit Courage Strength Bravery Honor Loyalty
>
> POPULAR T-SHIRT IN SUPPORT OF CHIEF ILLINIWEK

White University of Illinois students and Latino college students in general have one additional commonality. Both inherited traditions of dancing Indian that were constructed in earlier periods when Other-representation and unrestrained appropriation of Native culture by elites were normative. These traditions have enjoyed institutional support (including that of their respective states) during the intervening period between the moment of appropriation/creation and the present. This backing has had an ambivalent impact. Officialization brings resources and insulates Other-representation from contestation. It also fossilizes appropriated images of Indianness, making them less capable of adjustment with changing social circumstances. Common also is the tendency of formal institutions to deploy symbols to shape the perception and behavior of constituent individuals.

To further explore why the University of Illinois (and other U.S. institutions) have adopted imaginary Indians as key elaborating symbols, it is useful to consider adoption of Native leaders as heroes in another, foreign context. While researching institutional statements about the Chief, I was struck by their similarity to official Guatemalan state rhetoric about Tekun Umam, the K'iche' Maya military leader represented in the Dance of the Conquest. There are, no doubt, important and profound differences between Chief Illiniwek and Tekun Umam and their adopting institutions. However, comparing them reveals something about how images of Indians are used to create a sense of authenticity and become vehicles for indoctrination. Comparison also presents a fuller perspective on the cognitive and political difficulties that accompany appropriation.

As I explored in Part Five, universities in the United States have been charged with the task of completing the socialization of young people. Over time, the emphasis of college has varied from broad and idealistic goals of producing good citizens to more pragmatic career preparation. Whatever the ideology guiding the institution, the university has some common needs and challenges. First, a campus, like any place where human beings live in proximity, requires social control. Fostering college spirit and dedication to institution among students has obvious benefits in this area. Moreover, particularly in an environment of undependable state funding for education, the U.S. university needs loyal alumni. If students experience an intense sense of community, of connection to the collective identity of the college, they are more likely to return and to contribute. In the various ways that colleges promote attachment of individuals to institution, imaginary Indians have been particularly effective symbols. As Clifford (1988) observed, Native cultures are a source of authenticity and purity. Authentic symbols and the accompanying ideologies of the vanishing American and imperialist nostalgia have generated uncanny dedication among some students and alumni.

As do colleges, military institutions socialize members in a way that can profoundly shape identity and experience. Social control, of course, is a primary institutional function of an army. The Guatemalan army needs obedient soldiers and officers and during the early 1980s deployed them in pursuit of genocide. Under such circumstances, individuals within the military require an ideological mechanism that works to distance soldiers from the vulgar reality of state violence and terror. Tekun Umam becomes a confusing and compelling figure. As a martyr, he is a dead Indian who is a good Indian. Moreover, his sacrifice to Guatemalan freedom necessitates loyalty in return. Venerating a K'iche' warrior of the distant past within an institution that recently killed many K'iche' civilians convolutes the distinction between self-sacrifice and murder. This cognitive paradox became social reality in acts under military orders or military coercion whereby Maya soldiers or militarized Maya civilians killed other Mayas.[5]

Table 14.3. Dance forms compared

Form	*Dancers*	*Audience*	*Challenges*	*Representation in Dance*
K'iche' Traditional Dance	Maya	Maya, with some nonindigenous	• Colonialism • Lack of political autonomy • Ethnocide • Recent attempted genocide	• Strategies of interethnic relations • Material for cultural continuity coded, part of a dual discourse
Native American Powwow	Native (North) American	• Diverse in urban settings • Indigenous on reservations	• Colonialism • Ethnocide, assimilation • Stereotyped, imaginary Indians • Pan-ethnicity	• Embodiment of local culture • Influence notion of generic Indian • Work on common and diverse paradox of pan-ethnicity
Latino Folkloric Dance	Latino (typically nonindigenous)	Latinos, some whites	• Anonymity • Discrimination • Transnationalism • Pan-ethnicity	• Indigenous Others of own country, region to create "authentic" and satisfying identity • Influence notion of Latino • Work on common and diverse paradox of pan-ethnicity
Sports Mascots Dancing	White	Mixed, largely white	• Lack of authenticity • Lack of a meaningful past • Seeming loss of privilege	• Unique "authentic" tradition through imagined Indians • Myths of identification that deemphasize colonialism and genocide • Protection of ethnic hierarchy by representing the indigenous Other

So these state-sponsored institutions with divergent culture and history found themselves with similar functions. Both adopted Indians as symbols to idealize their functions, framing Tekun Umam and Chief Illiniwek through the lens of imperialist nostalgia. Noble, dead Indians from a romanticized past are powerful symbols for people separated from kin and community who confront alienated and changing societies. Moreover, the identities that these institutions embrace are shaped by an ideology of identity that stresses loyalty to an entity that is nonfamilial and theoretically culturally homogeneous. The qualities that they attempt to inculcate are abstract and highly idealized. Who can argue against loyalty and courage? Cultural homogeneity is equated with unity, and abstract values with the symbolic Indian and its institution. The symbol comes to represent all that is good. The state, its institutions, and members are to manifest the good symbolized in the appropriated Indian. A criticism of either symbol or institution becomes an attack on goodness and on self.

In the end, however, the larger societies that host and support the University of Illinois and the Guatemalan military include Native people who are alive and much more complex than the noble savage. Their voices, competing with entrenched ideology buttressed by compelling symbols, generate cognitive dissonance. It is difficult to adjust a symbolic constellation that has been reinforced with the resources of the state and that proclaims a hold on all that is good and noble. Tekun Umam retains his official status, although his ritual and representation in monumental architecture seem to fade. Chief Illiniwek is no longer official, but students and alumni attempt to revive him through secular ritual (and object authenticity).

The social conflict resulting from the disjuncture of rigid reinforced symbols and complex social reality has roots in other, larger, and more tacit confusions. These I explore in the final chapter, moving beyond dance and back to the complex and stratified global reality of the twenty-first century.

NOTES

1. For more on such effects in ritual, see Lex (1975).

2. I am indebted to Marvin Cohodas for pointing this out while we attended a performance of the Dance of the Conquest in Momostenango.

3. Virtually all K'iche' dancers are male; comparison with female powwow dances is, accordingly, difficult.

4. There are interesting parallels as well in the Ajitz character in the Dance of the Conquest and the healer-originator of the Grass Dance. Both reference fire and are spiritual mediators who are also warriors. Moreover, the connection between Ajitz and Kawil with his snake/fire-drill foot is reminiscent of the Grass Dance originator, who had a deformed foot but was an apt dancer.

5. For more on the complexity of murder during *la violencia*, see Sanford (2003).

Fifteen

Confusions and Conclusions

Representational dance, as secular ritual, is a conceptual means to address conflicted topics. Drawing on Shay (2006), I have examined how people of differing societies express ethnicity and often attempt to control images of identity through representational dance. Additionally, representations in dance reflect social inequality. These two issues, ethnicity and inequality, are salient in the global era. We encounter Others of greater diversity more often. In the process great social and economic inequality is more directly revealed. Not surprisingly, such expression and contestation of ethnicity are occasionally subject to controversy. Three basic confusions frame the conflict over Other-representation and the controversy of insistent expression of unique identity: (1) the confusion of personal and stable for authentic, (2) the confusion of de jure and theoretical equality with real and pervasive inequality, and (3) the facile equivalence of one's ideas of identity with those of ethnic Others.

PERSONAL AND STABLE CONFUSED WITH AUTHENTIC

In this book I have outlined various problems with authenticity, identifying it as the folk theory about the folk. I discussed its assumptions that real culture is unchanging culture. I explored how authentic voice is judged by a standard—a unique and original creation—that is not possible (or at least not attested) in actual individual expression or cultural traditions. These idealized standards of truth and purity in expression and material production are applied and judged in ways that represent, in an ongoing process, the colonial origins of authenticity. Given the difficulties of authenticity, we are left to ponder why people seek it. In particular, it is the denizens of large wealthy complex societies, the "modern" ones, that seek authenticity. James Clifford succinctly captured much of the critical thought on modernity in *The Predicament of Culture* (1988). Clifford contends that, in essence, modernity lacks authenticity. There are two basic problems of modernity that make it seem inauthentic. First, we should concede that modernity is market capitalist modernity. Modern societies feature systems of mass production that are governed largely by the market (or, more bluntly, by the desire to maximize material wealth). Such systems produce objects through complex, impersonal processes. The vast majority of people involved in such processes leave no personal mark on objects turned out identically in large masses. Furthermore, the systems of distribution are anonymous as well; we may catch a glimpse of someone stocking the shelf or driving the truck to the store, but the process is absent direct face-to-face human interaction. Add the scale of modern society to its alienated production and lives marked by wealth and security become quite impersonal as well.

As Carrier (1990:590) has pointed out, a system of wholly impersonal manufacture and delivery of material culture is a recent phenomenon in human history. In small-scale societies—those similar to the ones in which human beings evolved—production, distribution, and consumption of food and objects are personal. Though most indigenous groups are integrated into the global market, some production is personal, an artisan connected to the product she makes, a farmer to the food he grows. As a result of such production (among other factors), objects made by an indigenous person become, for some consumers, "authentic" objects. More sophisticated seekers of authenticity may demand objects made to the standards of a particular moment in time, no matter how much style and function may have evolved before or after.

Alienated, impersonal production is only one characteristic of market-based large-scale society. It is also rapidly changing. Spaces, subject to changing value determined by market forces, are targets also of frequent destruction and reconstruction. Citizens in pursuit of better work or dislocated by loss of work live life in shifting social networks rather than more constant social groups. As a result, in addition to its impersonal qualities, modern society impresses a sense of instability. Much as we label personally moving experiences as authentic, so do we find authentic the sense of stability created by the enactment of tradition. In the end, faced with the challenges of alienation and instability inherent in modernity, some find relief in experience that is personal and seems stable. The expectation that Others (or reworked versions of their cultures) provide "authenticity" has varied implications, opportunities, and risks.

The experience of some of the people involved in Totonicapán's sustainable tourism project illustrates one problem of seeking authenticity. Since the advent of Mel Gibson's *Apocalypto*, K'iche' Maya tourism hosts have encountered visitors who ask to be shown the "real Maya." One guide reports being told that he was not Maya because he did not conform to images in the film (despite the fact that even *Apocalypto*'s inaccuracies depict the Maya *of the past*). Beyond the obvious inability of film audiences to distinguish between history and fiction and the power of film to shape perceptions of "truth," social inequality is evident. First, the person telling an ethnic Other that he is not authentic in his identity seems unaware of the impact of such a statement. This stems from not having experienced such pronouncements about the speaker's own identity. When was the last time someone had to defend the authenticity of his whiteness or modernity? Second, those enjoying positions of social and economic privilege within the wealthy core countries seem comfortable with the notion that they hold the authority to judge the authenticity of poor people, even when they are familiar with the specifics of a culture through only a film or a guidebook. The act of judging the authenticity of the Other is one that confirms and asserts social and economic advantage. Moreover, as Little (2004) illustrates in more depth, tourists come with the expectation that actual people will conform to the constructs of tourism websites, pamphlets, and guidebooks. They expect, having spent money for such an experience, that they deserve to receive it. Though uncertain about Mayas working for cash in nontraditional fields, some tourists seem comfortable with the commodification of the authenticity that they seek.

As I have stressed, authenticity is a contradicted and subjective concept. In its uncertain and shifting semantic components, labeling something "authentic" masks the satisfying dimensions of the experience. In the end, more than authentic, what we seek is personal, human, and stable. Human beings are apt to equate a profound sense of social connection (Turner's *communitas*) with the transcendent truth of the ideas enacted in ritual. So are we capable of labeling objects, acts, and experiences that resist alienation as "authentic."

ACTUAL SOCIAL INEQUALITY AND IDEAL SOCIAL EQUALITY CONFUSED

If seeking authenticity drives audiences to representational dances, the reality of social inequality motivates dancers to self-expression of ethnicity. The insistent expression of cultural distinctiveness in turn generates another response rooted in gaps between ideal and real. Modern states and countries that aspire to modern statehood embrace the notion of equality of their respective citizens. This imagined equality has social and cultural dimensions. Legal equality, even when statutes and principles are not enforced, presumes in the minds of the privileged the actual social equality it idealizes. Moreover, large gaps in access to power and wealth encourage emphasis on the ideals of equality (including equality of opportunity). As states promote ideal social equality, they also embrace ideologies that equate nation and state, presuming cultural homogeneity where actual cultural diversity is pervasive. These two areas of ideal equality contradicted with actual social inequality generate cognitive dissonance. As is the case with cognitive dissonance in general, our reactions vary. We can pretend ideal is real and ignore inequality, or we can adjust our cognitive models and accommodate real inequality, or we can work to change social reality to better approximate our ideals.

After decades of neoliberal rhetoric, working to reduce gaps in power and wealth does not have a broad popular base. As a consequence, making social reality better approximate ideal wealth and power equality seems unlikely to occur soon (if it all). The other ideal equality, that of identity, has a different history. Interestingly, the failure and unintended consequences of government policies aimed at homogenizing culture have not made it into the public consciousness. We are readily skeptical that government can address socioeconomic inequality but blind to the disastrous results of government-sponsored programs of cultural assimilation. The facile equivalence of unity with "adopt my culture" enjoys widespread support.

The cognitive dissonance generated by this pair of confusions (of real social inequality with ideal equality and of real cultural diversity with cultural homogeneity) has consequences in the way representational dance is created and read. People of ethnic privilege who believe themselves equal members of culturally homogeneous society find persistent expression of distinctiveness irksome. Those who self-represent in dance find their identities ignored or made invisible, while they continue to face real social inequality rooted in ethnicity. Other-representation faces similar issues. Dancers appropriate the culture of long-lost or soon-to-disappear peoples who nonetheless persist. They dance Indian, arguing that in a free and equal society all are free to dance what they please. Those whose culture is appropriated struggle to influence how their Otherness is presented, lest they be subject to further discrimination and marginalization.

NAÏVE REALISM OF IDENTITY

Implicit in the assumption of equality of expression is a naïve realism about identity. Beyond the problem of being represented by powerful or privileged Others is the presumption that all identity is the same everywhere. People who live away from the margins, in the mainstream, enjoy security that is the product of state action and policy. In return, whether or not they actually provide security and protect rights, states demand loyalty. Combined with nationalist ideologies that equate polity and people, states promote the notion of unitary identity. Individuals are foremost (if not exclusively) citizens of states, and complexity of identity, especially if it involves attachment to groups culturally distinct from the official ethnicity of state, is threatening. Indigenous people and ethnic minority groups, however, by virtue of power inequality inhabit multiple ethnic selves and reference varied norms of discourse, depending on social setting.

Beyond the way that political and social inequality fosters multiplicity of identity, there are cultural differences in how identity is conceptualized. Within the states explored in this book (Guatemala and the United States) are indigenous traditions that stress multiplicity of identity. People have robust kin ties, senses of connection to local communities and landscapes, and particular indigenous identities and live within polities largely controlled by ethnic Others. Across this cultural diversity, indigenous peoples in both states also tend to value both individual autonomy and cooperation with group. Accordingly, identity within group and between ethnic self and Other is multiple.

Unfortunately, state policy and Other-representation generally stress homogeneity of complex diverse groups. Folkloric dance emphasizes uniformity in dress and step in its representations of indigenous Mesoamerican cultures. Sports mascots suggest that hundreds of Native nations can be represented by one kind of Indian. The assumption of Other-representers reflects their nationalist-influenced notion of identity. Indigenous response seeks to protect and express diversity of identity and persistent cultural distinctiveness. Given these contradictory notions and the power that backs imagined cultural homogeneity while maintaining social inequality, it is no surprise that indigenous and nonindigenous perform and witness secular rituals about their identities. Human beings turn to ritual enactment when closely held ideas are cognitively difficult or when social reality diverges significantly from core values.

A primary goal of cultural anthropology is to reveal and explore the tacit dimensions of one's own culture. The question, then, is what to do with the resulting enhanced understanding of collective self. In the present case, I have emphasized beliefs about society, culture, and identity that diverge from social reality. When such gaps are persistent they carry a cost. In this case, what we say we seek (unity or authenticity) is undermined by policies and actions that seek to make the ideal of uniformity real. Coercing cultural homogeneity often generates greater attachment to diverse identity. Moreover, when state institutions are the mechanism of cultural homogenization, it undermines states' claims to offer equal protection (or protection of any sort) to all of their respective citizens. So in unloading and examining ideals of nation and state we must confront a seeming paradox: a sense of loyalty to state and fellow citizens is possible only when diversity is valued. Similarly, recognizing that we label things "authentic" that are better termed "personal and stable" introduces another paradox. Such experiences are generated through living culture enacted by groups of complex human beings. The resulting social reality is messy and inherently changing.

Representational dance is a predominant secular ritual of our globalized era. Not unlike more conventional forms of human ritual, it deals with the conflicted and difficult areas of human experience. The forms of this secular ritual explored herein sort into two broad types: self-representation and Other-representation. In closing I summarize the basic motivations behind representative dancing relative to self and Other. When discussing Kayapo politics, Terence Turner stresses that power is created in the act of representation (2002:246). We can influence others to action, whether or not they share our ethnic identification, through representation. So in our final go-round of the dance genres discussed in this book, I explore the motivations for the creation of power through representation among various dancers.

It is obvious why indigenous people strive for self-representation. Their representations by Others, whether in legal matters, state politics, financial matters, or image, form a history of misrepresentation and misery. Self-representation is a means of decolonization and of influencing powerful Others. Dance is associated with both tradition and indigeneity; it is compelling beyond its regular power to embody social order and cultural identity. Moreover, leaving representation and its attendant power to Others risks having that power exercised in ways corrosive to Native community and culture.

Clear also is why immigrants dance to self-represent. Despite the ideal of equality of rights, states tend to meet the needs of some segments of society better than others. Immigrant groups (and indigenous groups) are among those underrepresented in the protections and benefits distributed by states. Moreover, just as there is political strength in the Native American (enacted in powwow dances), so is there strength in the Latino (enacted in folkloric dances). The anonymity of U.S. society adds to the need to self-represent. Here, the power created through representation works against the imposition of overly broad and stereotyped constructions. Immigrant dancing works to influence those within the pan-ethnic category of Latino and those outside it.

It emphasizes and works to resolve the paradox of commonality and diversity for various kinds of insiders and outsiders.

Most difficult to understand is persistent Other-representation by advantaged and powerful individuals and institutions. However, Other-representation is not unconnected to self-representation by indigenous dancers. Construction of meaningful identity and social inequality are the primary factors in both cases. Other-representation makes alienated more authentic through images of Indianness. More, however, is in play than appropriation of culture to construct authenticity. Appropriated imaginary Indians (and the ability to represent them) assert and confirm ethnic hierarchy. Other-representation manifests the privilege to construct the authenticity of Others. What evinces ethnic and political power more than being able to determine how another people is conceptualized? Other-representation is not about challenging inequality, but about asserting and protecting it.

As a consequence, those whose culture is appropriated work to contest the construction of their identities through dance. The insistence on self-expression (often annoying to the privileged) works as much to counter-appropriate as to be obstinately different. So long as deep social inequality and ideal equality coexist, Other-representers will be inclined to protect social privilege. The Others they represent will struggle to contest it. These representations and counterrepresentations become parallel forms, appropriation and counter-appropriation, manifesting a certain cogenesis through conflict.

Works Cited

AIC (American Indian Center of Chicago)
2006 "53rd Annual Powwow: Honoring the Heartbeat of Mother Earth." Event program. November 17–19.

Albers, Patricia, and Beatrice Medicine
2005 "Some Reflections on Nearly Forty Years on the Northern Plains Powwow Circuit." In *Powwow*, edited by Clyde Ellis, Luke Eric Lassiter, and Gary H. Dunham, 26–45. Lincoln: University of Nebraska Press.

Amik (Larry Smallwood)
N.d. "The Jingle Dress as Dreamed: The Story of the Jingle Dress." Electronic document, http://www.millelacsojibwe.org/cultureColumn.asp?id=115, accessed July 29, 2008.

Anderson, Benedict
1983 *Imagined Communities: Reflections on the Origin and Spread of Nationalism.* London: Verso Editions.

Anderson, Jack
2000 "Amalia Hernández, 83; Led Ballet Folklorico de Mexico." *New York Times*, November 7: C23.

Angrosino, Michael

2002 "Civil Religion Redux." *Anthropological Quarterly* 75 (2): 239–267.

Applegate Krouse, Susan

2001 "Traditional Iroquois Socials." Theme issue, Maintaining Identity in the City. *American Indian Quarterly* 25 (3): 400–408.

Arens, William

1975 "The Great American Football Ritual." *Natural History* 84 (8): 72–82.

Arndt, Grant

2005 "Ho-Chunk 'Indian Powwows' of the Early Twentieth Century." In *Powwow*, edited by Clyde Ellis, Luke Eric Lassiter, and Gary H. Dunham, 46–67 Lincoln: University of Nebraska Press.

Associated Press

2007 "Internet Threat Yields No Charges." *Chicago Tribune*, January 30: Metro p. 3.

Axtmann, Ann

2001 "Performative Power in Native America: Powwow Dancing." *Dance Research Journal* 33 (1): 7–22.

Ballet Folklórico de México

2005a "About Us." Electronic document, http://balletamalia.com/quienese.html, accessed August 1, 2006.

2005b "Facts." Electronic document, http://balletamalia.com/noticiase.html#2, accessed August 1, 2006.

2005c "School." Electronic document, http://balletamalia.com/escuelae.html, accessed August 1, 2006.

2006 "Amalia Hernández's Ballet Folkórico de México." Event program. September 23–24.

Baumann, Roland

1995 "The 'Moors and Christians' of Valor: Folklore and Conflict in the Alpujarra (Andalusia)." PhD dissertation, Department of Anthropology, Tulane University, New Orleans.

Bauxar, Joseph

1978 "History of the Illinois Area." In *Handbook of the North American Indians*, edited by Bruce G. Trigger, 594–601. Washington, DC: Smithsonian Institution.

Blasingham, Emily J.

1956 "The Depopulation of the Illinois Indians, Part I." *Ethnohistory* 3 (3): 193–224.

Bode, Barbara

1961 *The Dance of the Conquest of Guatemala*. New Orleans: Middle American Research Institute, Tulane University.

Burke, David

2001 "Dance Pioneers." *Quad City Times*, September 28. Electronic document, http://qctimes.com, accessed August 4, 2011.

Burkhart, Louise M., and Janine Gasco

1996 "Mesoamerica and Spain: The Conquest." In *The Legacy of Mesoamerica: History and Culture of a Native American Civilization*, edited by Robert M. Carmack, Janine Gasco, and Gary H. Gossen, 122–153. Upper Saddle River, NJ: Simon and Schuster.

Callender, Charles

1978 "Illinois." In *Handbook of the North American Indians*, edited by Bruce G. Trigger, 673–680. Washington, DC: Smithsonian Institution.

Carmack, Robert M.

1981 *The Quiché Mayas of Utatlán: The Evolution of a Highland Guatemala Kingdom*. Norman: University of Oklahoma Press.

Carrier, James

1990 "Reconciling Commodities and Personal Relations in Industrial Society." *Theory and Society* 19 (5): 579–598.

Castañada, Gabriel Aneel

1965 *Monumento a Tecún Umán*. Guatemala City: Tipografía Nacional.

Chief Illiniwek Educational Foundation

2004 "Brief History." Electronic document, www.chiefilliniwek.org, accessed July 9, 2007.

Clifford, James

1988 *The Predicament of Culture: Twentieth-Century Ethnography, Literature, and Art*. Cambridge, MA: Harvard University Press.

Cojtí Cuxil, Demetrio

1996 "The Politics of Maya Revindication." In *Maya Cultural Activism in Guatemala*, edited by Edward F. Fischer and R. McKenna Brown, 19–50. Austin: University of Texas Press.

Conrad, Geoffrey W., and Arthur A. Demarest

1984 *Religion and Empire: The Dynamics of Aztec and Inca Expansionism*. Cambridge: Cambridge University Press.

Cook, Garrett W.

2000 *Renewing the Maya World: Expressive Culture in a Highland Town*. Austin: University of Texas Press.

Davis, Laurel R., and Mavina T. Rau

2001 "Escaping the Tyranny of the Majority: A Case Study of Mascot Change." In *Team Spirits: The Native American Mascots Controversy*, edited by C. Richard King and Charles Fruehling, 221–240. Lincoln: University of Nebraska Press.

Deloria, Philip J.

1998 *Playing Indian*. New Haven, CT: Yale University Press.

De Shane, Nina

1991 "Powwow Dancing and the Warrior Tradition." *Studia Musicologica Academiae Scientiarum Hungaricae* 13 (1): 375–391.

DesJarlait, Robert

1997 "The Contest Powwow versus the Traditional Powwow and the Role of the Native American Community." *Wicazo Sa Review* 12 (1): 115–127.

Duncan, Jeffrey

1998 "Illiniwek Irony." *Chicago Tribune*. March 13: Voice of the People, 24.

Eber, Christine, and Janet Tanski

2002 "Women's Cooperatives in Chiapas, Mexico: Strategies of Survival and Empowerment in Times of Struggle." *Social Development Issues* 24 (3): 33–40.

Ellis, Clyde

2005 "The Sound of the Drum Will Revive Them and Make Them Happy." In *Powwow*, edited by Clyde Ellis, Luke Eric Lassiter, and Gary H. Dunham, 3–25. Lincoln: University of Nebraska Press.

Ellis, Clyde, and Luke Eric Lassiter

2005 "Introduction." In *Powwow*, edited by Clyde Ellis, Luke Eric Lassiter, and Gary H. Dunham, vii–xv. Lincoln: University of Nebraska Press.

Ferguson, Brian R.

1990 "Blood of the Leviathan: Western Contact and Warfare in Amazonia." *American Ethnologist* 17 (2): 237–257.

Fischer, Edward F.

1999 "Cultural Logic and Maya Identity: Rethinking Constructivism and Essentialism." *Current Anthropology* 40 (4): 473–499.

Fisher, Donald M.

2001 "Chief Bill Orange and the Saltine Warrior: A Cultural History of Indian Symbols and Imagery at Syracuse University." In *Team Spirits: The Native American Mascots Controversy*, edited by C. Richard King and Charles Fruehling, 25–45. Lincoln: University of Nebraska Press.

Fowler, Loretta

2005 "Local Contexts of Powwow Ritual." In *Powwow*, edited by Clyde Ellis, Luke Eric Lassiter, and Gary H. Dunham, 68–84. Lincoln: University of Nebraska Press.

Fox, Richard G.

2004 "Continuities, Imputed and Inferred." In *Pluralizing Ethnography: Comparison and Representation in Maya Cultures, Histories, and Identities*, edited by John M. Watanabe and Edward F. Fischer, 291–298. Santa Fe, NM: School of American Research Press.

Freidel, David, Linda Schele, and Joy Parker
1993 *Maya Cosmos: Three Thousand Years on the Shaman's Path*. New York: Quill/ William Morrow.

Ganter, Granville, ed.
2006 *The Collected Speeches of Sagoyewatha, or Red Jacket*. Syracuse, NY: Syracuse University Press.

Garippo Louis B.
2000 "The Chief Illiniwek Dialogue: Intent and Tradition vs. Reaction and History." Report to the Board of Trustees of the University of Illinois. Champaign: University of Illinois. Electronic document, www.uillinois.edu /trustees/dialogue/repat-files/toc.html, accessed August 4, 2011.

Gathering of Nations Powwow
2009 "2009 Contest Information." Electronic document, http://www.gathering ofnations.com/powwow/2009/contest.htm, accessed July 13, 2010.

Geertz, Clifford
1973 *The Interpretation of Cultures*. New York: Basic Books.

Gelo, Daniel J.
1999 "Powwow Patter: Indian Emcee Discourse on Power and Identity." *Journal of American Folklore* 112 (443): 40–57.

Goetz, Delia, and Sylvanus G. Morley, trans.
1950 *Popol Vuh: The Sacred Book of the Ancient Quiche Maya*. From Spanish translation by Adrian Recinos. Norman: University of Oklahoma Press.

Goldenstein, Taylor
2010 "The Next Dance Event Perseveres." *Daily Illini*, October 22. Electronic document, www.dailyillini.com/index.php/article/2010/10/the_next_dance_ event_perseveres, accessed August 4, 2011.

Gossen, Gary H.
1996 "The Religious Traditions of Mesoamerica." In *The Legacy of Mesoamerica: History and Culture of a Native American Civilization*, edited by Robert M. Carmack, Janine Gasco, and Gary H. Gossen, 290–320. Upper Saddle River, NJ: Simon and Schuster.
2004 "Everything Has Begun to Change." In *Pluralizing Ethnography: Comparison and Representation in Maya Cultures, Histories, and Identities*, edited by John M. Watanabe and Edward F. Fischer, 127–161. Santa Fe, NM: School of American Research Press.

Gow, David D., and Joanne Rappaport
2002 "The Indigenous Public Voice: The Multiple Idioms of Modernity in Native Cauca." In *Indigenous Movements, Self-Representation, and the State in Latin America*, edited by Kay B. Warren and Jean E. Jackson, 47–80. Austin: University of Texas Press.

Graham, Laura R.

2002 "How Should an Indian Speak? Amazonian Indians and the Symbolic Politics of Language in the Global Public Sphere." In *Indigenous Movements, Self-Representation, and the State in Latin America*, edited by Kay B. Warren and Jean E. Jackson, 181–228. Austin: University of Texas Press.

Grand River Powwow

2010 "Grand River 'Champion of Champions' Pow-wow Website." Electronic document, http://www.grpowwow.com/Main.html, accessed July 13, 2010.

Grandin, Greg

2000 *The Blood of Guatemala: A History of Race and Nation*. Durham, NC: Duke University Press.

Green, Linda

1994 "Fear as a Way of Life." *Cultural Anthropology* 9 (2): 227–256.

Grube, Nikolai

1992 "Classic Maya Dance: Evidence from Hieroglyphs and Iconography." *Ancient Mesoamerica* 3: 201–218.

Hale, Charles R.

2006 *Más que un Indio: Racial Ambivalence and Neoliberal Multiculturalism in Guatemala*. School of American Research Resident Scholar Book. Santa Fe, NM: School of American Research Press.

Harjo, Suzan Shown

2002 "The Real Fightin' Whities." *Indian Country Today*, April 18.

2006 "Note to Congress: Stop Shielding 'Indian' Mascots and Start Defending Indian People." *Indian Country Today*, June 9.

Harris, Max

2000 *Aztecs, Moors, and Christians: Festivals of Reconquest in Mexico and Spain*. Austin: University of Texas Press.

Hispanofest

2011 "Mission." *HispanoFest*. Electronic document, http://hispanofest.org/#/about-us/4550338649, accessed August 4, 2011.

Honolulu Star Bulletin

1999 "Hispanic Christmas Celebrated." *Honolulu Star Bulletin*, December 20: Island Images section.

Honor the Chief

N.d.a "Frequently Asked Questions." Electronic document, http://www.honorthechief.org/faq.html, accessed July 13, 2007.

N.d.b "History." Electronic document, http://www.honorthechief.org/history.html, accessed July 13, 2007.

Howard, James H.

1976 "The Plains Gourd Dance as a Revitalization Movement." *American Ethnologist* 3 (2): 243–259.

Intertribal Indian Club of Tulsa (IICOT)

2007 "30th Annual Powwow of Champions." Event program. August 10–12.

Jung, Patrick J.

2007 *The Black Hawk War of 1832*. Campaign and Commanders series, 10. Norman: University of Oklahoma Press.

Kaiser, Robert L., and Meg McSherry Breslin

2001 "Illiniwek Controversy Gets Personal: Indian Youth Says Racism Drove Him from Champaign, Blames Acceptance of the University's Costumed Symbol." *Chicago Tribune*, March 5: Chicago Sports Final 1.

Kaquatosh, Yvonne

2006 "Smoke Dancers Take Lambeau Field." *Kalihwisaks: "She Looks for News,"* August 17.

Kearney, Michael

1972 *The Winds of Ixtepeji: World View and Society in a Zapotec Town*. Long Grove, IL: Waveland.

Keeler, Jacqueline

2000 "Thanksgiving: A Native American View." *Pacific News Service*, Saturday, January 1.

Keesing, Roger M.

2000 "Not a Real Fish: The Ethnographer as Inside Outsider." In *Stumbling Toward Truth: Anthropologists at Work*, edited by Philip R. DeVita, 107–112. Long Grove, IL: Waveland.

King, C. Richard

2001 "Uneasy Indians: Creating and Contesting Native American Mascots at Marquette University." In *Team Spirits: The Native American Mascots Controversy*, edited by C. Richard King and Charles Fruehling, 281–303. Lincoln: University of Nebraska Press.

King, C. Richard, and Charles Fruehling Springwood

2001a *Beyond the Cheers: Race as Spectacle in College Sport*. Albany: State University of New York Press.

2001b "The Best Offense . . . : Dissociation, Desire, and the Defense of the Florida State University Seminoles." In *Team Spirits: The Native American Mascots Controversy*, edited by C. Richard King and Charles Fruehling, 129–156. Lincoln: University of Nebraska Press.

Kracht, Benjamin R.

1994 "Kiowa Powwows: Continuity in Ritual Practice." *American Indian Quarterly* 18 (3): 321–348.

Krystal, Matthew
2008 "Colonialism and Continuity in the Guatemalan Dance of the Conquest." *Mesoamerican Voices* 3: 77–94.

Landreth, Mary
2001 "Becoming the Indians: Fashioning Arkansas State University's Indians." In *Team Spirits: The Native American Mascots Controversy*, edited by C. Richard King and Charles Fruehling, 46–63. Lincoln: University of Nebraska Press.

Lévi-Strauss, Claude
1966 *The Savage Mind*. Translated by John Weightman and Doreen Weightman. Chicago: University of Chicago Press.

Lex, Barbara W.
1975 "Physiological Aspects of Ritual Trance." *Journal of Altered States of Consciousness* 2 (2): 109–122.

Little, Walter E.
2004 *Mayas in the Marketplace: Tourism, Globalization, and Cultural Identity*. Austin: University of Texas Press.

Lloyd, Nora, Warren Perlstein, Joseph Podlasek, and David Spencer
2004 *Chicago's 50 Years of Powwows*. Chicago: Arcadia Publishing.

Maybury-Lewis, David
2002 *Indigenous Peoples, Ethnic Groups, and the State.* 2nd ed. Boston: Allyn and Bacon.

Mead, Margaret
1971 [1928] *Coming of Age in Samoa*. New York: Harper Perennial.

Merrion, Paul
2006 "Options Running Out for U of I's Chief Illiniwek." *Crain's Chicago Business*, May 12.

Milbert, Neil
2005 "No Victory Dance; NCAA Rules Illini Nickname Is OK but Chief Is Not." *Chicago Tribune*, November 12: Sports 1.

Miller, Mary, and Karl Taube
1993 *The Gods and Symbols of Ancient Mexico and the Maya: An Illustrated Dictionary*. London: Thames and Hudson.

Moffatt, Michael
1989 *Coming of Age in New Jersey: College and American Culture*. Piscataway, NJ: Rutgers University Press.

Montague, Susan P., and William Morais
1976 "Football Games and Rock Concerts: The Ritual Enactment of American Success Models." In *The American Dimension: Cultural Myths and Social Re-*

alities, edited by William Arens and Susan P. Montague, 32–52. Port Washington, NY: Alfred Publishing Company.

Montejo, Victor D.

2002 "The Multiplicity of Mayan Voices." In *Indigenous Movements, Self-Representation, and the State in Latin America*, edited by Kay B. Warren and Jean E. Jackson, 123–148. Austin: University of Texas Press.

2005 "Maya Identity and Interethnic Relations." In *Maya Intellectual Renaissance: Identity, Representation, and Leadership*, by Victor D. Montejo, 1–15. Austin: University of Texas Press.

Montoya, Matilde

1970 *Estudio sobre el Baile de la Conquista*. Guatemala City: Universidad de San Carlos.

Moore, Sally F., and Barbara Myerhoff, eds.

1977 *Secular Ritual*. Amsterdam: Van Gorcum, Assen.

Myerhoff, Barbara G.

1978 *Number Our Days*. New York: Touchstone.

Nabokov, Peter, ed.

1999 *Native American Testimony: A Chronicle of Indian-White Relations from Prophecy to the Present, 1942–2000*. Rev. ed. New York: Penguin.

Nahachewsky, Andriy

1995 "Participatory and Presentational Dance as Ethnochoreological Categories." *Dance Research Journal* 27 (1): 1–15.

Nájera-Ramírez, Olga

1989 "Social and Political Dimensions of Folklorico Dance: The Binational Dialectic of Residual and Emergent Culture." *Western Folklore* 48 (1): 15–32.

Nash, June

2004 "Beyond Resistance and Protest: The Maya Quest for Autonomy." In *Pluralizing Ethnography: Comparison and Representation in Maya Cultures, Histories, and Identities*, edited by John M. Watanabe and Edward F. Fischer, 163–198. Santa Fe, NM: School of American Research Press.

Nesper, Larry

2003 "Simulating Culture: Being Indian for Tourists in Lac du Flambeau's Wa-Swa-Gon Indian Bowl." *Ethnohistory* 50 (3): 447–472.

Newbart, Dave

2006 "The Last Dance: Under NCAA Sanctions, U. of I. Plans to Drop Chief after This Year." *Chicago Sun Times*, August 31: News 1.

Niezen, Ronald

2003 *The Origins of Indigenism: Human Rights and the Politics of Identity*. Berkeley: University of California Press.

Ortner, Sherry

1973 "On Key Symbols." *American Anthropologist* 75: 1338–1346.

Otzoy, Irma

1999 "Tekum Umam: From Nationalism to Maya Resistance." PhD dissertation, Department of Anthropology, University of California, Davis.

Peoples, James, and Garrick Bailey

2003 *Humanity: An Introduction to Cultural Anthropology*. 6th ed. Belmont, CA: Wadsworth Publishing Company.

Peoria Tribe of Indians of Oklahoma

2007 "History." Electronic document, http://www.peoriatribe.com/history.php, accessed March 26, 2009.

Preston, Julia

1997 "Transforming Mayan Mysteries into Fancy Footwork." *New York Times*, September 18: E2.

Prochaska, David

2001 "At Home in Illinois: Presence of Chief Illiniwek, Absence of Native Americans." In *Team Spirits: The Native American Mascots Controversy*, edited by C. Richard King and Charles Fruehling, 157–188. Lincoln: University of Nebraska Press.

Raxche' (Demetrio Rodríguez, Guaján)

1996 "Maya Culture and the Politics of Development." In *Maya Cultural Activism in Guatemala*, edited by Edward F. Fischer and R. McKenna Brown, 74–88. Austin: University of Texas Press.

Recinos, Adrian, ed.

1984 *Cronica Indígenas de Guatemala*. 2nd ed. Guatemala: Academia de Geografia e Historia de Guatemala.

Roberts, Kathleen Glenister

2005 "Beauty Is Youth: The Powwow 'Princess.'" In *Powwow*, edited by Clyde Ellis, Luke Eric Lassiter, and Gary H. Dunham, 152–171. Lincoln: University of Nebraska Press.

Robes Kipp, Darryl

2001 "Images of Native People as Seen by the Eye of the Blackbird." *Wicazo Sa Review* 16 (2): 29–34.

Rosaldo, Renato

1989 *Culture and Truth: The Remaking of Social Analysis*. Boston: Beacon Press.

Rosenstein, Jay

2001 "In Whose Honor? Mascots and the Media." In *Team Spirits: The Native American Mascots Controversy*, edited by C. Richard King and Charles Fruehling, 241–256. Lincoln: University of Nebraska Press.

Rosenstein, Jay, dir.
1997 *In Whose Honor: American Indian Mascots in Sports*. 47 min. New Day Films. Harriman, New York.

Ross, Murray
1971 "Football Red and Baseball Green: The Heroics and Bucolics of American Sport." *Chicago Review* 22 (2/3): 30–40.

Rostas, Susanna
2009 *Carrying the Word: The Concheros Dance in Mexico City*. Boulder: University Press of Colorado.

Sam Colop, Luis Enrique
1996 "The Discourse of Concealment and 1992." In *Maya Cultural Activism in Guatemala*, edited by Edward F. Fischer and R. McKenna Brown, 107–113. Austin: University of Texas Press.

Sanford, Victoria
2003 "The 'Grey Zone' of Justice: NGOs and Rule of Law in Postwar Guatemala." *Journal of Human Rights* 2 (3): 393–405.

Schieber, Barbara
2008 "Guatemalan Modern and Folkloric Ballet Make Los Angeles Debut." *Guatemala Times*, September 17. Electronic document, http://www.guatemala-times.com/news/world/364-guatemalan-modern-and-folkloric-ballet-make-los-angeles-debut.html, accessed November 9, 2008.

Scott, James C.
1985 *Weapons of the Weak: Everyday Forms of Peasant Resistance*. New Haven, CT: Yale University Press.
1990 *Domination and the Arts of Resistance: Hidden Transcripts*. New Haven, CT: Yale University Press.

Sexsmith, Pamela Windspeaker
2003 "The Healing Gift of the Jingle Dance." Electronic document, http://www.ammsa.com/buffalospirit/2003/jingledance.html, accessed July 29, 2008.

Shay Anthony
2002 *Choreographic Politics: State Folk Dance Companies, Representation, and Power*. Middletown, CT: Wesleyan University Press.
2006 *Choreographing Identities: Folk Dance, Ethnicity and Festival in the United States and Canada*. Jefferson, NC: McFarland & Company.

Smith, Carol A.
1990 "Introduction: Social Relations in Guatemala over Time and Space." In *Guatemalan Indians and the State: 1540 to 1988*, edited by Carol A. Smith, 1–30. Austin: University of Texas Press.

Speer, Mary Louise
2004 "Their Love of Dance Needs No Translation." *Quad City Times*, January 3.

Spencer, Herbert
1988 [1877] "The Evolution of Society." In *High Points in Anthropology*, 2nd ed., edited by Paul Bohannan and Mark Glazer, 6–28. New York: Alfred A. Knopf.

Spindel, Carol
2000 *Dancing at Halftime: Sports and the Controversy over American Indian Mascots*. New York: New York University Press.

Spradley, James, and David W. McCurdy, eds.
2009 *Conformity and Conflict: Readings in Cultural Anthropology*. 13th ed. Upper Saddle River, NJ: Pearson Prentice Hall.

Springwood, Charles Frueling
2001 "Playing Indian and Fighting (for) Mascots: Reading the Complications of Native American and Euro-American Alliances." In *Team Spirits: The Native American Mascots Controversy*, edited by C. Richard King and Charles Fruehling, 304–327. Lincoln: University of Nebraska Press.

Stack, Carol B.
1974 *All Our Kin: Strategies for Survival in a Black Community*. New York: Harper & Row.

Stone, Lyle M., and Donald Chaput
1978 "History of the Upper Great Lakes." In *Handbook of the North American Indians*, edited by Bruce G. Trigger, 602–609. Washington, DC: Smithsonian Institution.

Students for Chief Illiniwek
N.d. "The Next Dance." Electronic document, http://web.me.com/pauldschmitt/Students_for_Chief_Illiniwek/The_Next_Dance.html, accessed July 12, 2010.

Taube, Karl
1993 *Aztec and Maya Myths*. Austin: University of Texas Press.

Taube, Rhonda
2006 "Culture, Media, and Identity: Public Performance in Contemporary Momostenango, Guatemala." Paper presented at the Annual Meeting of the American Anthropological Association, San Jose, November 18.

Tedlock, Barbara
1992 *Time and the Highland Maya*. Rev. ed. Albuquerque: University of New Mexico Press.

Tedlock, Dennis
1993 *Breath on the Mirror: Mythic Voices and Visions of the Living Maya*. New York: HarperCollins.

Tedlock, Dennis, trans.
1996 *Popol Vuh: The Mayan Book of the Dawn of Life*. Rev. ed. New York: Simon and Schuster.

Thiesz, R. D.

2005 "Putting Things in Order: The Discourse of Tradition." In *Powwow*, edited by Clyde Ellis, Luke Eric Lassiter, and Gary H. Dunham, 85–109. Lincoln: University of Nebraska Press.

Tooker, Elisabeth J.

1975 "Ethnometaphysics of Iroquois Ritual." In *Symbols and Society: Essays on Belief Systems in Action*, edited by Carole E. Hill, 103–116. Southern Anthropological Society Proceedings, no. 9. Athens: University of Georgia Press.

Trimillos, Ricardo D.

1995 "More Than Art: The Politics of Performance in International Cultural Exchange." In *Looking Out: Perspectives on Dance and Criticism in a Multicultural World*, edited by David Gere with coeditors Lewis Segal, Patrice Clark Koelsch, and Elisabeth Zimmer, 23–39. New York: Schirmer Books.

Turner, Terrence

1992 "Defiant Images: The Kayapo Appropriation of Video." *Anthropology Today* 8 (6): 5–15.

2002 "Representation, Polyphony, and the Construction of Power in a Kayapó Video." In *Indigenous Movements, Self-Representation, and the State in Latin America*, edited by Kay B. Warren and Jean E. Jackson, 229–250. Austin: University of Texas Press.

Turner, Terence, and Vanessa Fajans-Turner

2006 "Political Innovation and Inter-ethnic Alliance: Kayapo Resistance to the Developmentalist State." *Anthropology Today* 22 (5): 3–10.

Turner, Victor

1969 *The Ritual Process: Structure and Anti-Structure*. Chicago: Aldine Publishing.

2001 *From Ritual to Theatre: The Human Seriousness of Play*. New York: PAJ Publications.

Twohey, Megan

2008 "Chief Illiniwek to Dance Again." *Chicago Tribune*, November 12: News 3.

Warren, Kay B.

1998 *Indigenous Movements and Their Critics: Pan-Maya Activism in Guatemala*. Princeton, NJ: Princeton University Press.

Warren, Kay B., and Jean E. Jackson

2002 "Introduction: Studying Indigenous Activism in Latin America." In *Indigenous Movements, Self-Representation, and the State in Latin America*, edited by Kay B. Warren and Jean E. Jackson, 1–46. Austin: University of Texas Press.

Wilhelm, Ronald W.

1994 "Columbus's Legacy, Conquest or Invasion? An Analysis of Counter-hegemonic Potential in Guatemalan Teacher Practice and Curriculum." *Anthropology and Education Quarterly* 25 (2): 73–195.

Wilkins, David E.
2002 *American Indian Politics and the American Political System*. Lanham, MD: Rowman and Littlefield Publishers.

Will, George
2006 "Chief among the Silliness." *Washington Post*, January 5.

Willard, John
2004 "Foot Fiesta." *Quad City Times*, September 15.

Wise, David W.
2003 "My Chief Concern: The Mothballing of Chief Illiniwek Would Be a Disservice." *Chicago Tribune*, November 18: Commentary 23.

Young, Gloria Alese
1981 "Powwow Power: Perspectives on Historic and Contemporary Intertribalism." PhD dissertation, Department of Anthropology, Indiana University, Bloomington.

Young, Ryan
2009 "Students Plan Chief's Next Dance as Yearly Event." *Daily Illini*, October 5. Electronic document, http://www.dailyillini.com/news/campus/2009/10/05/students-plan-chiefs-next-dance-as-yearly-event, accessed July 12, 2010.

Index

Page numbers in italics indicate illustrations.